W9-BZC-645

PREACHING CREATION

Throughout the Church Year

JENNIFER M. PHILLIPS

COWLEY PUBLICATIONS
Cambridge · Boston
Massachusetts

© 2000 Jennifer Phillips
All rights reserved.

Published in the United States of America by Cowley Publications, a division of the Society of St. John the Evangelist. No portion of this book may be reproduced, stored in or introduced into a retrieval system, or transmitted, in any form or by any means—including photocopying—without the prior written permission of Cowley Publications, except in the case of brief quotations embodied in critical articles and reviews.

Library of Congress Cataloging-in-Publication Data:
  Phillips, Jennifer M., 1952–
    Preaching creation: throughout the church year / Jennifer Phillips.
        p. cm.
    Includes bibliographical references and index.
    ISBN 1-56101-174-6 (alk. paper)
    1. Lectionary preaching—Episcopal Church. 2. Religion and science. 3. Technology—Religious aspects—Episcopal Church. 4. Environmentalism—Religious aspects—Episcopal Church. I. Title
    BX5979.5.P73 P45 2000
    251'.6—dc21   99-049302

Cynthia Shattuck, editor; Annie Kammerer, copyeditor
Vicki Black, designer

Cover art: "Earth Has Hope" (1995) by Ansgar Holmberg, CSJ

This book was printed in Canada on recycled, acid-free paper.

Cowley Publications
28 Temple Place • Boston, Massachusetts 02111
800-225-1534 • www.cowley.org

Preaching Creation

In thanksgiving

for H. Paul Santmire and Clifford Green
*who stirred my mind to think theologically
and my passion to love creation,
and*
Victor and Mavis Phillips
*who taught me how to tend and appreciate the earth,
having brought me to it.*

CONTENTS

PREFACE

This lectionary guide came about from a conversation with a clergy colleague who remarked to me, "I'd like to preach more often about creation and its care, but so few of the lections seem suitable." I took his words as a challenge. As fleshly creatures of an incarnate God in a whole creation redeemed by Christ's resurrection, wherever we start, surely we must come round again to our place in God's material world.

On the threshold of a new millennium, many churches are calling Christians to observe a Jubilee year, a time sacred to God in which we repent and turn our hearts back to our Creator, rededicate ourselves to honoring God's creation, and take concrete steps to do justice and kindness to one another—particularly those in great need and distress. Among the reflections here you will find calls to international debt forgiveness, to agricultural and marketing practices that favor the poorest people, and to repentance for our American consumption of far more than our share of the earth's resources. In the Episcopal Church, Presiding Bishop Frank Griswold has offered a Jubilee Proclamation directing us to labor and pray for these changes, and also to enter into the sabbath rest of God. Genesis describes how God rested from the work of creation, enjoying the goodness of everything that had been made. We, too, are summoned to lay aside our habits of overwork, overconsumption, exhaustion of natural resources, and burdening our neighbors in order to remember that all comes from and belongs to God. The gift is wonderfully good and sufficient when we enjoy it with justice, prudence, temperance, and courage.

I am the child of a research scientist and a nurse, and have been entranced with the world of science all my life. Still, I read science as one who loves it but comes to it as something of an outsider, asking the theologian's questions: How is God at work in all of this? What does the created world teach of its Maker? How does creation lift my heart in praise of God? I write, similarly, for fellow visitors to the realm of science who desire as people of prayer and as preachers to whet their own appetites and those of their congregations for more knowledge. The commentary in this volume offers tidbits to provoke wonder and curiosity. I do not pretend to objectivity. Like most of the sources I cite, I have strong opinions about environmental and technological issues, and they will emerge in the text. It is my great hope that you will seek out and read the books and journals to which I refer, if they pique your interest. As I write about science, I often feel like the young child who picks up some wondrous thing—a glittering rock, some pond weed, a many-colored moth—and calls out in wonder, "Look at this!" This volume is my little shout of praise.

With few exceptions, I have elected not to include commentary on the lectionary psalms. They deserve their own volume, though many of their creation themes are self-evident. You are of course free to borrow information from any lection that seems useful to apply to another, including the week's psalm. The scriptural index is intended to make the book adaptable to other lectionaries and for occasional use.

The work of a preacher is to be shamelessly seductive on behalf of God. Like the ambassador sent to arrange a marriage between a distant noble and a sought-after bride, the preacher seeks to inflame the bride's desire, to paint the suitor in such splendor that she could not think of looking elsewhere, to help love happen. The wonders of creation—the fresh discoveries from human wisdom and exploration about God's boundless imagination—can woo the most rational and reluctant bride. There has been space here only for small nuggets: teasers to entice interest, spice to provoke thought or stimulate prayer. Some of the connections made between the lections and the material are unabashedly tenuous, allusive, even elliptical and playful. It is my hope each might spark reflection, wonder, delight, surprise, prayer, concern, debate . . . and a sermon.

YEAR A

ADVENT

❧ 1 Advent

Isaiah 2:1-5 War turns plowshares into swords, meadows into minefields. The connection between war and the destruction of the environment can be seen in many places. How might we relate Christian stewardship and the defense budget? Cleaning up after war overlaps issues of economic justice, health, and the environment. Landmines both maim people and render farmland unusable. The burning oilfields of Kuwait darkened the sky with pollutants for many months after war ended there. Decaying radioactive or chemical weapons disposed of at sea now contaminate the fish stocks of Arctic waters on which northernmost people rely; toxins have concentrated in the fat of whales, seals, and birds—all creatures who prey on these fish—and in the bodies of Arctic people for whom they are the primary food source. Who should bear the costs of beating modern swords into plowshares?

Romans 13:8-14 Love is the fulfilling of the law. What does love for those who will come after us require? Consuming resources without renewing them might be defined as "stealing" from children and grandchildren. Might "gratifying the desires of the flesh" more usefully be applied to overconsumption than to sexuality when evaluating any long-term effects upon the world's people?

Matthew 24:37-44 Apocalyptic scriptures remind us of the potential for disaster, and not only on a cosmic scale, to which the Christian response is wakefulness and readiness. We must not be "sleepy"—unconscious, inattentive—when the reign of God breaks in unexpectedly. Disaster-preparedness requires that we organize resources and personnel for flexible, speedy response to catastrophe. I remember the old duck-and-cover training of the nuclear era. Even as a child, having seen the photographs from Hiroshima, it was clear to me that sitting in the school corridor with our coats over our heads was not going to be an effective strategy for surviving a nuclear war. Little was taught about the skills of negotiation and peacemaking that might prevent one in the first place. Apocalypse- preparedness asks that we have our souls in order and be about Christ's work when Christ returns. How do we set about this task?

❧ 2 Advent

Isaiah 11:1-10   Isaiah's peaceable kingdom envisions a harmonious creation, nursery-like in its simplicity. In actuality, the creation hangs in a fine, complex balance in which predation is necessary—not a violation of peace—and life, death, and new life all have a place. How do these two kinds of beauty compare, the idealized and the actual? What does each suggest about God?

Romans 15:4-13   "Live in harmony with one another," instructs the apostle. Within the scientific world a tempest of disagreement has arisen as sociologists in the field have raised some fundamental questions: How do scientists agree about what counts as truth? What is valid scientific method? How do people decide what will count as "knowledge"? These sociologists have raised questions about the conventional view of science as the search for ultimate truths—and have shocked some scientists.

Social phenomena have a large role in science. Science also generates some myths of its own that are not necessarily more valid than myths of other disciplines. Many scientists think of their work as building a complete and exhaustive account of the world, rather than seeing knowledge itself as a social construct; they fear encouraging the public in magical, superstitious ways of viewing the world. Sociologists hope that the public will become aware that human elements can and do color scientific knowledge, and must be taken into account.[1] How might we think about the "ultimate truths" of faith in light of these questions?

Matthew 3:1-12   John the Baptist is a dangerous man, this hot-tempered child of Elizabeth and Zechariah grown up like the Nazarite Samson: unshaven and rough-clad, itinerant in the wild country, camping by the river. Jesus' cousin and forerunner, he is the archetype of the wild man, the prophet as a force of nature, Gilgamesh's Enkidu. When John wades into the stream to baptize Jesus, I imagine nature itself is bemused that it should be called upon to purify the one who is Lord and Word of its creation, and yet a willing collaborator in the designation of the Holy One by water and a descending bird. By comparison, the enemies of Jesus appear as a brood of vipers—like that first serpent of Genesis—hoping to slip away out of sight before the cosmic Lord of the harvest shall appear with fire and a winnowing fan in his hand for the last baptism and purification of creation. How is it that John so engages us? How might he epitomize the prophetic stance in our own time? Who are the wild people of our day?

❦ 3 Advent

Isaiah 35:1-10 "Waters shall break forth in the wilderness," the desert itself and all its blossoms will sing for joy, and human healing will be just one part of this setting right of the whole creation. Astronaut Edgar Mitchell wrote of his trip into space:

> We went to the moon as technicians; we returned as humanitarians. . . . I experienced the universe as intelligent, loving, harmonious. . . . Only when a man sees his fundamental unity with the processes of nature and the functioning of the universe—as I so vividly saw it from the Apollo spacecraft—will the old ways of thinking and behaving disappear. [2]

Have recent views of our planet and others in the galaxy changed our way of seeing the earth and caring for it?

James 5:7-10 "The farmer waits for the precious crop from the earth, being patient with it until it receives the early and the late rains." In agriculture, timing is everything. In a startling discovery, German scientists have determined that if farmers plow their cropland at night, far fewer weed seeds brought to the surface will germinate than if they plow by day. Experiments with wheat fields showed so few weeds germinated in night-plowed strips that herbicides were virtually unnecessary. Researchers are pessimistic that farmers will rush to adopt this practice in place of using the chemical weed killers upon which they have grown dependent. Perhaps what is most amazing about this discovery is that despite all the centuries of farming and plowing it was not made sooner—though I remember one old landscaper in a small town where I lived who advised me to seed a new lawn at night in the dark of the moon.

With the advent of electric and gas power, our awareness of the rhythms of night and day, work and rest, has changed. While enhancing life in many ways, we have also lost some of our sense of patience, of waiting in darkness for light to return, of valuing our fallow time, of paying attention to the sky and the earth. We cannot rush

Christ's return in judgment. Nor can we hasten the growth of our own souls. We are called to tend them in patience—waiting, valuing the time. What disciplines equip us for this work of waiting? And what, today, are our expectations for God's future?

Matthew 11:2-11 Go and tell John what you see and hear: signs of life, signs of God nearby. What do we see and hear that tells us God is close by us, busy healing, liberating, spreading good news, feeding, and renewing? The setting of a broken arm, the amending of a life, a case of pneumonia cured, a troubled conscience salved by confession, a cataract removed—we hardly notice that these ordinary acts and events are marvelous; they are signs that God is near us, in our own locality, present to us in love and power. What have you seen and heard lately?

🌿 4 Advent

Isaiah 7:10-17 The young woman is with child. It seems the most ordinary of events—how then shall it be a sign? In the Eastern Orthodox liturgies for Christmas, the birth of Jesus returns the universe to paradise, reopening the locked gates and causing blossom to return to the tree of life:

> The prophecy of all the prophets is fulfilled,
> Christ is born in Bethlehem.
> Paradise is opened to those of Adam's race.
> Prepare, O Bethlehem,
> For Eden has been opened to all.
> Adorn yourself, O Ephratha,
> For the Tree of Life blossoms forth from the Virgin in the cave.
> Her womb is a spiritual paradise planted with the fruit divine;
> If we eat of it, we shall live forever and not die like Adam.
> Christ is coming to restore the image which He made in the beginning.[3]

Romans 1:1-7 Jesus is "descended from David according to the flesh." His lineage includes some surprising women: Tamar (who plays prostitute to become pregnant by her father-in-law), Ruth (a foreign woman who arguably seduces Boaz), Bathsheba (taken adulterously from her husband), and Mary (unmarried and pregnant). Nowadays, DNA can be traced from ancient hair and bones so that living people can claim their relationship to the bones of their ancestors beyond a doubt. In Jesus' day lineage was a matter of oral history, which makes it even more interesting that

Matthew names some female ancestors a person might want to sweep under the rug. The king and the outsider-woman share genes; the Messiah draws his flesh from a peasant woman's body. How has your own genealogy helped to shape your sense of self? What difference does it make to Christians that Jesus has such a checkered heritage?

Matthew 1:18-25   I have always thought of Joseph as a man of the urban world, but while reading Wendell Berry's wonderful book of essays I suddenly had an image of Joseph as a wilderness traveler—a pioneer venturing into an unknown landscape, estranged from social convention:

> The man who goes into the wilderness on foot, stripped of all the devices of the illusion of fixed order, finds his assumptions to be much shorter lived. Afoot, cut off from the powers by which men change things, he has made himself vulnerable to change. Whether he intends it or not, the wilderness receives him as a student. And what it begins to teach him is to live beyond his expectations; if he returns often and stays long perhaps it will teach him to live *without* expectations. It will teach him the wisdom of taking no thought for the morrow—not because taking thought is a bad idea, but because it is not possible; he doesn't know what thought tomorrow will require.[4]

We often hold up Mary as the model for a seeking soul. But what about Joseph as the person who steps into the unknown, wide-eyed and willing, trusting that God is faithful and that the wild country's unfolding landscape will become home?

CHRISTMAS

❧ *Christmas Day II*

Isaiah 62:6-12   Build up the highway for God! insists the prophet. We are also to make ready our inner highway for God's approach, for all we do in the outer world proceeds from our inner impetus.

> For twenty-five hundred years Buddhist meditators, along with their families and friends, have noticed a transformation of character—a gradual movement into ease, strength, and peace. How is it possible that such deep and lasting change could occur, belying theories that our nature is determined for life by heredity and early childhood experiences? Much current research into the neurophysiology of the brain suggests that the Buddha was not speaking metaphorically when he said that it is possible to eliminate, not repress, even deeply established patterns of reaction.... To a certain extent, we literally create the structural design of our brains by our mental processes, our habits of response.[1]

How do the paths of Christian prayer help us make way for God's coming?

Titus 3:4-7   Christ saved us through the water of rebirth. I once heard a missionary serving in a drought-stricken land of Africa describe baptizing a dying infant with his saliva because there was no water. "I am living water," says Jesus in John's gospel. Our bodies are two-thirds water; without water to drink in some form we quickly die. We understand with our bodies the sacredness of water. On this day (more or less), Mary's birth-water broke and brought forth life for the world.

Luke 2:1-20   Shepherds come to the stable where Jesus lies among the beasts. In *The Mirror of Perfection*, St. Francis expresses a particular gratitude for the creatures that kept the Christ child warm and companioned. He imagines asking the emperor for a special law to feed the birds on Christmas day, and

> that for the reverence of the Son of God, Who rested on that night with the most blessed Virgin Mary between an Ox and an Ass in the manger, whoever shall have an Ox and an Ass shall be bound to provide for them on that night the best of good fodder.

What purpose does it serve in Luke's narrative that Jesus is born in a stable among the humble creatures?

❧ *1 Christmas*

Isaiah 61:10–62:3   Under a deep blanket of snow, my winter garden is alive. Though the shrubs have scaled over their new shoots with tough armor and lie dormant, everything is by no means in suspended animation. Roots are pressing down into the soil below its frozen surface. Air and water are being exchanged through cell membranes—a great and quiet breathing is going on. The earliest bulbs are sending up points of hardy green to probe for the surface. I think of this pressure of life beneath the apparently static whiteness as a great movement of joy. Like the steady befriending and courtship, discovery and mutual vulnerability of lovers that finally erupts into the glad celebration of a public covenant of love, the winter earth is laying a groundwork for spring, when it will deck itself with garlands. Again and again scripture drops hints that the expanding of God's reign is seed-like; death and transformation are part of its life processes. "Love is come again like wheat that springeth green"[2] as the hymn says . . . and then comes the garland!

Galatians 3:23-25, 4:4-7   Many Christians wince when they hear the phrase "Mother Earth." Some fear that any such metaphor will lead us down the slippery slope into neo-paganism. God is our Father, they maintain; the earth is just his artifact. God as Mother raises many of the same hackles for a portion of the church. What is there about our relationship with our mothers that makes the metaphor alarming? Is it that for a time we have been utterly contained, contingent, dependent within a mother's womb? Yet that reality is aptly descriptive of our relationship with our planet and with our God. Are we afraid of the way our home planet gets under our skin, how deeply we love and need it, and how stunningly remote from it we sometimes feel, encased in our human-made houses, cars, and egos?

Galatians reminds us that Jesus as Son of God was born of a woman: he is a planetary, fleshly, and therefore creaturely being like us, but also the divine one through whom we gain adoption as children and heirs of God. Beyond our creatureliness we are invited to become divine children alongside our brother. We are drawn into deep intimacy with God, whom we may explore like the little child feeling her mother's or father's face with a tiny hand, not knowing just where we leave off and God begins. We may touch the earth in the same wondering way as God's gift of love for us.

John 1:1-18 The One who was before everything is the one through whom everything comes into being. In this season I see him in the arms of his mother, recalling a statue I encountered in my first congregation. She is the "Black Madonna" carved from darkest oak. Jesus, toddler-sized, has a look of older wisdom. He presses himself into the crook of her arm and holds in his hand the orb of royalty as a plaything. It seems to me that he is holding the whole earth in his tiny hand and gazing at it with a half-smile. He is not the usual toddler: I feel no anxiety that he might tire of it and hurl it aside. The earth seems so secure in his young hand, a precious thing. If I kneel on the prie-dieu beside this lovely Bavarian carving and look up at his face gleaming in the red-glow of a votive light, it seems he is looking over the rim of the tiny earth at me and saying, "Shall I hand it to you? Will you hold it for me?"

❧ 2 Christmas

Jeremiah 31:7-14 The returning exiles will be led home beside water brooks. These are the source of life for travelers in the arid Middle East, and even in the water-rich parts of the world like Missouri where I live, in big river country. Naturalist Edward Hoagland writes:

> Water is our birthplace. We need and love it. In a bathtub or by a lake or at the sea, we go to it for rest, refreshment and solace. "I'm going to the water," people say when August comes and they crave a break. The sea is a democracy, so big it's free of access, often a bus or subway ride away, a meritocracy, sink or swim, and yet a swallower of grief because of its boundless scale—beyond the horizon, the home of icebergs, islands, whales.[3]

How those exiles must have delighted in the image of their homeward trek refreshed by the springs of divine providence. Each raindrop, each tiny puddle in the streets of their captivity must have been a reminder of the promise of being led beside still waters. So today, sitting in my urban office and looking out on an asphalt parking lot turned Impressionist by patches of light and glossy darkness where the rain pools, I remember: God is faithful.

Ephesians 1:3-6, 15-19 Having the eyes of our hearts enlightened is a mysterious process. At times, by grace and God's design, we come to a flash of unprecedented, unprepared insight. Rounding a bend of the Missouri River, God's glory beams at me from the great white wings of a bald eagle in flight; my heart is brought to its knees. More often, enlightenment is the slow process of grace at work through the practice of discipline. One writer observes:

> A spiritual discipline is not just another something on your to-do list. It's not another task, like remembering your vitamins and flossing. It's the thing in which the tasks of life happen. It's the frame of life. For many of us, finding time for this "frame" simply doesn't seem possible. When I find myself struggling to make time for intentional prayer, meditation, and Bible reading, I recall the Benedictine novice mistress who said to one of her hurried and harried young charges, "You have all the time there is."[4]

My spirit becomes schooled and fluent in prayer by the same repetitive, orderly sort of learning that once helped me master a geometry proof in order to understand the relationship of angles and volumes in a sphere bisected by a plane. In what ways are patience, attention, and humility the building blocks of a more holy life?

Matthew 2:13-23 The Holy Family became refugees fleeing in fear of political reprisal. Other Jewish families must have fled as well if, as the story tells it, Herod's troops systematically killed Jewish boy children. In 1996, newsreels captured the slow procession of 450,000 Rwandan refugees from camps in Tanzania back to their homeland. Some 20 to 30 million refugees are on the move every year, according to the United Nations High Commissioner for Refugees, driven by fear, hunger, force, and hope. In 1998, over 300,000 people were residing in camps in Tanzania, having fled the Hutu and Tutsi conflict in Burundi. It is hard to imagine the daily lives of such floods of displaced persons, often separated from loved ones and having left behind whatever they once possessed. Joseph seems to have prospered well enough in Egypt as a craftsman; most refugees of war are not so fortunate, and this is a season to remember them.

EPIPHANY

❦ *The Epiphany*

Isaiah 60:1-9   Camels have a reputation for being ill-tempered and unintelligent beasts of burden, but without them, it is unlikely that the desert regions of Africa and the Middle East would have been explored and settled in ancient times; the whole history of trade and civilization might have been different. The camel has pads of thick fibrous tissue on its big feet to keep the heat of the ground from damaging them and to balance its weight on shifting sand. Two-humped camels (and related, speedier one-humped dromedaries) can eat thorny vegetation high in salt, travel 60 to 70 miles a day, and bear a load of some 600 pounds. For protection, their nostril flaps close during sandstorms. Dromedaries have three-chambered stomachs that hold up to 30 quarts of water. This enables them to go for five days in extreme heat or nearly a month in cool weather between drinks. Their humps are composed of fat that the animals can survive upon when food is unavailable. Their hair is used for clothing and tents, and their meat provides nourishment. Camels may have been indigenous as early as the time of Abraham, and here they are a sign of wealth and abundant trade.

Ephesians 3:1-12   The mystery hidden for ages is being made known, pronounces the author of Ephesians. Yet we are still filling in the details. Scientists quest for a "theory of everything" that would unify all the laws of physics into a cohesive whole. Stephen Hawking asks whether such a unified theory truly exists that we may someday discover—or perhaps we are just "chasing a mirage":

> Even if we do discover a complete unified theory, it would not mean that we would be able to predict events in general, for two reasons. The first is the lim-

itation that the uncertainty principle of quantum mechanics sets on our powers of prediction.... The second... arises from the fact that we could not solve the equations of the theory exactly, except in very simple situations.... Why does the universe go to all the bother of existing? Is the unified theory so compelling that it brings about its own existence? Or does it need a creator, and, if so, does he have any other effect on the universe?[1]

Matthew 2:1-12   The visit of the magi is a wonderful image for the meeting of cultures and the exchange of gifts. In our day of easy travel around the globe, we often forget the marvel of being able to converse with and visit people from distant places. Each of the three foreign wise ones brings something of value particular to his homeland. Each takes away gifts also: hope, expanded wisdom, new relationships, and the satisfaction of a journey of exploration brought to successful completion. As the church of the new millennium reflects about mission, it is clear that our encounters are not about bringing information to the ignorant, but rather about the exchange of holy gifts. Wherever we travel, God's star has already shone there, and though we bring news of what God is up to in our own place, we are sure to find God already at work and to hear this good news from those we meet through the partnership of mission.

❧ 1 Epiphany

Isaiah 42:1-9   Space travel has provided us with images of the heavens spread out like a tent, and the earth like a colorful canvas luminous with green and blue reflected light. Science writer Lydia Dotto reflects:

> We venture into space enclosed in a technological life-support system—a spacecraft—that can provide, in a limited way and for short periods of time, what the earth has provided for all life for hundreds of millions of years. In this way, a spacecraft is a microcosm of earth: a source of food, air, water, atmospheric pressure, and protection from the extremes of heat and cold found in space. Since these resources are severely limited in a spacecraft, we've learned to conserve and recycle them. We recirculate air and remove excess carbon dioxide from it so that the atmosphere can continue to support life. We carefully collect wastes and prevent dangerous chemicals from being released, because these would contaminate the life-support system and endanger the crew. We're extraordinarily careful about taking these precautions in space—and yet we

appear to be neglecting them on earth. Why? Perhaps because we haven't really thought of earth as a closed life-support system. . . . It has boundaries and limits. . . we are capable of pushing it to those limits and perhaps beyond.[2]

Acts 10:34-38; Matthew 3:13-17   Jesus is baptized in the Jordan. We often picture a deep flowing river, but the Jordan is now, much of the time, a stony, relatively shallow stream. Since the mid-sixties the bulk of Jordan river water has been diverted for human use, leaving the Dead Sea into which it empties dwindling and saltier. This sea is a terminal desert lake, that is, a basin with no outlets; each year more than a meter of fresh water evaporates from it, leaving salt behind. It is home to salt-loving bacteria found nowhere else. New plans are afoot to return more fresh water to the Jordan and its lakes—for the sake of tourism more than environmentalism.

When the Hebrew people first came down the arid hills and into the lush, green Jordan plain, what they described as a land flowing with milk and honey—with flocks and blossoms—was in fact a land flowing with sweet water which made all this abundance possible, prospering a city at nearby Jericho for over ten thousand years to the present day. In the Holy Land the landscape at every turn reminds one how vital water is to life, how it cannot be taken for granted, and how the pressures of population growth and agriculture are mining water from beneath the earth which cannot be replaced once it is gone. How does our own baptism call us to be stewards of water?

⚘ 2 Epiphany

Isaiah 49:1-7   "The Lord called me from the womb," says the prophet, "and in the body of my mother, God named my name." There is never a moment too early for us to belong to God. In Hebrew the word for compassion (*rachamim*) comes from the root of the noun for womb (*rechem*). The womb is the place of padding, warmth, nourishment, and fluids for the vulnerable fetus to take form and grow. The hospitable, roomy, womb-like compassion of God welcomes back sinners (Isaiah 54:7, Hosea 2:19, Zechariah12:10) and is merciful (2 Samuel 24:14). God's mercy—God's womb-ness—makes room for us, holds us in our weakness, nurtures us intimately, never abandons us. A deep respect for life, whatever one's thoughts about reproductive choices, is informed by compassion, the womb-quality we share with God. What happens to our images of God if we consider God with a womb?

1 Corinthians 1:1-9   "Grace to you and peace," is the apostle's greeting. Philosopher Charlene Spretnak defines grace as saving love, and suggests:

We are indeed created in the "image" of the participatory universe. We are of it—not by projecting our type of mental processes onto the universe, but by realizing that the human mind participates in the processes of the larger "mind." We are not apart from the dynamic cosmos. Experiencing grace involves the expansion of consciousness of self to all of one's surroundings as an unbroken whole, a consciousness of awe from which negative mindstates are absent, from which healing and groundedness result. For these reasons grace has long been deemed "amazing."[3]

John 1:29-41 The first time I heard a preacher talking about the pollution of groundwater in his region, saying, "Contaminated water is dead, it is not fit for baptizing," I felt tears come to my eyes. For us as Christians, that is the measure of our sin—that we render water unfit for baptizing. In scripture, *living* water means running water—clean, non-stagnant water that can sustain life. It is in living water that we baptize. As we cleanse and conserve the waters of the planet, we are effectively returning water to its sacred state as the water of baptism, as holy water.

❦ 3 Epiphany

Amos 3:1-8 Lions once inhabited the Holy Land, North Africa, and parts of Europe. The Persian lion, *Panthera leo persica*, was a small, bushy-maned lion indigenous to the Holy Land that became extinct in that area around 1300. Regarded as a royal beast by the Assyrians, the lion was portrayed in the decoration of Solomon's temple, and as the symbol for the tribe of Judah. It then became a fitting symbol for Christ in the book of Revelation (5:5). Lions and other great cats continue to dwindle in numbers as their habitats disappear in Africa and Asia. Perhaps in a few generations they will seem as "mythological" to our descendants as the biblical "leviathan" and "behemoth" seem to us. What would be lost if our descendants found "Christ the Lion of Judah" as incomprehensible as those other ancient creatures whose zoological identities we cannot even determine?

1 Corinthians 1:10-17 Factions are warring within the Christian community in Corinth: not a new problem! For the ancient Greeks, music, mathematics, and the forms of things in the created world—including the human body—all pointed to a set of ideal relationships and proportions that could be expressed in numerical equations. When rightly ordered, they expressed harmony. In *Against the Pagans*

Athanasius, bishop of Alexandria in the fourth century, borrows a metaphor from music:

> Think of a musician tuning a lyre. By skill the musician adjusts high notes to low and intermediate notes to the rest, and produces a series of harmonies. So too the wisdom of God holds the world like a lyre and joins things in the air to those on the earth, and things in heaven to those in the air, and brings each part into harmony with the whole.

What does this image suggest to us about bringing factions into harmony?

Matthew 4:12-23   Fishers in the Sea of Galilee today find an abundance of fish symbolic of God's plentiful harvest of souls. In our children's lifetimes, as the ocean's fish supply dwindles from overfishing and destruction of habitats, and freshwater fish dwindle from pollution and loss of species diversity, most fish for human consumption will be raised on farms. Perhaps we will need to rewrite our parables of fishing accordingly. Poor nations who rely on ocean fish as the protein staple of their diet are most at risk. For many of these countries, fish farming will be too expensive, or will consume too much land and fresh water and create too much pollution to be viable. How might the changing realities of fishing change our image of scripture or the way we pray?

❧ 4 Epiphany

Micah 6:1-8   "Do justice, love kindness, and walk humbly with your God," says the prophet. Justice, humility, and kindness pertain not just to human beings but to our relationship with all creation. The Anglican province of South Africa has started an environmental justice campaign called "Save Our Future." Its spokesperson, Bishop Geoff Davies of the diocese of Umzimvubu, warns: "The natural world is in a state of crisis, whether we like to admit it or not." He traces a direct relationship between economic exploitation and the degradation of the environment. The campaign challenges governments and all people of faith to work toward environmental education, sustainability, respect for the sanctity of all life, fair trade practices, wise legislation, reduction of military expenditure, development of renewable energy sources, protection of threatened ecosystems, recycling, and corporate regulation regarding the impact of tourism and trade on indigenous peoples. "We have to keep God at the center," says Bishop Davies, "and rediscover the centrality of God the Creator."[4] What else does the fact that God is *Creator* mean for justice with regard to the earth?

1 Corinthians 1:18-31 "God chose what is low and despised in the world...to reduce to nothing things that are, so that no one might boast in the presence of God." What could be less than nothing? Could "nothing" be more than we think? A vacuum in fact hums with its own kind of energy. The concept of a vacuum is modern: as late as the seventeenth century René Descartes maintained that it was by definition impossible to have nothing between two particles without them being joined together. Quantum theory, however, from Max Planck in 1911 onward, changed the understanding of energy, seeing it as contained in little packets or quanta. Vacuum energy was first proposed in mathematics and then supported by experimental data in the 1920s. Vacuums violate common sense: particles coming into being and vanishing, emptiness full of activity, pressure that perfectly matches and cancels its energy density. Even "nothingness" is dense with mystery; the more we learn, the more we are called into a reverent humility and thankfulness for God's ingenuity, for God's loving design. How in your experience has something tiny and insignificant turned out to be full of revelation, mystery, and importance?

Matthew 5:1-12 Jesus went up the mountain: for eons human beings have ascended mountains and hills seeking transcendence. I have done it myself a hundred times: panted up a steep incline, perhaps through a thick wood, placing my feet carefully. I have come out often onto a rocky ledge above a New England timberline where the air is cool, fresh, and moving and where the landscape is laid out below. I have sat down, weary, and felt the sun-warmed or frosty stone under me as a monumental stability, ancient and trustworthy, enduring and patient.

So I envision Jesus on a small mountain in his own place and time, experiencing the same solidity of ground, the movement of air, the wide panorama, and feeling the energy rise in himself to teach and to speak, in particular, a word of hope: "Blessed—fortunate, honorable, truly all right—are you poor, bereaved, yearning, striving ones, for God is supplying and empowering you, here and now. Feel it! Believe it!"

How have mountain landscapes influenced your own life of prayer and sense of God?

🌿 5 Epiphany

Habakkuk 3:2-6, 17-19 "God's glory covered the heavens, and the earth was full of God's praise. God's brightness was like the light, rays flashed from God's hand." The poet-prophet describes God as light, but also the one on whom plagues are attendant, and who stirs the tectonic motions of earth's rocks and magma to raise and lower mountain ranges. This image of God is both beautiful and terrible: God is clothed in the great forces of nature, constructive and destructive. It is not comfortable to connect radioactivity, volcanism, earthquake, and epidemic with God's activity, yet scripture makes this connection again and again. God is not cuddly and comfortable, but awesome and beyond our knowing. How can we look on the devastation of creation's forces of change and say, "Praise to you, God, who has made heaven and earth, and called all things good"?

1 Corinthians 2:1-11 "No one comprehends the thoughts of God except the Spirit of God," and yet there is much we may deduce about God's mind and imagination from God's image in creation. In *Against the Pagans* Athanasius writes:

> By his own wisdom and Word, who is our Lord and Savior Christ, the all-holy Father... like a skillful pilot guides to safety all creation.... For if the movement of the universe were irrational, and the world rolled on in random fashion, one would be justified in disbelieving what we say. But if the world is founded on reason, wisdom, and science, and is filled with orderly beauty, then it must owe its origin and order to none other than the Word of God.

How does the Spirit teach us of God in creation? And what is the curriculum?

Matthew 5:13-20 I gained a fresh appreciation for the salt of the earth after visiting the Dead Sea: the southern shores have towers of white crystal rising from salt deposits in a lovely but eerie landscape of death where virtually no plants or animals can survive. Yet we could not live without salt in our bodies. Our cells draw in or exude water to maintain a delicate balance—just the needed proportion for homeostasis. A teaspoon or two of salt on a hot day might need to be replaced, depending on one's activity level. The athlete who sweats out vital salts must replenish them or begin to die from their lack. The swimmer in the Dead Sea who exposes delicate mucous membranes to that super-salty water feels the sting of dying cells overwhelmed by salt. Salt preserves food from decay for long-term storage and perks our taste buds to enjoy the flavor of foods, but can overwhelm in injudicious quantities. Like salt, we disciples may give life and zest—sometimes even a sting—to society. How might we need to temper our actions so that they are life-giving and not withering?

🌿 6 Epiphany

Ecclesiasticus 15:11-20 "It was God who created us in the beginning and left us in the power of our own free choice." The sinful misuse of our wills puts us in need of repentance toward creation. A lovely expression of penitence comes from the Iona community:

> By the awareness of Thy good creation round us,
> by the intimations of Thy redemption in us,
> by the pulsing sense of Thy Spirit round about us and between us—
> what else is left for us to do but say sorry?
> For our earthiness and our laziness:
> for our blindness and forgetting.
> . . . .
> Give us life that we may be penitent.
> Penitent that we may live.[5]

1 Corinthians 3:1-9 We water, God gives growth. One of the small miracles of the gardener's year is to plunge small, dry, homely bulbs into the earth; cover them with soil; watch the ground freeze over them and the snowfall cover them; and then, come spring, see the first green shoots and, finally, blossoms. All winter, the roots press out from the bulb, the storehouse of carbohydrates needed to feed the new growth once the ground begins to warm and the days lengthen. After we have done our part in the planting, we sit in patience, wait for the miracle, and give thanks. We are co-creators with God, co-laborers in the work of creation. What role is ours and what is God's? Where are the limits of our responsibility?

Matthew 5:21-37 "If your right hand causes you to sin, cut it off and throw it away; it is better for you to lose one of your members than for your whole body to go into hell." Mark also repeats this strong admonishment (missing in Luke) that calls Jesus' followers to an even higher standard than the Torah of old. When I did my first work as a chaplain in a state psychiatric hospital, the supervisors gave strict instructions that this text was not to be read or preached about since at some point, in a state hospital somewhere, a psychotic patient had taken the advice literally and maimed himself. If today's congregations followed suit, the church would be full of one-eyed, one-armed people: our senses and, more crucially, our brains constantly lead us into sin. The translation of the Greek word *sympheri* is not "better," as rendered in the *New Revised Standard Version* of the Bible, but "more useful," "more profitable," "beneficial," even "more congruent."

So what might the gospels really be saying in this long list of admonishments? What does it mean for us to be *perfect* (or mature, whole, complete) as God is? The urgency of tone is clear, implying "strive with all your might" to live uprightly, as are the warnings that we should not expect God to do more kindly for us than we are willing to do for others. It requires a huge effort to pay attention to our acts and choices at every moment as though each one of them matters to us, to the world, to God. When I was a little child, I remember idly throwing a candy wrapper out the car window and having my dad pull over and say, "Imagine what the world would look like if everyone threw their trash in the street. Would you want to live in a world like that? Think about what you are doing."

❦ 7 Epiphany

Leviticus 19:1-2, 9-18   I grew up in the woods of New York state, and this was an ethic I learned before the age of seven: When you pick wildflowers, don't pick the protected ones (which I learned to recognize), and always leave a blossoming stem on the plant to go to seed so there will be more; never pick the only blossom in the neighborhood. For the sake of the poor, farmers are enjoined in Levitical rules to leave the edges of their fields unharvested so they may be gleaned. Our capacity to consume "the very last one" of a species is well known in the dynamic of overfishing, in the harvesting of wild bulbs for plant markets, and in the hunting of rare animals for trophies or products. If the poor end up being the harvesters of many of these scarce local resources, it is not infrequently to meet the appetites of the well-to-do. In the ancient laws, roots of social justice entwine with an environmental justice for which the ancestors had limited language. In what ways might we extend the metaphor and "leave the edge of our fields unharvested" for the benefit of those in need?

1 Corinthians 3:10-23   "You are God's temple. Your body is a temple of the Holy Spirit." As an adult, I am filled with wonder about all we do not yet know about just how our bodies work and how our selves are integrated with them. One of the major medical discoveries of the twentieth century slipped by in August of 1998 with hardly a ripple of media attention. Helen O'Connell, a urology surgeon at Australia's Royal Melbourne Hospital, carried out painstaking dissections of female cadavers and discovered that the internal structure of women's genitalia is entirely different—larger and more complex—than it has been portrayed in generations of medical textbooks. Her descriptions of female anatomy may save women having pelvic surgeries from ending up with damage to sexual function. Such nerve-sparing surgical knowledge was obtained decades ago for males, but the nerve and internal structures of females had never been mapped out, and were simply described in such terms as "a poor homologue" of the male's.[6] We are temples of God's presence, and yet our prejudices and assumptions often blind us to the evidence before our eyes.

Matthew 5:38-48 God sends rain on the just and the unjust; it is a resource and a blessing provided regardless of our deserving. In 1999 some good news arrived about rain: acid rain is diminishing in the United States thanks to reduced sulfur dioxide emissions at a low cost of about $1 billion a year. Flexible regulations are credited with helping speed improvement—particularly by power plants using an emissions trading system. Many plants have switched to low-sulfur coal and are using scrubbing systems to clean exiting emissions. Some parts of the east have seen up to 25 percent less acid rain since 1983.[7] Being perfect as God is perfect extends beyond our relationships with fellow human beings to our relationship with the whole earth. Those who are children of God give an extra measure of care to the creation in God's name, and pursue changes to ensure its environmental health.

🌿 8 Epiphany

Isaiah 49:8-18 "On all the bare heights shall be their pasture." I remember driving through the Rocky Mountain National Park on a winding road across the peaks until I reached an alpine meadow, where a sign instructed visitors to stay strictly on the path. Thousands of passing feet had beaten a little track across the slope, and to either side tiny, tough plants were covered with blossom. The plants—all of them—were leathery, hairy, or scaly to resist the drying winds, and small enough to withstand their buffets. They were deeply rooted in crevices of the rock through a thin skin of gravelly soil. Saxifrages can actually break the rock apart with their roots to get a toehold in this fierce environment. Human feet can wipe out tundra meadow plants with a few careless steps. For God to make a grazing field on a mountaintop is more amazing than putting the proverbial camel through the needle's eye. The delicate tundra and alpine meadow is miracle enough for me.

1 Corinthians 4:1-13 We are to be "stewards of God's mysteries." It is a priestly image, bringing to mind the great mystery of Christ present in the eucharist and the water and oil of baptism. But the priestly people of God are stewards of a wider set of mysteries than this. Former president Jimmy Carter writes on Romans 1:19-20:

Paul's point was that the glories of the world around us demonstrate God's existence. Like Paul, I see the glory of God around me in the unfathomable mysteries of the universe and the diversity and intricacies of creation. We stand in wonder at how a tree grows from an acorn, how a flower blooms, or how DNA can shape the appearance and character of a living creature....None of these discoveries contradicts my belief in an ultimate and superior being; they simply confirm the reverence and awe generated both by what becomes known and by what remains unexplained.[8]

Matthew 6:24-34   There is an essentially joyous vision underlying Jesus' words about birds and flowers and human beings. We are caught up together in one matrix of God's provisioning and love. God's care and design are not merely extended to us, but to all creation. In St. Basil's words:

O God, enlarge within us the sense of fellowship with all living things, our brothers the animals to whom thou gavest the earth as their home in common with us. We remember with shame that in the past we have exercised the high dominion of man with ruthless cruelty so that the voice of the earth, which should have gone up to thee in song, has been a groan of travail. May we realize that they live not for us alone but for themselves and for thee, and that they love the sweetness of life.

❦ *Last Epiphany*

Exodus 24:12-18   "The glory of the LORD was like a devouring fire on the top of the mountain." For the ancients, fire was a sign of purification, the element of warmth and energy, the agent of destruction. We are able to know fire more fully as a physical and chemical reaction that transforms matter and releases energy in combustion, during which oxygen combines with matter so rapidly that both light and heat are produced. The rusting of metal is as much an oxidation process as the burning of wood, but at a different rate of speed. Each combustible substance has a particular temperature at which combustion takes place, known as its kindling temperature. Spontaneous combustion can take place if a combustible substance that is a poor heat conductor rests in still air. And about God's kindling temperature...ah, we do not know!

Philippians 3:7-14   Paul describes himself as pressing on toward the goal, which includes deep knowledge of Christ with heart and mind and soul, and ultimately (as he says in 1 Corinthians) seeing face to face, knowing as he is fully known. As a well-schooled man he applied all his reason to this task, even as he was applying his great energy to service and proclamation. In us, too, faith seeks understanding and pushes us on toward greater knowledge so that our love also may be greater. Nineteenth-century Anglican theologian William Porcher DuBose describes the quest this way:

> But we do not . . . see God only in man: it is contrary to reason to try to divorce the meaning of man from that of his environment—to find in his outcome a reason and meaning for himself and not also for the process and conditions by which he has realized himself. The Logos of man is the Logos of nature, for it is nature that has produced and includes all that is natural in man. . . . It is the last reach of spiritual science to learn how all these and all other truths meet and unite and come to their fulfillment only in the truth of truths, the end of ends, the fact of the Incarnation, the self-realization of God in his creation, of the whole creation in God.[9]

Matthew 17:1-9   The transfiguration story brings us into a landscape of bleak rock, of lowering cloud that becomes an enveloping mist—the visible sign of God's "tenting" presence with humankind that is perfected in Jesus. Here, then, is a little recapitulation of God's appearances in history. We remember Moses coming down from a similar mountain, his face shining from having looked upon God's glory; the pillar of cloud that led the Israelites through the wilderness; Elijah hiding in the cleft of another mountain as God's glory passed by and spoke; and the description of Wisdom (Sirach 24:3f.) at work in creation: "I came forth from the mouth of the Most High, and covered the earth like a mist. I dwelt in the highest heavens, and my throne was in a pillar of cloud." The disciples want to build some shelter up there on the peak: they feel exposed, vulnerable, and disoriented—fogged in on the heights. These are the very conditions in which God most easily becomes known to us in God's creative energy and abiding presence: when all our usual references fail, when we cannot see where we are or what we should do, and we find ourselves simply listening.

LENT AND HOLY WEEK

❧ *Ash Wednesday*

Joel 2:1-2, 12-17; 2 Corinthians 5:20–6:10; Matthew 6:1-21 The litany for this feast says much about our poor stewardship of the material world and one another. Abuse and exploitation of creation might be a good preaching theme for the day. What are the hallmarks of "right relationship" with creation? What is the interplay between our private patterns of sin and corporate sinfulness? Exploitation due to policies of our nation and our economy, mass behaviors (waste creation, noise and light pollution, disruption of water above and below ground)—we are woven into these realities whether we will it or not. Do our small acts of restitution in light of this corporate sinfulness matter? How might your particular congregation act to put things right?

❧ *1 Lent*

Genesis 2:4–3:7 What does it mean that God was remembered as having established humankind in a garden? How do the two accounts of creation in Genesis (1:1–2:3 and 2:4–3:24) offer slightly different ways of thinking about the relationship of humans to the creatures and to each other? Our understanding of sexuality and gender is much more complex today. Many scientists now recognize those people whose experience of gender is not simply "male or female": transgendered and transsexual persons, those with XYY or XXY chromosomes, those with ambiguous or missing genitalia, those who feel throughout life they are inhabiting a body of the wrong gender, those who are homosexual or bisexual. How does the church make room for their stories and make welcome their lives?

Romans 5:12-21 "Where sin increased, grace abounded." There is a wonderful Celtic story that as Noah set sail in the ark he failed to realize that he had left out one crucial nail in the hull. The devil, distressed to have been left out of the cargo of creatures destined for survival, turned himself into a swimming serpent and tried to get into the boat through the nail hole. He became wedged in the hole and kept the ark from sinking during its stormy voyage, a sign that even the devil can be enlisted in God's work of salvation, can become a tool of grace.

Matthew 4:1-11 Temptation comes to Jesus in the wilderness. Heat, thirst, an empty horizon with no familiar landmarks, isolation—in just such a setting countless ascetics after Jesus also sought closer communion with God, but found themselves wrestling with their demons. As shimmering heat rises from the sun-baked ground, creating mirages of water and trees, Satan easily concocts visions of a shining city or stones turning into loaves of bread in the mind of a food- and water-deprived Jesus on a vision quest after the powerful spiritual encounter of his baptism. In the lives of most people of faith, certain landscapes have become teachers, places of encounter, outer reflections of inner reality, settings for realization of the numinous. Which landscapes have been transformative for you?

❧ 2 Lent

Genesis 12:1-8 Abraham's journey from Haran to Canaan (Phoenicia) takes him from the valley of the Euphrates River through what today is central Syria and Jordan, into Egypt, and back into south central Israel. What was the environment like through which he traveled? Abraham followed a watershed from the Transjordan across the hill country, following seasonal pastures, oases, and streams, and stopping in major urban centers for provisioning and trade. Rain was seasonal, soil shallow, and famine a constant threat if the rains should fail. The west wind off the ocean brought moisture and growth; the east winds off the great deserts brought only parching heat. While the landscape was often harsh, he was following a trade route frequented by other caravans as well as by the armies of invading peoples.

The earliest extant map of the environs of Jerusalem is the Medeba map, a floor mosaic from the sixth century labeled in Greek. The routes of ancient travels are pieced together by looking at water sources and topography, archaeological remains where they exist, the preservation of ancient place and family names, and identification of sites in later documents. How do the environs of our travels influence our spiritual lives? How might we map our interior journey of faith?

Romans 4:1-17 God calls into existence the things that do not exist. Creation is a dynamic process, continually unfolding from the mind of God. Antimatter is one of the amazing discoveries of the twentieth century. Few things in our universe slip into and out of existence as swiftly and elusively as antimatter—and a good thing for us, since if there were a lot of antimatter around it would be busy meeting and annihilating an equal amount of matter. Scientists have demonstrated that all types of particles have antimatter doubles. Why then didn't matter and antimatter, if present in the early stages of the universe in equal amounts, just annihilate each other entirely, leaving only the photon remnants of their collisions as radiation? In fact, some portion of matter survived, while antimatter vanished in our universe and we do not know why as yet. To this mystery of asymmetry, we owe the existence of the material world.

John 3:1-17 Can a man be born when he is old? New reproductive technologies seem to suggest that the answer is not an emphatic no, even in the natural world. From the moment of the cloning of Dolly the sheep, the possibility has been accepted that a human being might be cloned from an adult cell of another, and could be made genetically identical.

So the language of the modern church that speaks of our responsibility and power as co-creators with God, whether comfortable or not, has new reality. Are these new reproductive technologies good, we ask? Are they godly—that is, merciful and just, righteous and compassionate? How does this new reality change us? What obligations does it carry? What does it tell us of God? And, finally, are there circumstances in which I myself, or someone close to me, might need to make a decision about using this technology? How would we choose?

✤ 3 Lent

Exodus 17:1-7 Moses strikes the rock and water comes out; how can this be? We think of rock and water as being about as opposite as substances can be. Yet geologists believe that enough water for ten earth oceans lies deep under earth's surface within the very rocks—droplets in the crystal lattices of minerals mingled into the mantle in molecular form. Our planet is wetter even than the "blue planet" photographs from space suggest. Water in these forms acts as a lubricant along fault lines to help tectonic plates slide against one another. We know more about the underground aquifers that carry lakes and rivers of water deep below the surface and that we tap with wells for irrigation and domestic use. Even under the sands of high desert, water may flow beyond the reach of plant roots. Though there is no need to explain away the lovely description of Moses' miracle, it is wonderful to think of the hidden water—part of the planet's life processes beyond our sight.

Romans 5:1-11 Suffering produces endurance and character, says Paul. This may be true for some types of suffering, but others erode character. For people who endure chronic pain, there may be not only physical disability but also depression, irritability, loss of patience, isolation, cynicism, loss of faith, family strife, and an increased rate of suicide. Attributing meaning to suffering, such as improvement of character and strength, is best done by the sufferers themselves. To have someone else interpret one's suffering can be intrusive. One young man who was wasting away with AIDS, his feet and legs too painful to be touched, said to me, his hospital chaplain, "I mourn the man I used to be. Now I am a disease inhabited by a man, not a man with a disease. I am disappearing and nothing seems to matter much anymore." Does your congregation help teach people to sit with suffering persons and gently inquire what they are making of their own suffering? Or how to manage our own helplessness in the company of those for whom nothing tangible can be done?

John 4:5-42 The woman said to Jesus, "Sir, give me this water, so that I may never be thirsty." The well where Jesus encounters the Samaritan woman was a center for town life. Its site, now some twenty feet below ground and enclosed in a little church within a church, is still commemorated as Jacob's well in the once Samaritan town of Nablus. It is a deep vertical shaft from which clear water can still be drawn and drunk after millennia of use. The ancient people of the Near East were skilled at locating and harvesting water. Miles of hydrologically sophisticated underground tunnels have been discovered in the hills to the west of Jerusalem that are over 2000 years old. These were carved through dolomite to carry spring and aquifer water to terraces where crops and fruit were grown until modern times. As modern communities were built, some tunnels were destroyed and replaced by nonsustainable wells. But as water grows scarce, interest in the old waterways that were once able to bring flowing, living water through the thirsty land is increasing. What does this renewed interest in ancient ways of thinking say about our society today?

❦ *4 Lent*

1 Samuel 16:1-13   The anointing of David is just one of many instances in Hebrew scripture in which God singles out the smallest, humblest, and youngest to be the agent of deliverance and the particular servant of God. Therapist and rabbi Edwin Freedman writes:

> The position we occupy within the sibling constellation of our nuclear family of origin foreshadows our expectations of the opposite as well as of the same sex, our degree of comfort with our own various offspring, and our style of leadership in succeeding nuclear groupings.

He cites Walter Toman's work in the field of psychology and birth order, which suggests that "parents tend to have the most sympathetic relationship with the child whose sibling position is closest to their own."[1]

What does your own experience of birth order in families contribute to your understanding of David and his gifts and liabilities? (Or Joseph, Jacob, Rachel?)

Ephesians 5:1-14; John 9:1-38   For the author of Ephesians, light and darkness are analogous to good and evil conduct. But in John's gospel, which is also much taken with images of light and darkness, the man has not been born blind because he was bad or because his parents sinned, but rather so that God's goodness might be revealed through his healing. Vision is a delicate function. When a photon of light reaches a rhodopsin molecule in your retina, a neuron fires its message and your brain perceives light. In a perfectly dark room, the dark-adapted eye can see one single photon. Unlike our ancestors of the first century, we know that there is a vast spectrum of light that is invisible to our eyes, of either too long or too short a wavelength to be seen.

Light for many people is reassuring, orienting. But darkness—unlike evil—has its own virtues and can be perceived as embracing, hospitable, restful. Standing in the long tradition of mystics who found God in the darkness, T. S. Eliot wrote in his great poem "East Coker" in *The Four Quartets:*

> I said to my soul, be still,
> and let the darkness come upon you
> which shall be the darkness of God.

What are your images and experiences of darkness?

❧ 5 Lent

Ezekiel 37:1-14   The valley of dry bones is stirred to life by the power of God. Bones do not tend to live again, in our experience. Yet thanks to anatomical research, painstaking measurement, and, most recently, sophisticated computer graphics, forensic artists can now take a human skull and make a sculpture or drawing that looks just like the person did in life. This technique helps identify decomposed remains, and also fleshes out history. We can at last get a fairly accurate picture from mere bones of what our stone-age ancestors and even some historical figures looked like when they were alive.

Romans 6:16-23   "Whatever you yield yourselves to, that enslaves you." I began some years ago keeping an Advent discipline of quiet by doing all my Christmas planning and shopping before the start of Advent. A great sense of peace came from not going to the malls during the holiday crush. When I did not walk the aisles filled with merchandise, when I did not flip the pages of the enticing catalogues that arrived in the mail those weeks, I spent very little money—and did not miss shopping much. Now, I try to keep Lent the same way: staying out of malls and catalogues, limiting household purchasing to the essentials. In monastic life until fairly modern times, religious were taught to "keep custody of the eyes." It was a way of preserving a contemplative solitude in a crowded building by avoiding the temptation to idle communication, keeping the appetites from being stirred, and respecting the silence and space of one's sisters or brothers. We too can choose to keep appetites simple and reserve our gaze for God, practicing a kind of conservation that helps the earth as each of us takes a smaller share of its resources.

John 11:1-44   Lazarus comes bound out of his tomb. What might he have felt and thought, suddenly reimmersed in the stream of life after having been in a place apart? He finds himself in the same old, tired body, yet somehow newborn and vulnerable, naked before the intense sunlight, the noise of amazed voices, the return of sensation to numbed limbs—perhaps like a person waking from a coma. Going on retreat into solitude, deep prayer, and silence and then reemerging into the bustle of the usual world makes me feel a bit like Lazarus, stunned on re-entry. Wendell Berry describes a wilderness retreat in similar terms: "The man who walks into the wilderness is naked indeed. He leaves behind his work, his household, his duties, his comforts—even, if he comes alone, his words. He immerses himself in what he is not. It is a kind of death."[2]

❧ *Palm Sunday*

Isaiah 52:13–53:12 The suffering servant remains a shocking image of human being deformed by illness or injury. Though Christians came to read this passage as a presaging of Jesus Christ, the description it offers is the very converse of what we think the Christ ought to look like: strong, healthy, full of vigor and beauty.

Consider this suffering servant, this Jesus mocked, scourged, and crucified; made blemished, fleshly, earthy—ultimately physical; exposed to the gaze and touch of strangers by force; weak and helpless. Consider him as a "feminized" man: bleeding, in a process that several of the ancient theologians likened to birthing; giving forth from his side water and blood, which they likened to lactation; giving his very body in an ultimate act of nurturance and love. In him the broken and estranged parts of human being are made one. Even genders are reconciled into a new resurrection body. If the images shock us, they are intended to do so, to bring us to look upon the one whom we have pierced.

Philippians 2:5-11 "Grasping equality with God" passes through my mind as I stand watching water pour through a crack in my basement wall and run into a near-by floor drain. It is March: rain and tornado season in Missouri. The mighty Mississippi where it rounds the bend enclosing St. Louis grew wide and shoaly, and a great shipping canal was built in the last century so that barges and riverboats might bypass the white water safely. But in flood season, all that careful engineering is humbled by the brown torrent that carries away whole trees, rips boats from their moorings, and reminds us of how feeble our illusion of control over nature is. It is a good season to ask oneself: "How am I grasping for equality with God? What am I trying to control? Where is this useful and where is it vanity and foolishness? In what way can I open my hands and heart and let go, taking the form of a servant?

Matthew 26:36–27:66 The landscape of the passion moves from garden to barren hilltop and back to the garden of the sepulchre. In the wonderful ancient sermon for Easter Eve that my congregation and I read each Holy Saturday at the noonday office, the unknown author writes in the voice of Christ speaking to Adam as he pulls him up from the grave into resurrection:

> For you, I your God became your Son; for you, I the Master took on your form, that of a slave; for you, I who am above the heavens came on earth and under the earth; for you, man, I became as a man without help, free among the dead; for you who left a garden, I was handed over... from a garden and crucified in a garden.... I slept on the cross and a sword pierced my side, for you, who slept

in paradise and brought forth Eve from your side. My side healed the pain in your side; my sleep will release you from your sleep in Hades; my sword has checked the sword which was turned against you. But arise, let us go hence. The enemy brought you out of paradise; I will reinstate you, no longer in paradise, but on the throne of heaven. I denied you the tree of life, which was a figure, but now I myself am united to you, I who am life.

❧ Maundy Thursday

Exodus 12:1-14   Years ago, when I was a young hospital chaplain, I remember listening to a medical colleague giving eloquent testimony about his work with AIDS patients. He likened his role to that of the angel of the Passover, reviewing in his mind's eye the dozens, the hundreds of afflicted people—the ones smitten down by illness and those astonishingly spared. "It's not that I believe God sends this plague on anyone," he said, "but that I feel called upon to remember, to give witness to what I have seen, to those I have loved, to all who have died, that they may not be forgotten."

This season calls us all to remember and bear witness. As we break bread together in the eucharist and remember Jesus' self-giving love in its institution, as we kneel to wash each other's feet, we bear witness to our precious humanity: how vulnerable, how particular each one of us is, how deep God's love for us is, how the passion (the suffering, enduring, pouring ourselves out) of each stirs the compassion of our neighbors. We are called to observe the great commandment: to love as we are loved.

1 Corinthians 11:23-32   I always extend this reading to include the next two verses, which describe just what the early church members were doing that brought judgment against them. Arriving hungry at the eucharist, they took more than their share of bread so there was not enough to go around. They were, in short, dishonoring the community and so dishonoring God. We have a sobering reminder, then, that it is not enough to come to the Lord's Table decorously and have our morsel of bread and sip of wine unless we honor by our whole conduct the community of our sisters and brothers. Chiefly, Galatians reminds us that in God's provision there is enough for all to partake if none gobble more than their share, if none forget that there are others coming after them to be fed.

Luke 22:14-30   One of our new eucharistic prayers contains an echo of the words still heard in the Roman rite, stemming from a Jewish *berekah,* or blessing: "presenting to you these gifts your earth has formed and human hands have made, we acclaim you, O Christ." There is a wondrous collaboration between earth, humankind, and God in the making of the elements that become our sacrament of communion. Matter, mind, and spirit—all are present. There is a trinitarian mingling of the three that points us toward God the Blessed Trinity, who is known to us through our body, mind, and spirit. God, who has given these things, makes use of them to present Godself to us. We make use of the stuff of creation to present ourselves back to God. Creation gives of itself beyond our making in an oblation to its Creator.

⚶ *Good Friday*

Genesis 22:1-18   Some scholars think that the binding of Isaac is the narrative that communicates Israel's complete renunciation of human sacrifice. But try hearing the text in another way: as a call to consider consecrating, offering up, the thing that to us is most precious, about which we have particular passion, in which we feel most called and blessed. This offering is not in order that something dear be destroyed, burned to cinders, but rather that it be purified and wholly dedicated to God; that we undertake it, we tend it, with a single-hearted love that serves only God.

What if we were to love and offer our earth in just this way? How would we behave in order to consecrate the planet—earth, air, water, plants, and animals—as a holy offering to its Creator? How would we lay hands on it, or forbear laying hands? How would we purify it for God's delight?

Hebrews 10:1-25   We who are far from all these cultic practices may find that the image of Christ as sacrificial animal does not take us far into the mystery of the incarnation. And so I pass along another Christ metaphor, also in its way strange, but evocative to anyone who has turned the soil of a garden:

> The most exemplary nature is that of topsoil. It is very Christ-like in its passivity and beneficence, and in the penetrating energy that issues out of its peaceableness. It increases by experience, by the passage of seasons over it, by growth rising out of it and returning to it—not by ambition or aggressiveness. It is enriched by all things that die and enter into it. It keeps the past, not as history or as memory, but as richness, new possibility. Its fertility is always

building up out of death into promise. Death is the bridge or the tunnel by which its past enters its future.[3]

We need not fear new metaphors for the divine life if they open fresh understandings, fresh appreciation for God's saving work.

John 18:1–19:37 "This is the wood of the Cross on which hung the Savior of the world; come let us worship" say many of us on this day, venerating in some fashion the instrument of Jesus' death. Ancient hymnists and theologians have found depths in the image of the cross itself: the Tree of Life from the garden of Eden, abased by human violence, hewn and erected as a gallows-tree, yet bearing into life the whole creation through Jesus' dying. In a Holy Week hymn we sing the words of sixth-century Ventantius Honorius Fortunatus:

> Faithful Cross! above all other,
>   one and only noble tree!
> None in foliage, none in blossom,
>   none in fruit thy peer may be:
> sweetest wood and sweetest iron!
>   sweetest weight is hung on thee.
> Bend thy boughs, O tree of glory!
>   Thy relaxing sinews bend;
> for awhile the ancient rigor
>   that thy birth bestowed, suspend;
> and the King of heavenly beauty
>   gently on thine arms extend.[4]

❧ *Holy Saturday*

> Today a grave holds him
> who holds creation in the palm of his hand.
> A stone covers him who covers with glory the heavens.
> Life is asleep and hell trembles
> and Adam is freed from his chains.
> Glory to your saving work by which you have done all things!
> You have given us eternal rest,
> your holy resurrection from the dead.[5]

EASTER

𝗹 The Great Vigil of Easter

This service is comprised of assorted readings from salvation history. The little history of the earth finds its fulcrum and center point, index and future in the history of Jesus. The cave of the earth can finally no longer contain the resurrection glory of God that breaks out, with angels and women as its witnesses. There follows a very tender moment in which the risen but not yet ascended Jesus goes among his dearest, intimate friends to give them hope and to say good-bye in the body. It is a time when the veil between incarnation and transcendence is thinned, and when touch can be both too confining and utterly confirming.

In baptism, the primary sacrament of this night, transcendence and immanence again touch as the candidates enter the water of death and rebirth to begin their resurrection life. The rest of life, like that tender transition for Jesus, is a time when glory shows through but sin still pains, when we are part of the life of God yet still intimately bound to the earth and one another's earthly lives—when we too are in some sense "risen but not yet ascended." And so in this baptized life we break bread and tell God's stories on the road in order to touch Christ's wounds and glimpse the Savior among us.

𝗹 Easter Day

Acts 10:34-43 Those disciples of Jesus who ate and drank with him after his resurrection become the founders of the churches. In both Judaism and Christianity, ritual meals form a central part of community life. In fact, the single aspect of early

Christian communities most central to their identity was that they ate and drank together, across the boundaries of social status and ethnic and religious affiliation, in memory of their risen Lord.

In my experience, different congregations have their own habits around community meals—both sacramental and social—and these have symbolic weight. In a congregation where many feel insufficiently loved, the parish Easter potluck may feature chips and bread and no protein. Another congregation may feel no meal is complete without lavish supplies of alcohol. One may have many cooks, but no one to clean up. One may set the altar table carelessly so it looks like an unmade bed; another may fill the altar with such a jumble of fancy silver vessels that it is impossible for the congregation to see that a meal of bread and wine is being blessed and served. One may tolerate sour wine and stale hosts; another may have lovingly home-baked bread almost every Sunday.

What are the customs and meanings of food and its service in your congregation? Does the practice fit what the congregation desires to communicate about itself and God to members? To visitors?

Colossians 3:1-4 "Set your minds on things that are above," says the author of Colossians—on Christ enthroned in the heavens. "The heavens declare the glory of God," says the psalmist. Abram is told to look up and number the stars in order to understand the scope of God's plan for Israel. Medieval Christians envisioned the cosmos like a set of nesting dolls: concentric crystal spheres ranged around the earth, with God on the outside of them all. Looking at the sky has always helped human beings to think about and revere a divinity otherwise unimaginable. Today astronomers and physicists study the cosmos by telescope, by computer, and by mathematical theory to try to "understand the mind of God" and figure out how the whole system works together.

John 20:1-18 Mary Magdalene mistakes the risen Jesus for the gardener. The great Anglican preacher Lancelot Andrewes wrote on an Easter day in the eighteenth century:

> Christ may well be said to be a gardener, and indeed is one...the gardener planted of Paradise, as God makes all our gardens green in yearly spring....He it is who gardens our *souls* too...who made such a herb grow out of the ground this day as the like was never seen before, a dead body to shoot forth alive out of the grave....By virtue of this morning's act [He] will garden our bodies too, turn all our graves into garden plots; yes, one day will turn land and sea and

all into a great garden, and so husband them as will in due time bring forth live bodies. . . . This Gardener will look to it, that man will have his spring.[1]

❦ 2 Easter

Genesis 8:6-16, 9:8-16 Was Noah's flood an historical event passed down in oral tradition? Scientists recently went looking for evidence of an ancient flood that might have given rise to the stories of Noah and Gilgamesh, 1000–2000 B.C.E.; they believed that the flood might have been a deluge of the Black Sea Basin some 7000 years ago.

During the great ice age the Black Sea is thought to have been a landlocked freshwater lake. When the earth warmed and glaciers melted, ocean levels rose and created huge pressure on the Bosporos strait separating the Black Sea from the Mediterranean until abruptly it broke through, submerging huge areas of land—up to 100,000 square kilometers. There are indications that the sea rose swiftly within a number of days to cover dried mud and land plants. In the higher levels, Mediterranean native sea creatures suddenly appeared; snails from this fossil transition layer date to 7000 years ago, fitting the flood scenario exactly. The banks of the Black Sea were populated in that era. It is possible that such a flood was remembered by the descendants of those who fled south to Mesopotamia where the Gilgamesh story developed, and north into eastern and southern Europe.[2]

1 Peter 1:3-9 The refining of gold offers romantic images to those of us who have not dealt close-up with the dirty reality of the furnace or the toxic waste of the pit mine. Gold mining in the Amazon region is one of the most hazardous professions. Miners dig holes in the mineral-rich ground, pump them full of water, add quantities of mercury to concentrate the gold, and sift through the resulting toxic sludge looking for the precious metal. If they do not die of mercury poisoning first, they will likely be stricken with malaria. Infected mosquitoes thrive in the murky water.[3] The ugly reality of gold refining might point us back toward the ugly reality of the cost of God's love for us and how precious a possession we are in God's eyes: God mines for us, refining us from the toxic environment of our sin and violence and hatred.

John 20:19-31 The gospel describes sins released and subdued by the authority of the community. Elsewhere, we are reminded to remove the log from our own eye before worrying about the splinter in our neighbor's eye. How do we find the proper balance between intervening to release or subdue sin for the sake of our own community and humankind in general, or the oppressed neighbor, given competing values and interests?

In 1996 a French genetic engineering company gained permission from the Chinese government to gather genetic data from China's 1.2 billion citizens, looking at indicators for disease or abnormality. Couples so marked who wish to marry must agree to be sterilized or practice abortion. China regards the well-being of the general population as a much higher priority than individual rights, and sees eugenics as socially useful. The French researchers hope to learn more about disease from their wide sampling. Is the benefit worth the cost? Is there a middle ground to be found between the high regard for individual rights in this country and the Chinese perspective that collective good supersedes all other concerns? What does the gospel suggest about such discernment? What is the responsibility of Christians outside France and China to involve themselves in this matter, to name or subdue sin?

☙ 3 Easter

Acts 2:14, 36-47 The Acts of the Apostles shows us early Christian communities pooling their goods and reaching out to the poor around them. In *On the Love of the Poor,* Gregory of Nazianzus makes an argument for a wider human generosity not just to fellow humans but to the whole creation:

> You have been made a child of God, co-heir with Christ. Where did you get all this, and from whom?...Who has made you master of everything on earth?...Is it not God who asks you now in your turn to show yourself generous above all other creatures and for the sake of all other creatures? Because we have received from him so many wonderful gifts, will we not be ashamed to refuse him this one thing only, our generosity?...Friends, let us never allow ourselves to misuse what has been given us by God's gift....We shall hear St. Peter say: "...Resolve to imitate God's justice and no one will be poor."

1 Peter 1:17-23 Seed is both fragile and tough. Grain buried in ancient Egyptian pyramids has been successfully germinated after millennia in that dry, airless environment. Yet if seed becomes damp, it can be quickly destroyed. Many nations have established seed banks to try to preserve local plant species that might otherwise disappear. Sometimes such indigenous plants can be hybridized with imported varieties to add resistance to local climatic conditions or to strengthen the stock. In Africa a bold plan is underway among several small nations to move seed from one country to another in the event of war or natural disaster: plant varieties would then be preserved to the potential benefit of all. So far, the United States has been slow to help fund seed banks. We are a major exporter of new seed varieties, so there are competing interests at work.

Luke 24:13-35 As they near Emmaeus, the disciples describe the burning of their hearts within as the sign of Christ's presence. We may conclude that what they experienced was not just a physical sensation of excitement and heat, but also a kind of unitive vision. This is common to those who encounter the numinousness of God—a sudden insight that the whole universe is shot through with meaning and beauty, that it hangs together cohesively and with purpose. As they heard familiar scripture recited by their beloved teacher, perhaps they were overtaken with the sense that all *works together* for God's glory: their own lives intersected and extended that story of divine salvation into the present moment and filled the future with hope. Both scientists and poets have described moments of holy unitive vision—like the mathematician Mandlebrodt's dream in which a lattice of strings suddenly shifted from an image of chaos into one of repeating patterns, small to large, suggesting an ordered universe. Or Gerard Manley Hopkins' poem "God's Grandeur," which begins, "The world is charged with the grandeur of God." What have been your own glimpses of God? Do we provide an opportunity for sharing our encounters with the holy in our congregations?

❦ 4 Easter

Nehemiah 9:6-15 The story of Israel's salvation is told in brief: God hears the cries of the oppressed, delivers them from bondage, leads them into a place of promise, builds up the new city, establishes justice. Many of the biblical authors, Jewish and Christian, share this same concern: to look for the pattern of divine activity.

A computer program called "Swarm" was developed a few years ago at the Santa Fe Institute to recreate the patterns of individuals flocking together, such as schools of fish, traffic jams, insect swarms, flocks of birds, or crowds of pedestrians. With no central leadership or organization, these mobs of individuals nonetheless follow complex patterns of collective behavior and abide by rules. Social scientists have used similar programs to reproduce the rise and fall of historic societies—such as the Assyrian and Byzantine empires—with surprising accuracy. Behaviors may seem random in individuals but patterns emerge when seen collectively.

Though the reasons for the sudden downfall of a society may be unknown, scientists hypothesize that when wealthy individuals in power begin to hoard too much of the society's resources, a crisis may result. Social contracts then unravel. Eventually it is hoped that this computer modeling technology will provide answers for historians about social trends in past and present civilizations. It may allow the testing of certain political and economic strategies to see if they will help or hinder human development, or predict the migration of refugees, the stressing of resources, and patterns of violence in conflicts of peoples and cultures.[4] These days doomsayers predict the downfall of the church and the end of Christendom. Looking for the ancient patterns of God's destroying and rebuilding, deliverance and promise, might renew our hope.

1 Peter 2:19-25   He bore our sins in his body on the tree. The embodied God is crucified on the tree of life; creation dies in him and is resurrected. Anglican theologian Sallie McFague speaks of God's transcendence:

> The model of the universe as God's body radicalizes transcendence, for *all* of the entire fifteen billion-year history and the billions of galaxies is the creation, the outward being, of the One who is the source and breath of all existence. In the universe as a whole, as well as in each and every bit and fragment of it, God's transcendence is embodied. We do not see God's face, but only the back. But we *do* see the back.[5]

If we were to understand creation as Christ's body, what would be the implications for our relationships with its elements? How might we pray differently?

John 10:1-10   "I am the door of the sheep." Surely this is as homely a metaphor as Jesus could have attached to himself, plain as a split-rail fence. It is as though Jesus, in our time, were to say, "I am the garage door-opener." But what could be more homely than for God, in Jesus' human flesh, to say, "I am this"? The concreteness, the domesticity, the finitude of the incarnation is everything in expressing God's unstinting love for us.

> Human nature is. . . but a hazy devotional idea until Christ is seen in the world and in relation to particular creatures: the homes at Nazareth and Bethany, the mountain top and wilderness, the water that turned into wine and the stones that did not turn into bread, the doves in the temple, the fish in the boat, the

palms before the ass, and the withered fig tree; how tremendously important these things are![6]

❦ 5 Easter

Acts 17:1-15 The crowd to whom the apostles are preaching turns into an angry mob bent on violence. When a large group of individuals suffers general dissatisfaction or distress within a disorganized social structure, crowd hysteria may result. Individuals in crowded circumstances are measurably more stressed, have higher blood pressure, report disliking people more often, become more withdrawn and less interactive, are more suggestible, become more aggressive (men in particular), and are less able to think critically. Delusionary thinking, or a manifestation of certain behaviors or symptoms, may spread rapidly through a crowd, causing individuals to act in a manner they would not adopt under other circumstances. The positive energy of a crowd—at an athletic event or concert, for example—can quickly turn to rage or panic or erupt in violent behavior if there is a precipitating crisis. Within a congregation, a milder form of contagious negative thinking can gain momentum unless leaders and individuals become aware of their behavior and change it, communicating with others in the process.

1 Peter 2:1-10 "Living stones": what a compelling image. In the summer of 1998 we were all riveted by reports that a meteorite from Mars appeared to contain fossils of living organisms. Could it be that the soft bodies of tiny worm-like creatures had been trapped in sediment until crystals replaced the molecules of their bodies, reproducing them in the stone? There was debate back and forth over months. The conclusion was inconclusive: probably not life, merely mineral deposits that happened to be stringy like worms. Part of our bodies, like those of all living creatures, is "stone." If all the water were removed, we would consist of four or five pounds of minerals—mainly calcium from our bones with traces of other metals. Without minute amounts of these trace elements, we soon sicken and die, just as with an excess of many of them we are poisoned to death. So we are *living* stones.

John 14:1-14 In my Father's house are many mansions, many dwelling places. This is an image of hospitality to the multiplicity of persons in God's domain. In God's world are many ecosystems with room for a great variety of creatures. Like the rooms of a house, the cells of a monastery, or the homes of a neighborhood, somehow there is an organizing principle, a unity of parts that contains all. One scientist speaks to this unity:

> Once dismissed as little more than New Age mysticism . . . today, researchers are viewing Gaia and the whole notion of the [earth as] superorganism in the light of modern mathematical theory of complexity. Although a precise definition is elusive, a superorganism can be thought of as a group of individual organisms whose collective behavior leads to group-level functions that resemble the behavior of a single organism.[7]

He cites a beehive or an ant colony as examples of a superorganism. Those who agree with this definition for the earth look to the emergence of stable, repeating patterns in diverse ecosystems. Though the earth does not reproduce and has not evolved in the same way as other organisms, it is a hugely complex system of interrelated parts— a house with many dwelling places.

❦ 6 Easter

Isaiah 41:17-20 "I will make the wilderness a pool of water," says God to the prophet; it will be a sign of divine life revivifying the creation. In the Asian heart of the former Soviet Union lies the once-huge Aral Sea. In the thirty years since its two feeder rivers began to be diverted for irrigating vast cotton fields, the sea has lost two-thirds of its water and continues to shrink at the rate of 27 cubic kilometers a year. As it has dried up, a fishing industry has been lost. Wind carrying lake-bed dust, toxic with pesticides and fertilizers along with salt, sweeps over a vast terrain as far as Pakistan. As the water level drops, nearby aquifers have also become polluted; drinking water is causing illness in the region. In twenty years no sea will remain. The cost for making this desert bloom briefly has been higher than anyone anticipated.

Acts 17:22-31 Paul gives a name and identity to an unknown God worshiped in Athens. I am reminded of the way science butts up against its limits when thinking about the origins of the universe—and must stop short of being able to identify a creator—bounded by the limits of time. In *The Confessions*, fifth-century Augustine describes the universe created "with time" rather than "in time": in his view it was not meaningful to talk about time before creation, when time did not exist, though God existed outside time. These days scientists also point out that it is impossible to talk about time before the quantum fluctuation that began the universe. From their perspective, it is impossible to speak scientifically about God outside time. For many scientists, in the beginning there was some sort of unified force that divided into the four forces of our universe after the big bang: strong and weak nuclear forces, electromagnetic force, and gravitational force. These shaped the physical universe of matter: subatomic particles first, then atoms, gas clouds, stars, planets, complex molecules, and ultimately, living organisms. The origins of all begin in the mystery of eternity before time—where the unknown God operates, whom we name and proclaim as Creator, Word, and Spirit.

John 15:1-8 The health of the vine is maintained by grafting and pruning. Pruning diverts the plant's resources from dead, diseased, or barren branches to the other healthier ones. Grafting brings together plants of different varieties so that a shoot of one is snipped, shaped, and inserted into a cut in the other as it grows. The new shoot (the scion, or cion) then begins to draw resources from the old plant and becomes a part of it as the cut surfaces heal together; it may confer disease resistance, vigor, and a new sort of fruit to the old plant. In turn, the old plant offers a strong established rootstock, hardiness, and adaptation to local soil and climactic conditions. To graft successfully, two plants must be congenial, that is, able to adapt to each other. Sometimes a chunk of stem from a third species can be interposed between two uncongenial plants to help them accept one another.

This is a lovely analogy for the great variety of ways new members join a community and add to its life. Are they readily accepted, or do they require extra mediation to settle in? Perhaps these grafting designs will bring to mind some issues related to acceptance and fruitfulness in your own congregation.

❦ 7 Easter

Acts 1:1-14 Looking up to heaven is an activity that seemed to be distracting the men of Galilee from their proper business of getting on with being apostles. We, on the other hand, may not spend enough time looking up to heaven to be reminded of the marvelous imagination and intelligence of the one who created such glory. Journalist Timothy Ferris describes the experience of looking through a telescope:

> The human retina is constructed upside down . . . so that the optic nerves . . . converge and drop back toward the brain through a hole near the center of the retina. The brain pretties things up by paving over the hole with a concoction of portraiture borrowed from the immediately surrounding part of the visual field, so in day-to-day life we don't notice that there's a black hole in the cen-

ter of everything we see. But the trick is exposed when peering through a telescope at the night sky: dim things disappear if you look right at them. Deep-space observers combat this effect by employing averted vision, meaning that they look slightly away from the objects of their attention. Averted vision is the deepest vision.[8]

Might we explore an "averted" spiritual vision—seeing indirectly and thus more accurately?

1 Peter 4:12-19 We have a faithful Creator whom St. Anselm celebrates in this twelfth-century hymn:

> All nature is created by God and God is born of Mary.
> God created all things, and Mary gave birth to God.
> God who made all things made himself of Mary,
> and thus he refashioned everything he had made.
> He who was able to make all things out of nothing
> refused to remake it by force,
> but first became the Son of Mary.
> So God is the Father of all created things,
> and Mary is the mother of all re-created things.

John 17:1-11 "They are in the world but do not belong to it." The gospel speaks to the experience of the little Christian community named after John who felt besieged and threatened by the culture around them and sought to keep separate and pure. By comparison, Bishop Leo reveals a more grounded and comfortable sense of the relationship of the faithful and the world in his fifth-century "Sermon for the Nativity":

> Rouse yourself and recognize the dignity of your human nature. Remember that you were made in God's image: though corrupted in Adam, that image has been restored in Christ. Use creatures as they should be used: the earth, the sea, the sky, the air, the springs and rivers. Give praise and glory to their Creator for all that you find beautiful and wonderful in them. . . . Our words and exhortations are not intended to make you disdain God's works or think there is anything contrary to your faith in creation, for the good God has himself made all things good. What we do ask is that you use reasonably and with moderation all the marvellous creatures which adorn this world.

❧ *The Day of Pentecost*

Ezekiel 11:17-20   Our fleshly hearts are more wondrous than we suppose. Contrary to popular thought, the healthy heart does *not* beat in a perfectly even rhythm; it is diseased hearts that tend to adopt rigid, regular rhythms. The natural rhythm of the heart is complex, even chaotic—irregular but not random. The heartbeat is regulated by a node of cells that generates an electrical impulse to contract the heart muscles in sequence. Research into heart rhythms is raising questions about all the body's dynamic patterns, suggesting that disease is a failing of a complex dynamic set of processes into less dynamic and more predictable patterns.

Acts 2:1-11   Hearing the Word of God in our own languages is an eschatological experience: all the impediments to understanding will finally be cleared away and the Word alone will be heard. Hearing is a marvelous function of our senses, the loss of which may bring disruption of relationships not just with other people, but with the entire natural world of sound. Most people know that the inner ear contains three little bones that sense vibrations in the fluid within the eardrum and pass along nerve impulses to the brain, which then interprets them as sound. Less well known is the role of 30,000 sensory hair cells called stereocilia on the cochlea, a little spiral organ of the inner ear. As the fluid vibrates, it brushes the hairs, whose protein molecules lever open ionic channels inside the hair. This enables potassium ions to flow from tip to root, triggering an electrical message through the nerve.

Those who have never had hearing teach us that communication is still richly possible: the word may be transmitted eloquently by signing, image, or the movement of lips. God's Word will be made known to us in our own languages. As Meister Eckhart describes it, "God is constantly speaking only one thing. God's speaking is one thing. In this one utterance God speaks the Son and at the same time the Holy Spirit and all creatures." Together, we are the speaking of God.

John 20:19-23   "Peace be with you," says Jesus. Peace is not just an absence of conflict; from its Jewish roots, *shalom* refers to prosperity, completeness, wholeness, balance, fulfillment, harmonious relationships, and the abiding presence of God making all of this possible. Peace always carries an eschatological meaning as it leans toward that perfection in which God will be all in all. *Shalom* encompasses not just people, but also the land and its creatures. There can be no peace while humankind and the earth are in conflict. In the fulfillment of God's *shalom*, all things will be unified in Christ, who holds all things in unity (Colossians 1:15-17) and who is their destiny in God's "plan for the fullness of time" (Ephesians 1:9-10).

🌿 *Trinity Sunday*

Genesis 1:1–2:3 The creation of the cosmos. In 1927 Abbé Georges Lemaître theorized backward through his mathematical calculations from an expanding universe to its origin: a dazzling fireball—the explosion of a "primeval atom" or cosmic egg of hot, compressed matter—that scattered the galaxies into a new universe. He wrote, "Standing on a cooled cinder, we see the slow fading of suns, and we try to recall the vanished brilliance of the origin of the worlds."[9] From his thought developed the theory of the origin of the physical universe we know as the big bang.

2 Corinthians 13:5-14 "Examine yourselves; show improvement," instructs the apostle. Relationships of every sort are to be set right. This process of self-monitoring and making an effort to change is akin to athletic training. I tend to think of athletes as preoccupied with their own bodies and performances in an inward-turned way, so I was surprised to read this observation of a trainer:

> Most runners I know have a sincere concern for preserving the environment. It occurs to me that their environmental awareness might be a natural outgrowth of their interest in fitness. We run in order to return ourselves to fitness. The aim of the environmental movement is to perform the same kind of recuperative work on the earth itself: to achieve, or restore, its physical fitness.[10]

Why not ask all the athletes in the congregation to talk about the way their training relates them to the earth, to their sense of the creation, and to the human community?

Matthew 28:16-20 "Go make disciples of all nations," says the gospel. Meditating on the text in a wider frame, I find myself thinking about all that we—as Americans, as Episcopalians, as Christians, as human beings with unearned privilege—export to other countries. Whether we will it or not, something of who we are and what we believe about God and our neighbors is communicated in those products. Among other things, we export tobacco. If, as predicted, one in every three young men in China will die from a smoking-related illness, this will mean 100 million deaths in the next few decades—a staggering number. The latest research suggests that smoking acts synergistically with other disease processes and environmental and biological conditions to cause illness. In the United States, lung cancer is the leading smoking-related cause of death; in China, other respiratory diseases kill a larger proportion of smokers, and tuberculosis is also a major contender. Those to whom we should be exporting love in God's name are receiving from us instead early death in the name of our economy.

THE SEASON AFTER PENTECOST

❧ *Proper 1*

Ecclesiasticus 15:11-20   Choose life or death, says the ancient voice of wisdom. We make such choices daily when we develop land and so drive organisms into extinction. When rare species become extinct, are we merely losing curiosities of marginal value? From a biologist's perspective, rare species have many values. Rare relatives of common medicinal or food plants may contain more potent genes that could enhance their domesticated kin. Wild American grapes recently saved European wine grape stock from a plague of root-destroying phyoxera lice that threatened to destroy the whole wine industry. Much prized domestic flowers like sunflowers have been bred by crossing genes from wild varieties that are now dying out in the south. Botanists argue that loss of rare plants in the United States alone could be worth billions of dollars a year.

For Christians money is not the only issue. The diversity of creation reflects the mind and will of the Creator, and therefore is a source of knowledge about God. When we willfully drive species out of existence we are, in some sense, putting out our own spiritual eyes and choosing to know less of our Creator than we should. We are throwing away God's gifts to us still wrapped and unexamined, and we are squandering our descendants' heritage—choosing death over life.

1 Corinthians 3:1-9   Some need milk, not solid food, writes Paul. Milk has its place. Recent research suggests that mothers do well to breastfeed for at least a year if they are able: their babies suffer fewer infections and allergies and have lower risk of diabetes as they mature, and mothers are less likely to develop ovarian and breast cancers and osteoporosis in later life.[1] In the spiritual life, too, simple, well-balanced, digestible instruction helps the neophyte. But as we grow in our lives in Christ we are expected to become more sophisticated in our theological thought, to make more careful discernments, to seek nuance, and to accept more of the asceticism—the self-control and discipline—that go with adult life.

Matthew 5:21-37 Be reconciled to your neighbor before you approach God. Where is our relationship with global neighbors most in need of reconciliation? The most stunning example of corporate reconciliation I know is that of post-apartheid South Africa, with its commitment to rebuilding justice through forgiveness. One commentator writes:

> When the people of South Africa's new democracy find themselves still required to pay back debts which the apartheid regime incurred in order to buy the tanks and guns that killed those engaged in the struggle for liberation, we know we are dealing with a scandal.... The real cost of imagining the release of the debts of the poorest nations is our fear: fear that the whole system of relying on owing for survival might collapse... that we might have to trim our spending to what we have today.[2]

❦ *Proper 2*

Leviticus 19:1-2, 9-18 Do not reap to the border of the field. As a very small child in Britain, I developed an abiding love for hedgerows, those impenetrable shrubby walls enclosing pastures and crops. After World War II, huge numbers of hedgerows were dug up and replaced with modern fencing so that crops might be grown to the edges of the fields. In the four decades before 1985, 96,000 miles of hedgerow were lost—enough to circle the earth four times—and another 53,000 from 1985 to 1990. But the trend is finally reversing as conservationists and farmers alike recognize the value of these complex ecosystems.

Some existing hedgerows are unimaginably old. Ditches and dikes in Cornwall topped with shrubbery date to the Bronze Age. One Cambridgeshire farmer keeps a hedgerow planted by a niece of William the Conqueror that is some 900 years old. The age of a hedgerow can be estimated by the number of species in a length: about 100 years for each species in a 100-foot length of naturally populated hedge. Hedgerows are thick with wildflower, insect, and animal species. If you sit beside one, you can hear the rustling and gnawing, chirping and squeaking of creatures. More than 800 kinds of wildflower have been identified in British hedgerows. Small rodents rely on them for winter shelter, and small birds for nesting cover. Under the roots burrowing creatures find safety and food.[3]

1 Corinthians 3:10-23 "You are God's temple," says the apostle. Paul is not speaking here primarily of the physical body as a temple, but of the spiritual formation, the sound theology, the discipline of prayer and right behavior that together make up the spiritual human being. The proper care of the body, for Paul, is never an end in itself, but always in order that God may be honored in it and with it. We are neither to idolize nor to deprecate our bodies, but to practice discipline out of thankfulness for what we have been given. Writing in the late fourth century, Gregory of Nyssa comments:

> In our human life bodily health is a good thing, but this blessing consists not merely in knowing the causes of good health but in actually enjoying it. If we eulogize good health and then eat food that has unhealthy effects, what good is our praise of health when we find ourselves on a sickbed?[4]

Matthew 5:38-48 Rain falls on the just and the unjust. In the 1970s acid rain became a household topic of concern, and throughout the 1980s stringent controls on emissions of sulfur and nitrogen oxide came into practice. Nonetheless there are indications that the nearly 50 percent drop in emissions will not solve the acidity problem or save threatened ecosystems. American emission controls so far have proven far less expensive than predicted, while tradable pollution permits have played a useful though modest role in reducing the costs of compliance with clean air standards. Switching to cleaner fuels has been cost effective, though the use of low-sulfur coal has resulted in the burning of larger quantities. As a result, more carbon dioxide is emitted, contributing to the greenhouse effect; one problem is exchanged for another. Generally, controlling acid rain has been good for business, not injurious.[5]

🌿 *Proper 3*

Isaiah 49:8-18 Can a woman forget her nursing child? God never forsakes us, but Isaiah notes that a mother might, under some circumstances, forsake her infant. We so idealize the relationship between mother and infant that we often overlook the stresses and strains of this new relationship, making it difficult for new mothers to express their negative emotions. One book on the postpartum experience estimates that "from 50 to 80 percent of all new mothers experience some short-lived negative feelings that can be classified as the 'blues'," involving weepiness, exhaustion, irritability, and sleeplessness in the first couple of weeks after giving birth. For a small percentage of women these postpartum symptoms are acute, even life-threatening, but all, with appropriate help, are treatable.[6]

1 Corinthians 4:1-13 Bringing to light the things now hidden is the task of Christ at the end time of judgment. Because we have minds in the image of Christ, it is our predilection and delight to be also seekers of what is hidden in our world, to be endlessly curious. Our knowing is minute before the wisdom of creation. In the microscopic world, for example, biologists have to date identified around 5,000 species of bacteria, only a fraction of the probable millions that abound in earth, air, and water. Some are brand new forms of life, more different from one another than a person is from an elephant. No one yet knows what function these strains serve in their ecosystem, nor how so many exist side by side in a small space. Some bacteria are ubiquitous, while others are tailored for remarkably specialized environments like a hot spring or a sub-oceanic steam vent.

Every animal that goes extinct likely takes with it into oblivion several species of microbes that live in or on it exclusively. Why should we care about bacterial extinction? First, because these organisms play vital roles within their habitats. Second, because they may contain new antibiotics and chemicals of great potential use to us. And finally, because they also are God's remarkable creatures and reveal some aspect of divine wisdom.

Matthew 6:24-34 What were these "lilies of the field"? Flowers in biblical times had common collective names and it is difficult to pinpoint which one is intended. The white *Lilium candidum* grows in Israel, lifting its strong vertical stems of trumpet-shaped blooms out of the summer pasture. This was likely the lily (*shushan* in Hebrew) described in the Song of Songs: "I am a rose of Sharon, a lily of the valleys. As a lily among brambles, so is my love among maidens" (2:1–2). Matthew's *krina* in Greek denotes these white lilies, which came to be associated with Easter and with Jesus himself, the "Lily of the valley." Jesus might also have been referring to wildflowers in general—the tulips, poppies, anemones, daisies, and crocuses that cover the more fertile meadows by the Sea of Galilee to this day.

❦ *Proper 4*

Deuteronomy 11:18-28 "May the days of your children be multiplied" is an ancient blessing and wish. Human beings do live longer than other primates. One study of indigenous peoples of Tanzania described how women past menopause continued to gather large amounts of wild food even after their own children were grown and independent, and that this surplus was given to feed grandchildren. Researchers theorize that by insuring these grandchildren did not starve before reproducing, transmission of the grandmothers' genes down the generations increased. Natural selection, so it seems, would favor families with longer-lived and altruistic grandmothers. Aside from the biological argument, it is interesting to consider how "grandmotherly" cooperation in resource sharing has the potential to prolong life for all the world's children.

Romans 3:21-28 Paul's comments on the restrictions of the law invite us to consider the limited ability of institutions to hold and express dynamic truth. Similarly, we might ask in what way structures and their formal or traditional ways of thinking and acting toward creation prevent us from letting the fresh wind of the gospel stir us in new directions. How do national church initiatives help or stifle local enthusiasm and efforts for the care of creation? Has your local congregation participated in the national care of creation agenda by reviewing legislation from General Convention, or sending legislation up to it from the parish or diocese? Are there materials you could share? Are there local success stories that need to be told as good news for the wider church? Environmental missionaries you could send visiting? Perhaps there are local pains and problems that could use help, prayer, and intervention from the wider church. How do the structures of which you are a part, religious and secular, relate to the stewardship of the earth?

Matthew 7:21-27 The wise are those who build on the rock in the parable, but a good many cities are built on shaky ground, where the plates of earth's deep structure are in motion. We are well aware of the San Andreas fault in California and the whole network of subsidiary faults in that area. The New Madrid Fault running near St. Louis gave rise to the largest measured earthquake in U. S. history: in 1812 a series of three earthquakes that measured 8.4 on the Richter scale leveled the town of New Madrid and rang church bells as far away as Boston. The Mississippi River changed its course. Today there are six cities in the vicinity of the fault. A quake as small as 7.6 could kill an estimated 3,000 people and do $38.2 million in damage, according to the Central U. S. Earthquake Consortium. There is an 86 percent chance of a major quake in the area in the next fifty years. All our wisdom seems small compared to the complexity around us.

❧ *Proper 5*

Romans 4:13-18 For our medieval ancestors, earth was the center of nesting crystal spheres carrying the sun, the moon and planets, and the stars beyond, each ruled by a rank of angels, with the great empyrean of God on the outermost layer. In the same era, Jewish mystics of the Kabbala envisioned God as having ten aspects or *sephirot*, with the *Ein Sof,* the unknowable One from whom proceeded the initial light and matter of the universe, beyond them all. These ideas correspond strikingly with modern theories of initial dramatic inflation and ongoing expansion in the universe. Kabbalists describe the first *sephirah* as *Keter,* God's infinite potential to create; the second as *Hokhmah,* the bursting of the physical universe from the potential universe; and the third as *Binah,* a steadily expanding cosmos within the eternal womb.[7]

Early astronomers were almost invariably theologians, and to this day it is only a small number who insist that in science there is no room for a creator. Nearly 40 percent of American scientists polled by *Nature* believe in a personal God to whom they pray, close to the same number who expressed this belief in a survey of 1916.[8] An even larger number might be expected to claim some less-defined religious belief.

Hosea 5:15–6:6; Matthew 9:9-13 "It is God who has torn, and God will heal us," says the prophet Hosea. And we read in Matthew: "Those who are well have no need of a physician, but those who are sick." We call God our divine physician and the author of healing, and the church the hospital of souls. Religion is good for our physical and emotional health, too, and there is data to confirm it. A study of 400 elderly poor residents of Connecticut concludes that three psychological variables are significant in predicting mortality: religiousness, happiness, and offspring. Another study found a consistent pattern of lower systolic and diastolic blood pressures among frequent church attenders compared to infrequent attenders, independent of variations in smoking, age, obesity, or socioeconomic status. The researchers theorize that church attendance is connected to maintenance of hope; regulation of depression, fear, and anxiety; and protection of social-personal integration—all related to physical arousal patterns that affect blood pressure. In a community health survey, active (attending religious services at least once a month) rather than passive religious allegiance was correlated with a decrease in symptoms of illness.[9]

🕮 *Proper 6*

Exodus 19:2-8 God bears us up on eagles' wings. Well, vulture's wings actually! There is a good bit of imprecision about birds in the Bible. In detailing birds that may not be eaten (raptors and scavengers), Leviticus 11:13 lists several kinds of vulture. The word (*nesher*) appears twenty-six times in the Bible. The authors of *The Theological Wordbook of the Old Testament* suggest that "eagle" is the best translation in passages that emphasize the bird's strength, swiftness, and care of the young, but another term is used for a "lesser breed of bird"—those who ate carrion flesh.[10] An interesting case of prejudice overcoming scientific observation!

Romans 5:6-11 The Greek word we translate as "reconciliation" might also be properly translated "put into friendship with." It is a word from diplomacy establishing council, affection, mutuality. Theologians including Gregory the Great, Gregory of Nyssa, and Alcuin wrote of our friendship with God and God's with us. Less has been written in early Christian theology about our being friends with creation. For that we must listen hard to Francis, Julian, and even the Celtic Christian Pelagius, dismissed by many as a heretic, who saw God's spirit in all living things and cautioned against using our power in abusing animals and plants. In one of his letters Pelagius notes, "When our love is directed toward an animal or even a tree, we are participating in the fullness of God's love." How then shall we practice reconciliation with creation in our own place and time, and not in a naive way, but with maturity of understanding and generosity of spirit?

Matthew 9:35–10:15 "The harvest is plentiful, but the laborers are few." The work of mission is often very ordinary, unglamorous, and humdrum, so we find ourselves reluctant to do it. We hope for more interesting work than the same old round of our office or home, or of the church community: visiting the sick, giving food to the hungry, encouraging the imprisoned, caring for the marginalized, advocating for those oppressed. Surely there must be some more spiritual work, our minds whisper to us. But Julian of Norwich offers this firm advice:

> Be a gardener. Dig a ditch, toil and sweat and turn the earth upside down and seek the deepness and water the plants in time. Continue this labour and make sweet floods to run and noble and abundant fruits to spring. Take this food and drink and carry it to God as your true worship.

❧ *Proper 7*

Jeremiah 20:7-13 "I must shout, 'Violence and destruction!'" cries the prophet among people who fear the violence they see around them. Many in our culture, too, are frightened by what they interpret as increasing violence, though it becomes difficult to sort out whether violence is increasing or just gets more publicity in our time. A 1993 study found a positive correlation between exposure to violent incidents on film and children's tendency to push one another, and adults' use of abusive actions. The study also noted that those who watched violence in the media became more afraid of being a victim of violence and developed a greater appetite for watching violence on television.

Perhaps the cycle of increasing violence could be broken if we could respond to our fears rationally—by gathering accurate information about crime statistics, for example, instead of just buying more home security devices, or by setting up a neighborhood watch program instead of staying inside behind locked doors— and cultivate our own compassion by listening to the stories of others and choosing to help. How might congregations work to break the cycle of violence, both actual and perceived, in their own neighborhoods and homes?[11]

Romans 5:15-19 One man's act of righteousness sets right the cosmos. It summons us to grow into responsibility for how we use our one "wild and precious life," as poet Mary Oliver calls it. In the realm of science, most of the great contributions are made by professionals who spend decades honing their skills. Astronomy, however, is an arena in which amateurs not infrequently make significant discoveries of new things. Anyone with some knowledge, a telescope, persistence, and good fortune might identify a new supernova, or a comet not formerly recorded.

In California John Dobson is the maven of amateur astronomy. Featured on television news spots and in magazine human interest columns, Dobson's goal is to help everyone get a look through a telescope at the wonders of the sky. To this end, he sets up his own use-worn telescope on the streets of San Francisco, invites passers-by to have a look, and fills them with information about what they are seeing. It was another amateur, David Levy, who with Eugene and Carolyn Shoemaker discovered the comet bearing their names that crashed so dramatically into Jupiter in 1994. Such exciting discoveries are delightful reminders of the value of one person's devoted effort, and the joy of commitment to building up the sum of human knowledge.

Matthew 10:16-33 Not a sparrow will fall to the ground apart from God. In fact, from observation one might conclude that God takes good care of sparrows, gifting them with the innate knowledge necessary for survival. What is the natural wisdom of birds? Ornithologists in India discovered that sparrows line their nests with leaves of a tree rich in quinine, even if they have to fly some distance to obtain them. Previously the same sparrows lined their nests with another leaf. The switch to new housing material coincided with the outbreak of malaria in the area; scientists suspect the birds now choose leaves that help kill the malaria parasite.[12]

Proper 8

Isaiah 2:10-17 The cedars of Lebanon and the oaks of Bashan were cut down over 2000 years ago, victims of deforestation before the word existed. The World Conservation Monitoring Centre in Cambridge, England has reported that 10 percent of tree species around the world are in danger of extinction—some 976 species. Up to 300 insect species may be dependent on a single species of tree, so tree loss can initiate a cascade of extinctions. Together these studies support warnings that habitat destruction is significantly impacting life on our planet. Few endangered trees are in protected lands or subject to any conservation efforts. Almost every nation has some trees in danger, though 80 percent of all species are tropical, so losses in those areas—especially Malaysia, Indonesia, Brazil, India, and Hawaii—threaten to be largest. Conservationists recommend that every country protect 10 percent of its forests from timber loss.

Romans 6:3-11 We are baptized into Christ's death, and so we become those to whom death is never merely an enemy but always the path through which we travel into our full birthright of resurrection. This does not mean we do not fear death, of course, or wish to postpone it until a necessary and fitting time, but we rejoice that death does not have the last word over us. We also look death in the eye, prepare for it as a spiritual discipline, and practice decency and humaneness toward those facing death.

"The Dying Person's Bill of Rights," formulated at a workshop on the terminally ill and their caregivers, includes the right to participate in decisions, to be free from pain, to expect honesty, to maintain hopefulness, and to have help in facing death.[13] Are there other potential rights and universal desires for the dying person? What is the role of churches in intervening at medical institutions on behalf of patients, particularly those facing death?

Matthew 10:34-42 A cup of cold water is a gift of infinite value in time of thirst. As water grows scarcer around the world, we may have to begin paying attention to our indirect use through consumption of foods that require large amounts of water. Cornell scientist David Pimental has assessed the water used to produce a range of foods. Rice requires 1,900 or more liters per kilogram to grow, compared to 500 liters for potatoes. Wheat and alfalfa both consume 900 liters, while soybeans consume 2,000. Chicken requires 3,500 liters per kilogram, and beef a huge 100,000 liters per kilo, which works out to 11 cubic meters of water per quarter-pound hamburger! In the future, even in America, we will need to consider our stewardship of limited water supplies in the production of food.[14]

❧ *Proper 9*

Zechariah 9:9-12 It is no accident that dominion is "from sea to sea, and the river to the ends of the earth." Control of the coastline meant ensured commerce abroad, and control of the great rivers secured not only a transportation route, but also water to drink, irrigate crops, and support dense populations in prosperity. In our time, too, control of the waterways and their adjacent lands is a source of conflict in that part of the world: Egypt and Ethiopia are struggling for control of Nile water. Previously, Egypt had control over most of it with their great Aswan dam, but now Ethiopia wants to dam Lake Tana—the source of the Blue Nile—and could potentially divert most of Egypt's water supply. Egyptian political leader Boutros Boutros-Ghali was recently quoted in newspapers as saying "the next war in our region will be over the waters of the Nile." The Hebrew scriptures reflect times in which conquerors simply took the spoils of war—no longer an adequate way to settle disputes.

Romans 7:21–8:6 Spirit and flesh live in an uneasy relationship for Paul, as they did for Augustine a few centuries later: both men seem to have wrestled with sins of the flesh, but neither was content to separate flesh and spirit. In Romans, Paul uses flesh and spirit to name two categories of experience: the mortal and the immortal, the sinful and the godly. Yet he also uses the metaphor of the body and its parts in wholeness as the primary image of human relatedness in the church. And in *The Confessions* Augustine writes:

> So I saw plainly and clearly that you have made all things good, nor are there any substances at all which you have not made. And because you did not make all things equal, therefore they each and all have their existence; because they are good individually, and at the same time they are altogether very good, because our God made all things very good.

Matthew 11:25-30 "Come to me, all you that are weary," says Jesus, and yes, we as a society are weary! Sleep disorders affect huge numbers of people, and have been labeled by some as America's largest health problem. Ranging from rare forms of life-threatening insomnia to the average person's tendency to burn the candle at both ends, sleeplessness is increasing. Third shifts and double shifts tax even sound sleepers. Workers who are interrupted often during the night, like medical residents, begin to experience "microsleeps" after twenty-four hours on the job, losing consciousness for moments at a time without even being aware of it—a dangerous situation for a surgeon, a truck driver, or an equipment operator. Doctors, many of whom suffer from severe sleep disruption themselves, frequently fail to diagnose sleep ailments in their patients, even when these people present with chronic fatigue. Christ offers relief for the weariness of our souls, but it is a spiritual as well as a health discipline for us to take responsibility for the weariness of our bodies and for finding a sane and holy pace of life.

🌢 *Proper 10*

Isaiah 55:1-13 God's word goes out like the rain and the snow to give life to the seed and the sower. In a mystical vision recorded in *Scivias* Hildegard of Bingen hears God say:

> I hold the green land in my power. I never gave that power to you, did I, O person, so that you might make it grow whatever fruit you pick? And if you sow seed in that land, you are not able, are you, to bring that seed forth into fruitfulness? No. For you do not bring forth the dew, nor send forth the rain, nor allot the moisture in the greenness of the land. You do not give the warmth of the burning sun.... Similarly, you are able to sow words into the ears of a person. But you are not strong enough to pour into the person's heart—which is like my land—neither the dew of penitence, nor the rain of tears, nor the moisture of devotion, nor the warmth of the holy Spirit. In all of these, the fruit of holiness buds forth.

Romans 8:9-17 By baptism we receive a spirit of adoption. In his thirty-fifth letter, fourth-century Ambrose of Milan expands our view of this kinship far beyond our individualist thinking: "This adoption is that of the whole body of creation, when it will be as it were a child of God and see the divine, eternal goodness face to face."

The creatures become our siblings in this adoptive family, not our property to domi-
nate and subdue.

Matthew 13:1-23   In the "postscript" to Matthew's parable, the prudent sower works
to sow the seeds in accordance with their requirements for growth. In our time, however, genetic engineering of plants is rapidly developing. Before long, many characteristics of plants may be manipulable. Seeds may be made more versatile, able to
tolerate poor soil and low nutrients. Flowers could be given new colors and scents,
programmed to set blossoms on every shoot and to bloom at a preset time. Square
tomatoes? Lavender-scented grass? Entire forests developed as clones, growing to
ideal bulk for timber harvesting in just a few years?

The new technology most urgently needed by poor farmers, however, is in the
form of drought- and salt-resistant food crops and varieties of grain suited to particular climate and soil conditions. Most genetic engineering efforts will benefit wealthy
farmers who can afford to buy expensive seed. New agricultural technologies, like the
ancient ones, must balance our knowledge with a respect for the environment and its
limitations on us. How will these developments change our appreciation of nature?
Our sense of how God is active as Creator?

❦ *Proper 11*

Wisdom 12:13-19   The righteous must be kind, and true strength lies in forbearance, in holding back strength so as not to injure others. This is one aspect of temperance: not consuming more than our share, limiting ourselves for the well-being of
others. *How might we be righteous if we practiced not-doing?* How hard it is to withdraw
even briefly from the continual flood of activity that drives us. Not-doing is a practice
of accepting limitation in order to make room for others, for God. The universe does
not depend upon our action for its well-being every moment—it can all go on
without us, and someday soon, it will. How about a fast from consumption, for the
planet's sake: could any one of us go for seven consecutive days without buying anything (even if we except our electricity and water)? How might we practice the prayer
of simplifying our lives, even a little?

Romans 8:18-25   The creation is groaning in labor—a wonderful image of its collaboration with the Creator God to accomplish its redemption through Christ. One
theory of the origin of the cosmos called "Intelligent Design" (ID) maintains that reason allows for the possibility of a coherent design in the plan of the cosmos, that is, a

structure for ordering the ingredients of the universe. It is not inherent to those ingredients, but employs them in its interaction. Some scientists and theologians dismiss the theory, but proponents of ID argue that the inference of design stops short of theology and can be supported by evidence. Some knowledge gaps, they explain, are not simply pieces of data yet to be collected, but data that is by nature uncollectable—such as what happened before the big bang and the start of time.[15] For many Christians, ID is a theory appropriate to include in the public school curriculum on origins of the cosmos, while church and family can be the locus of teaching our belief that God is the designer and creator beyond the definition of material sciences.

Matthew 13:24-43   Weeds and wheat must be left to grow up together, lest by wrenching out the weeds, the wheat is pulled out also. Weeds also do service by adding shade and stabilizing soil, though they compete with the crop for water and nutrients. In the ancient world, darnel, or tares (*Lolium temulentum*), a common field weed, was a valuable fuel at the end of the season. Its stalks and seeds closely resemble those of wheat; when the seeds of wheat and darnel are mixed, being of similar size and shape, they are difficult to separate and produce a poor quality flour. New research suggests that where farmers are willing to let some weeds grow among their crops, the crops actually grow up stronger and bear more fruitfully than fields where every last weed has been poisoned with herbicide. For the gardener, weeds are useful for the compost heap, where they decay to nourish the new year's crop, or as mulch when left to rot between plants—all good botanical support for the idea that we should not rush quickly to judgment about who or what is of value in the complex order of God's creation.

⚜ *Proper 12*

1 Kings 3:5-12   Solomon is asking for understanding and moral wisdom—an insight into the mind of God. Inspired by the medieval English ascetic Hugh of St. Victor, modern theologian Martin Thornton looks to creation in his quest for the mind of God:

> We must get right through the symbol to the real purpose of creation; and so with all created things, with all scientific research, with all work and life. The moral implications of such a process are obvious and far reaching. No single ascetical point could be more important to-day when... the world's goods are so exploited and yet more rightly enjoyed by more people than ever before;

when honest affluence pertains in one half of the world and starvation in the other.[16]

Part of wisdom, then, is a sense of balance or temperance, of not consuming more than one's share; another part is justice—rendering to all their due. Prudence adds good sense—dealing with the world as it really is, not as our appetite paints it; and last comes fortitude—the courage to act rightly even at a cost. Do we teach these ancient principles of morality, the cardinal virtues, to our children? In our church?

Romans 8:26-34   "All things work together for good for those who love God." Today our awareness of the interconnectedness of all things in the goodness of God's creation is broader than it was for the apostle. The more we learn of the universe, the more it is apparent that all its parts are interconnected in complex ways. Years ago a person emptied a pail of Nile perch fry into Lake Victoria, perhaps hoping these fish would multiply as a food source. They did, and are now helping to sustain the fishing trade on the lake. But they also outcompeted indigenous fish, which in turn dwindled, including a species that kept algal blooms in check. These blooms in the lake now flourish, leading to still more loss of local varieties. Whether this introduction was an asset for the local economy or the start of an ecological disaster is not yet clear, but doubtless the effect of this one individual's action reached far beyond his imagining. The limits of our knowledge must lead us to proper humility and care in our actions, for they always bear the possibility of consequences we cannot imagine.

Matthew 13:31-49   The mustard seed of the parable came from the tall, wild, yellow-blossomed annual plant *Brassica nigra,* black mustard, which was extensively cultivated as a medicine, a cooking spice, and a source of oil in ancient times. Its seed is about pinhead-sized, but its flavor is large and pungent. So much for the seed; now for faith.

Physicans have long known that patients given inactive substances in place of a medication often show remarkable improvement of symptoms—a testimony to the healing power of the mind itself as it believes a benefit is taking place. This practice, known as the placebo effect, could allow doctors to reduce the dosage of some medications while still providing their patients full benefit, though the medical profession has yet to recognize and accept it as a part of ethically acceptable medical treatment. The variables include the patient's knowledge and expectations about an illness, and degrees of suggestibility. Still, for centuries we have had reports of healings experienced by patients with maladies of all kinds through faith in God and in the healer. It seems reasonable to suppose that the mysterious biochemical processes of our own brains may be one of the ways through which divine healing comes.

❧ *Proper 13*

Nehemiah 9:16-20   Manna and water were God's provisioning for the Israelites, with nothing left over for the following day, except on the sabbath. How might we care for the earth if we assumed that in its essential elements, including the organisms it supports, God has supplied the whole planet with just what is needful? Might we mourn the destruction of species more urgently? Artist and botanist Dugald Stermer has been drawing and painting endangered plants for over fifteen years, preserving a record of each plant's beauty, usefulness, history, and current status. In his wonderfully illustrated text he writes that

> the difference between a natural extinction and an unnatural, or untimely, one is that nature provides an almost instant replacement for the former, while the latter leaves a vacuum forever.... If we continue, through overconsumption, overdevelopment, and overpopulation, to destroy an ever-larger number of life-forms, we will surely unravel the complex systems that keep us alive. [17]

Romans 8:35-39   Who shall separate us from the love of God? "O God, our atmosphere" I once found myself praying, with that same sensibility in which the poet-theologian once addressed God "in whom we live and move and have our being"—God in whom we swim, our native element, whom we hardly notice, so thoroughly are we acclimatized to God's presence. God is to us like water to the fish and air to the bird: life, environment of motion, taken for granted and utterly reliable—that and more. Another poet puts it this way:

> O God, who art the tunnel in which we walk,
> all things express a thought that was not ours before
> we seized it from the air, the forest floor.[18]

God is ours and we are God's before we know it. Faith only adds the element of knowing and joy and thanksgiving to this truth.

Matthew 14:13-21   Five loaves and two fish leave no room for waste, though all have enough. No camper would eat the provisions for a whole journey on the first day, yet collectively we hardly hesitate to continue consuming a food source until it is completely exhausted, rather than rationing and harvesting prudently for the long haul. Last year, 100 chefs across America and a major cruise line agreed to drop swordfish from their menus as an attempt to raise awareness of the depletion of this popular food fish of the North Atlantic. A swordfish must be five years old to reach the size for reproduction, and some 40,000 fish are caught under the 44-pound harvest size and must be thrown back each year, of which many die from the trauma.[19] Cod have grown scarce, along with haddock and flounder; sharks are now being over-fished to fill the gap. Yet there is still strong resistance both to harvesting quotas and to the employment of fishing methods that do not destroy young fry, or tear up the hatching grounds and shelters for young fish. How might we change our thinking about food so as to value leaving "leftovers" rather than consuming as much as we have available just because it is there? Are we willing to alter our buying and our voting patterns to support sustainable fishing?

🔥 *Proper 14*

Jonah 2:1-9   For Jonah the bottom of the sea is a place of despair and fear, but for biologists it is a place of wonder. Charles Paxton of the Oxford University Animal Behavior Research Group has used computer statistical methods to try to determine how many as yet undiscovered sea monsters (creatures greater than two meters in length) might exist. Beginning with a 1758 text of Carolus Linnaeus that identifies twenty-three species, he did a literature search by year for new species and measured the declining rate of discovery versus the number of species found. Paxton concluded that there are an estimated forty-seven new species waiting to be discovered. These almost certainly will include a few new species of whale, he remarked, though he would be happy with "a couple of new totally weird sharks."[20]

Romans 9:1-5   Paul mourns his estrangement from his fellow Jews and praises their wonderful heritage. His inner division could serve as a metaphor for our own modern estrangement: there are many within our own churches who do not have a great abundance, but even those of modest means in the United States take for granted many gifts of creation. What would it take to feel Christ steadily pulling us away from our attachment to our luxuries of daily life? How do we even make a beginning at simplifying, at consuming less, at leaving less of a personal footprint on creation? What if we took the concept of the tithe—set it at any percent to begin with—and applied it to each area of our expenditure as a reduction goal: 10 percent less heating and cooling, less gasoline burned in the car (a more efficient vehicle?), a simpler diet?

Matthew 14:22-33   Jesus walks on the water. The only large creatures that walk on water in nature as we know it are 90-gram basilisk lizards, whose splayed feet slap the water so fast they create an air pocket above the water that keeps them on the surface.

A human being of 170 pounds or so would have to run 108 kilometers per hour and exert superhuman effort and energy to accomplish the same feat!

What do the stunning miracles of the gospels communicate to us about the relationship of God and nature? Some see this miracle of water-walking as a symbolic experience of Jesus' followers written back into the life of Jesus—their resurrected Lord coming to save them in a time of crisis. For others it expresses the first-century Christians' sense of Jesus' identity as the Son of God. Does it matter whether Jesus was a miracle-worker apart from the exorcisms and healings we might be able to interpret out of twentieth-century science?

❧ *Proper 15*

Isaiah 56:1-7   Do not let the eunuch say, "I am just a dry tree." In an age and culture preoccupied with sexuality, this ancient text points us back to a broader construction of human reproduction. Those who are just, even though they be infirm or maimed of body, shall be fruitful in building up the community. In our time, there are so many technological aids for those who are infertile but desire children that it can be very difficult for those who have exhausted medical options to hear that there is no solution for them but adoption, and doubly so for those who may not be accepted as adoptive parents. These are not the only options for fertility, for nourishing new life, however. The just person is not a tree that will quickly wither in drought, but is deep-rooted—like the tree in the first psalm "planted by streams of waters," able to withstand adversity and deprivation with strength, and still give shade and beauty of itself. To this justice we are all called. Where is new life needed in your particular community? In the wider world? How do people deepen their roots in justice? What supports are there for those who cannot give birth in the way they would prefer?

Romans 11:13-32   The gifts and calling of God are irrevocable. In my experience in the church, we are quick to value the gifts of educators, healers, even managers and administrators, but many of us give less attention to the gifts of scientists. I am grateful for Richard Feynman's clear explanation of the distinct gifts and calling of physicists and mathematicians:

> Mathematicians are only dealing with the structure of reasoning, and they do not really care what they are talking about. They do not even need to know what they are talking about, or, as they themselves say, whether what they say is true.... Mathematicians prepare abstract reasoning ready to be used if you

have a set of axioms about the real world. . . . But in physics you have an understanding of the connection of words with the real world. It is necessary at the end to translate what you have figured out into English, into the world, into the blocks of copper and glass that you are going to do the experiments with. [21]

Matthew 15:21-28   Throwing the children's food to dogs is a complex, unpleasant metaphor for giving the message intended for the Jewish people to a Gentile outsider. Matthew rebukes his fellow Jews who had not accepted Jesus, pointing out that since they will not come to the divine feast, outsiders will take their place at the table.

But this curious statement about children's food reminds me of how problematic eating is for many children in our society. Dr. Mary Pipher writes movingly of adolescent girls and their struggles with bulimia in *Reviving Ophelia*:

> It starts as a strategy to control weight, but soon it develops a life of its own. Life for bulimic young women becomes a relentless preoccupation with eating, purging and weight. Pleasure is replaced by despair, frenzy and guilt. Like all addictions, bulimia is a compulsive, self-destructive and progressive disorder. Binging and purging are the addictive behaviors; food is the narcotic. . . . Bulimic young women have lost their true selves. . . . They have a long road back. [22]

How might the church become a place that concretely models a healthy relationship with food, the body, and the self?

❧ *Proper 16*

Isaiah 51:1-6   I once visited a quarry on the Greek island of Paros where the white marble for much of Europe's Renaissance sculpture, including Michaelangelo's *Piéta*, was cut. A small tunnel leads into the hillside; you could walk by it and hardly notice, though below is an impressive set of human-made caverns. What a contrast to my last flight over West Virginia, when I looked down over great gashes in the green hillsides that stretched black and barren for mile on mile! Strip mining is cheaper, faster, safer indeed than the old man-dug mines, and mechanized so that fewer jobs are provided. But we do not even bother to evaluate its cost to the forest ecosystem: a loss of habitat, watershed, topsoil, microclimate, and the loveliness of the woods, all of which have a real value. In the difficult discourse about mining and conservation, about jobs in poor rural areas, about the need for fossil fuels at low costs, perhaps the best honor we can pay the creation is to do our best to count the real cost of our choices. We need to know the actual price, as nearly as we can calculate it, so that we do not exchange our birthright for "a mess of pottage," as the King James version described Esau's bowl of soup.

Romans 11:33-36   "From him and through him and to him are all things"—the apostle bursts into a paean of praise. Creation shows forth the mind of God; from ancient times theologians have understood that its loveliness leads human minds toward God. The mystic John of the Cross writes in "The Spiritual Canticle":

> My Beloved is the mountains,
> And lonely wooded valleys,
> Strange islands,
> And resounding rivers,
> The whistling of love-stirring breezes,
> The tranquil night,
> At the time of rising dawn,
> Silent music,
> Sounding solitude,
> The supper that refreshes and deepens love.

Matthew 16:13-20   Peter is described as a rock. What fun it is to speculate about what kind of rock Jesus might have had in mind. If they were standing near the Sea of Galilee, the rock was a hard limestone. Laid down layer by layer under ancient seas or rivers, limestone is the sediment made up of calcium bits from the bodies of aquatic creatures. If it is pressed hard enough for long enough it becomes marble, carrying the colors of the sediment that comprised it, seamed with irregularities or intrusions of other minerals, and fine and hard enough to be polished to a great luster.

Or maybe Jesus happened to be standing on one of the great black basalt boulders that litter that part of Galilee. Ejected from an ancient volcano, basalt is very light for its bulk, rough, and porous like a sponge. It was shaped into urns and grinding pots and stones—some are visible in the ruins of nearby Capernaum. From fiery temperament to grinding and shaping force to receptive vessel: that might fit the character of Peter.

Or did Jesus have in mind that less common rock, granite? Granite was carried some distance to be shaped into columns and foundations for important buildings in the Holy Land. In it are visible the flecks and grains of many minerals that began in the fire of earth's core, and over time were pressed into stone by the weight of mountains. The granite-like Peter would stand fast against eroding powers of wind and water, and catch up and combine all the fragments of experience into a unified whole. Whether sedimentary (layered by water), igneous (fire-made), or metamorphic (changed under pressure), Peter would bring considerable strength of character to the founding of the church!

Proper 17

Jeremiah 15:15-21 The prophet describes a wound that will not heal. I was meditating today on some photographs of refugees in Kurdistan (part of Iraq) living in tents—made of blankets and bedspreads—in a field of mud among a few stripped winter trees, without toilets, fuel (those trees will not last the winter!), or clean water. Even if their homes become safe from bombing so that they can return, their lands are littered with landmines. For them as for others in places of war, killing will go on for years, even decades after the formal conflict ends. Worldwide, some 60 million landmines are buried in 57 countries.[23] These mines continue to kill and maim—with children, farmers, and animals particularly at risk—long after peace treaties have been signed and active warfare has ended. Like a toxic waste, they render land unfit for agriculture or development. Removing them puts lives at risk and is beyond the economic means of poor nations. Our nation is a major manufacturer of landmines. What is the church's responsibility regarding their creation, use, and removal?

Romans 12:1-8 In this wonderful metaphor of the body and its members Paul shares his vision of the diversity and the interconnectedness of the gospel community. Flying over the midwest at night, reading this passage, I thought about the net of connections among people in community resembling the cobweb of lights across the dark landscape below. The electric power grid is a concrete reminder of the ways we are connected, both with one another and the environment. For nearly all of us, our power comes from somewhere else. If you live in the northeast, your electricity probably comes from Hydro Quebec, a chain of dams in James Bay, Canada. If you live in Los Angeles, your electricity travels from the great Hoover Dam in Nevada. So it is easy to forget to ask what impact our consumption has on those environments. The loss of wildlife habitat because of dams does not stir many hearts.

Belief in the reality of global warming has finally moved energy corporations to invest more substantially in solar power. Solar energy equipment is not cheap, yet when we add into the equation the real costs of fossil and nuclear power—to the climate, the environment, and our quality of life—it becomes a better bargain.[24]

So are those who build homes with independent energy systems "off the grid" of community? Far from it. By disconnecting, they seek to further the good of the whole community and the earth. Their connection with neighbors simply becomes less tangible than the matrix of underground cables that carry power.

Matthew 16:21-27   What shall we give in return for our life? Can a price be put on a human life? There was great outcry a few years ago when an intergovernmental panel on climatic change tried to assess the costs of global warming. They based their valuation of human loss of life upon average expected earnings: a resident of the United States or western Europe would be worth $1.5 million but a resident of a poor country only $150,000. Estimates suggest there may be five times as much loss of life in the developing world as a result of climatic change, but less "absolute loss of value." As scientists and economists try to measure the costs of various courses of action versus the risks of others, Christians along with believers of other faiths call out for the full dignity of every human being as equally made and loved by the Creator and therefore of equal, incalculable worth.

❧ *Proper 18*

Ezekiel 33:1-11   Take warning, says the prophet. Listen for the sound of the trumpet and take action! Did you ever think of that irritating cry from an infant as a trumpet warning helpfully calling you to action? (This might save you some fruitless rage.) A baby's cry has evolved with a particular intensity and range to command the attention of its parents, even to rouse them from sound sleep. A shrill cry measures 96 decibels; if sustained, it could damage hearing. Crying is a survival mechanism for both the individual and the species. Attentive parents quickly become attuned to interpreting the cause of their child's cries, whether wetness, fear, pain, hunger, overstimulation, exhaustion, or rage.

Romans 12:9-21   "Do not claim to be wiser than you are," instructs the apostle. "I think, therefore I am," said Descartes. Here we are, endlessly thinking beings. Because we think, and our inquisitive selves love to collect information and formulate explanations to help us manipulate our world and control it (not always a bad thing), we hunger to *know everything*. And at certain moments in our lives many of us think we do, or at least we behave that way. In fact, our inner scientists are reminded too often for comfort that we hardly know anything.

How often do we gather into our practice of prayer a meditation on the limits of our knowledge, practicing *not-knowing*, as it were? How afraid are we of practicing ways of prayer that require us to learn to stop thinking and imagining and speaking and being self-aware? What a wonder, what we do not know! How feeble and small is our knowing before the vastness of God and creation. We learn to honor God when we let ourselves fall into the fear of God, into awe.

> Awe is a soul word. Humility is an ego word. Together they are synergistic, they mean more than either alone. Awe expands the soul as humility causes the ego to retreat to manageable proportions.[25]

Who are we to wreck the creation without even knowing the consequences?

Matthew 18:15-20   Matthew proposes a structure for the discipline of the community—a kind of peer-review to pressure the wayward into right behavior. In the past few years, fraud in research science has caught the public eye. Often such fraudulence is driven by pressure to collect publishable data from successful experiments, and by competition for jobs, funding, and peer approval. Scientists—especially those who mentor others—must clearly communicate their commitment to ethical standards and create an environment in which research is valued for itself, not for its successes. Theories not upheld by study, methodologies tried and found faulty, or experiments that fail should also be greeted with appreciation by scientists, the press, and the public. These efforts, as well as the successful ones, increase the span of human knowledge, direct the future flow of interest, and steer others away from fruitless work. Is it time for a journal of unsuccessful research that publicizes the unglamorous contributions of dedicated researchers?

🔥 *Proper 19*

Ecclesiasticus 27:30–28:7   Can anyone who harbors anger against someone else expect healing from the Lord? Our attitudes affect our ability to receive the blessings God would give us. A negative attitude obstructs good health. This ancient wisdom has been finding fresh support: research suggests forgiveness is good for the body, while anger and resentment negatively affect health. Mike McCullough of the National Institute for Healthcare Research reports that those who practice forgiveness of others suffer less depression, anxiety, and sleep disturbance than those who do not, and also enjoy a lower risk of heart disease.[26] Psychotherapists would add that repressing anger—pushing it out of consciousness—is not a solution, for it festers and erupts in places it does not belong. Anger is the psyche's defense against threat. It serves a good purpose if it is directed suitably and moderately, and not allowed to become a chronic state. How then do we best express anger in Christian community to prevent injustice, while maintaining health for all concerned?

Romans 14:5-12 "Some judge one day better than another, while others judge all days to be alike." What an odd statement! It brings to mind weather forecasters now politely known by their formal title: meteorologists. Have you noticed that meteorologists on TV relish announcing "bad" weather: "You're not going to like this one!" they say with some glee, and then we hear about rain, wind, snow, heat, or cold. Gradually, this forecasting forms our expectations: inclement weather seems like doom. In fact, rain and snow water the plants and give us water to fill our reservoirs. Heat may wither, but it also ultimately gives life; if the sun went out, so would we. Even the frigid cold kills microorganisms that need controlling—allergens, insect pests, disease vectors—with a sanitizing effect. Wind warms and cools us; moves moisture our way then dries us out again; brings down dead wood from the trees; moves topsoil around for better or worse; and distributes seeds, spores, and baby spiders on their silk threads. What would our sense of weather be like if we woke up and said, "Thank you, God, for the blessing of today's weather!"—whatever it might be?

Matthew 18:21-35 Forgiving debts as we are forgiven is a hallmark of the one who knows forgiveness from God. Debt is not just an individual matter. Of forty-one nations considered by the International Monetary Fund and the World Bank to be "heavily indebted poor countries," thirty-three are in Africa. Payment of debt interest diverts scarce money from education, public health, roads, agriculture, and business development. Soil is depleted to grow cash crops; opium is more lucrative than grain. Overfishing, deforestation, and strip mining abound. Most of these debts are already so discounted that they could be relieved for relatively little cost, some at only 10 to 15 percent of the original loan. Jubilee 2000 Campaign is an international movement toward debt cancellation for about forty impoverished nations supported by dozens of religious organizations worldwide, including the Episcopal Church.[27] What would debt relief teach us about our relationship to our neighbor?

❧ *Proper 20*

Jonah 3:10–4:11 Jonah and the *kikayun* plant make a humorous tale. What was this odd plant that came and grew huge and died in a day? Some sort of castor bean, perhaps? The plant is a sign of the foolishness of a self-centered view of the universe: Jonah did not plant or water it, but he is personally insulted when it dies and no longer shades him from the sun. The creation exists not just for our comfort and our use, but ultimately to serve God's purposes. Can we still learn from what we may not be able to explain?

Philippians 1:21-27 "Striving side by side for the gospel": the image brings to my mind pairs of great draught horses team-pulling at the Missouri State Fair. These horses, weighing a ton or so themselves, pull a wooden sled loaded with increasing numbers of cinder blocks. Ultimately a load several times their own weight is shifted tens of feet. They are well fed and groomed with care, equipped with the best harnesses and tack. In each pair, one is the leader and the other fine tunes its response to the first so that the pulling is marvelously synchronized: an off-center pull squanders energy. These horses must love the work: they seem to put their hearts into it as they toss their heads and prance toward the start, pull their loads single-mindedly, and then strut away after they have done well. What can their enthusiasm, focus, and discipline teach us who strive for the work of the gospel?

Matthew 20:1-16 God's hiring of laborers for the vineyard upsets our sense of what is just and fair. Surely the latecomers should earn less than the conscientious early birds. But God does not deal with us out of an economy of scarcity in which there is only a fixed amount of blessing to be portioned out. God's blessings are poured out upon us endlessly, regardless of our deserving. If our ancestors stood beside us they would be shocked to realize that compared to all the resources of the earth they consumed in a millennia, we modern folk have consumed not only as much in a few centuries, but more.

> Human civilization is characterized by modification of the environment—beginning with fire and then agriculture—but until fairly recently we did not profoundly alter the planet as a whole. Over the past few centuries, however, the sheer expansion in the number of earth's human inhabitants and the growth in our technological ability to modify the landscape and exploit the earth's bounty of minerals, water, and fossil fuel have profoundly changed the entire earth system.[28]

Just imagining the speed and magnitude of the change to the planet's systems is difficult, something that takes work and study to realize. How shall we cultivate a holy imagination, informed by sound data? How shall we pray about our own impact on earth?

🔥 *Proper 21*

Ezekiel 18:1-4, 25-32   "The parents have eaten sour grapes, and the children's teeth are set on edge." This is a metaphor for all the ways that the behavior— including the sin—of one generation has consequences for future generations. At a recent conference called "Engineering in the Human Germline" biophysicist Gregory Stock presented research poll results that show a substantial number of parents—nearly 20 percent—see nothing improper about manipulating their offspring's genes to give them a competitive edge. Future geneticists might be able to affect whether a child is likely to develop bipolar disorder, left-handedness, even perhaps a particular sexual orientation. Yet it is possible that "disease" genes or other genes deemed undesirable might couple with other genes to form complex characteristics such as artistic ability, wit, or creativity. Such engineering knowledge *will* develop, sooner or later. What will we do with it? Who will decide which characteristics are valuable and which are not?

Philippians 2:1-13   In this text, believed to include a quotation from one of the earliest Christian hymns, *kenosis* is the Greek word for the self-emptying of God in Jesus. Theologian Matthew Fox writes:

> The early Christians who sang this hymn are employing the cosmology of the Hellenistic world of their time, the threefold division of the universe into heaven, earth, and the under-the-earth realm. Jesus rules all. Jewish theology is also employed here. Jesus "being in the form of God" alludes to "the image and likeness of God" motif according to the original Adam in Genesis 1:26-27. But Jesus was emptied and treated as a "servant" or "slave." Christ's cosmic rule is paradoxically that of the wounded slave. The one seeming to be the lowest and most wretched of creatures is, in fact, one and the same divinity as the Creator of all.[29]

How might this paradox affect our thinking about our own role as servants and stewards of the world in which we live?

Matthew 21:28-32   Which son does the will of the father? Doing and talking about doing the right thing are two different courses—neither son in this parable seems to be getting it just right! This brings to mind for me the endless debating I have heard in churches about the use of Styrofoam cups versus china or paper ones, or whether it is better to recycle waste paper or to burn it. These issues are more complicated than they seem. Matthew Leach, a British energy policy analyst, has published a study weighing all the alternatives and, surprisingly, concludes that two-thirds of waste paper should be burned, with only the poorest grades of paper composted or landfilled. So handling waste paper is a complex issue that requires consideration of hidden environmental costs, and the conclusion sometimes challenges common green assumptions. It may be harder to be completely righteous in our handling of resources than we think, but in any case it will be better to *do* than simply to *talk* about conservation.

❧ Proper 22

Philippians 3:14-21 "Their god is the belly": this could be an insult aimed at many of us in America. Why do we overeat? Normal hunger prompts us to replenish burned calories. Many physiologists think that a certain amount of fat circulating in the blood signals the brain that we should stop eating because we are full, but this signal seems to be easily ignored. We also eat to satisfy psychological needs for nurture and comfort, and to be socially agreeable; we even stretch our stomachs by chronically overeating so it takes more to make them feel full. For some, food craving is an addictive process: many find recovery through a disciplined twelve-step type program or psychotherapy.

The practice of fasting—not just ceasing to eat, but restricting the diet to certain foods, varying foods in different religious seasons, or limiting intake to small quantities—is a part of nearly every religious tradition. It is a way to honor God and the body by becoming mindful about eating and by shifting usual rhythms and patterns of life to mark sacred time. A meatless or alcohol-free Lent; a Maundy Thursday *agapé* meal of bread, wine, cheese, and dried fruit; a foodless Good Friday and Ash Wednesday all help Christians remember that we do not worship our bellies but the Giver of food, our Maker, for whose sake we moderate our appetites.

Isaiah 5:1-7; Matthew 21:33-43 Consider that God has made us tenants of the vineyard of planet Earth. Consider our management of just one of its natural resources. The United States currently imports more petroleum products than ever before, the largest portion of it from the volatile Persian Gulf nations. Though OPEC's world market share dropped from its highest level of 55 percent in 1973 to 30 percent in 1986, it has been expanding again and now stands at 43 percent. It seems that we learned little about conservation from our experience of the 1973 embargo by OPEC following the Yom Kippur War between Israel, Syria, and Egypt. During the six-month embargo, oil prices fluctuated wildly, gasoline was rationed, and there were lines at fuel pumps. In the next twenty years, oil imports are predicted to rise to 62 percent of domestic consumption in the United States.[30] The legislature also continues to consider plans for oil prospecting in the fragile Yukon and Arctic wilderness areas, while our vehicles increase in size, decrease in fuel efficiency, and are driven more recreational miles than ever before. And so I ask, "What sort of tenants are we of the vineyard that God has entrusted to us?"

❧ *Proper 23*

Isaiah 25:1-9 A feast of fat things sounds a bit alarming to our low-fat conciousness. To those who lived on a lean diet and ate mainly grains and vegetables with only small quantities of meat (one that sustains many people in the developing world to this day), fatty foods were the epitome of abundance and health. Even prosperous areas of the ancient world experienced occasional famines, and in such places plump, well-fed people were (and still are) regarded as particularly attractive. Isaiah's vision of the divine banquet loses some of its punch for readers in a society that wavers between junk food and diet food. How might the table be spread in our vision of the heavenly banquet?

Philippians 4:4-13 Think on these things for your edification, says the apostle. In a fifth-century sermon, Leo the Great preaches that creation itself is a teacher that can edify the faithful:

> Dear Friends, at every moment "the earth is full of the mercy of God," and nature itself is a lesson for all the faithful in the worship of God. The heavens, the sea and all that is in them bear witness to the goodness and omnipotence of their Creator, and the marvellous beauty of the elements as they obey him demands from the intelligent creation a fitting expression of its gratitude. [31]

What else does creation teach us about the nature of God?

Matthew 22:1-14 Creation itself is spread out before us like a banquet of delight to nourish and rest us, inspire and protect us, challenge and companion us. Are we grateful for the invitation to come and share? Or too busy to notice? And do we wear our wedding garment—Christ, the clothing of our baptism—as we attend the feast? Do we act and live out of that identity which is Christ in us?

❧ *Proper 24*

Isaiah 45:1-7 "I form light and create darkness, I make peace and create evil: I the LORD do all these things." Here is a wonderful declaration of the radical wholeness in God, in whom all polarities are reconciled. Human beings, like most living things, need darkness as much as light: some new studies suggest that human modification of the light/dark cycles may even have health consequences. The brain hormone melatonin helps reset the body's clock during darkness, and in turn reduces estrogen production. Two Norwegian studies suggest that there may be a connection between night illumination and some types of cancer. "Light is a drug," says neuroendocrinologist Russel J. Reiter, and "by abusing it, we risk imperiling our health." Melatonin is an antioxidant and anticarcinogen. One study found a strong correlation between reduced breast cancer risk and diminishing vision in women, though this has not been supported by further research. Tumors in rats grew much faster in animals exposed to even small amounts of light at night than those in complete darkness. While the link is not proven, it does suggest that the natural rhythms of the body have a role in our health and disease patterns that warrants careful examination.[32] How might we imagine God as darkness as well as light?

1 Thessalonians 1:1-10 By becoming imitators of God, the faithful serve as examples to one another. The marketing of products in our culture relies on the examples of the famous and attractive to woo ordinary people, especially young people, to buy. The latest development: Nike shoes now feature small sacs of sulphur hexafluoride in the soles of running shoes to cushion the feet of runners. The large molecules of this gas are less likely to leak than the air cushions used by other manufacturers. But as a greenhouse gas, sulphur hexafluoride is 35,000 times as potent as carbon dioxide and when shoes rot or are punctured, the gas escapes into the atmosphere. Nike is looking for an alternative, but when their patent expires this year, other manufacturers may begin using the polluting gas. How shall we nurture our children to examine the examples of prominent and popular figures and imitate those who care for creation?

Matthew 22:15-22 Paying taxes to the emperor is one way of dealing with the world as it is, respecting its rules, living pragmatically. To do this is to practice the classic virtue of prudence, honoring creation and dealing with it sensibly and reasonably. Sustainability is one aspect of prudence: it is living within the limits of nature so that the most people may thrive for the longest duration in the greatest degree of harmony possible. This is not the same thing as accommodating to corrupt systems of power—perhaps the interpretation Jesus' opponents expected him to place on their question about taxes. What "taxes" do we owe creation?

☙ *Proper 25*

Exodus 22:21-27 "You shall not exact interest." This imperative appears several times in scripture but in modern life is conveniently overlooked: we hardly give a thought to our credit cards, mortgages, and the justice of collecting what others owe us. But consider the consequences of debt on a larger scale, for our personal debt in the wealthy world is directly connected to the debt of the poor of the earth. For example, Mozambique spends 50 percent of its national budget on interest for its international loans, compared to our 14 percent. The per capita debt in Mozambique is $223, compared to an annual average income of $80.[33] What would it mean to take the biblical imperative at face value?

1 Thessalonians 2:1-8 Paul describes his ministry to the church at Thessaloniki as tender, like that of a wet nurse to an infant. St. Anselm picks up this image of nurture and applies it to both Jesus and Paul. The wet nurse is a particularly apt metaphor for the apostle who tends a community he did not necessarily bring into being, yet knows intimately. In these days of infant formula, wet nurses have almost disappeared in the United States, though some lactating women still donate breast milk to milk banks to nourish premature infants whose own mothers are not producing milk or have died. Breast milk is far superior to formula, especially for the most vulnerable babies.

Some adoptive mothers feel so strongly about wanting to nourish their infants from their own bodies that they go through the sometimes-painful discipline of putting the child to the breast to suck for prolonged periods every day until their hormonal systems begin to respond by milk formation. I am reminded of the deep human desire to nurture, leading to the patient, daily effort that is able to transform the body itself. What a powerful metaphor for the apostle who devotes great time and tenderness, self-giving and persistence, and allows his or her own life to be transformed into the shape of a wet nurse of the gospel.

Matthew 22:34-46 The great commandments call us to an over-arching ethic of love, for the same love which is God in us draws us to love God and our neighbor. This is the activity of the Trinity in and for us. How is this love manifest in dealing with our planet? Gro Harlem Brundtland, director of the World Health Organization, writes:

> The very real possibility that our actions are depleting the earth's genetic resources, changing the climate and the composition of the atmosphere, and upsetting the chemical balance of our lakes and waterways proves that if we all do as we please in the short run, we will all lose in the long run.... We have an opportunity to break the negative trends of the past. For this to happen we need new concepts and new values based on a global ethic. We must mobilize political will and human ingenuity. We need closer multilateral cooperation based on the recognition that nations are increasingly interdependent.... It is politically, economically and morally unacceptable that there is a net transfer of resources from poor countries to rich ones.[34]

❧ Proper 26

Micah 3:5-12 Corrupt prophets exist in every age, and thus discerning true prophecy from false becomes the task of every generation of faith. Consider the voices competing to define our relationship with the environment in our own time and place: journalist Bruce Selcraig describes a major effort now underway by anti-environmental concerns—including Exxon, The American Coal Foundation, Dow Chemicals, International Paper, Caterpillar Equipment, and many others—to pour large amounts of funding into curriculum materials and free hand-out publicity pieces for schools. Their goal is to convince children and teachers that "environmental problems" associated with their industries are fabricated or trivial. Global warming, open-pit mining, acid rain damage, clear-cutting forests, overpopulation, dioxin dangers, petroleum pollution, and the like are downplayed or dismissed as erroneous.[35]

The best environmental education takes children out of the classroom into the natural world, even if this is the vacant lot across the street, and teaches them to observe, record, question, analyze, and appreciate what they find. It is up to parents and other adults to pay attention to the materials their children are being given as hard data; to notice who is footing the bill and what is being left out of the curriculum as cash-poor schools accept propaganda as information. In my own urban multi-class parish I have encountered third graders who think milk is made in a bottle and know nothing of the cow, or who believe that all vegetables grow on trees. What is the responsibility of church classrooms to address environmental issues as a matter of faith as well as good science, and for members to become aware of what the congregation's children are learning or not learning? How might we teach discernment of truthful versus corrupt prophets of science?

1 Thessalonians 2:9-20   "As you know, we dealt with each one of you like a father with his children." Paternalism is the term given to a system under which a person claims the status to make judgments and take actions on behalf of another based on superior wisdom and knowledge. Modern medicine in the west has evolved rapidly through and away from paternalism as practiced by physicians; at one time doctors were expected to make decisions about treatments with little disclosure of their patient's medical situation, prognosis, or rationale for treatment. Paternalism is often now considered an inappropriate and arrogant assumption of a "fatherly" role over a patient who is an adult competent to make his or her own decision.

Physician Peter Marzuk offers a persuasive alternate viewpoint about medical paternalism. He argues that a patient's emotional reaction may compromise judgment, and that wide access to medical information, accurate and not, may cause a patient to plead for treatment that, in the physician's best judgment, is not indicated or safe.[36] Physicians faced with patients' refusals of treatment need to consider the source of that decsion. Treatment is not just about "rights" and "free choice," but also about careful discernment, effective communication, and trust. These are, finally, the hallmarks of the good—as opposed to the tyrannical—father, epitomized by God.

Matthew 23:1-12   Compare the hypocrisy of the scribes and Pharisees "who do not practice what they preach" to the humility expressed in this passage about the natural world:

> I need to watch the sun, to calculate the hours that I should pray to God. But the blackbird who nests in the roof of my hut makes no such calculations: he sings God's praises all day long. I need books to read, to learn the hidden truths of God. But the blackbird who shares my simple meals needs no written texts: he can read the love of God in every leaf and flower. I need to beg forgiveness, to make myself pure and fit for God. But the blackbird who drinks with me from the stream sheds no tears of contrition: he is as God made him, with no stain of sin.[37]

Proper 27

Amos 5:18-24 "Let justice roll down like waters." This phrase suggests a great flood unleashed, like a rain-swollen torrent pouring down an arroyo in the desert, sweeping everything in its path away. But much of the might of waters consists in their power to rearrange the landscape little by little. There are occasional cataclysms, but for the most part rivers alter their courses incrementally. Little by little a stream becomes a lake, becomes a peat bog, becomes a forest. Little by little a delta pushes out into the sea, or a sandbar island erodes through into a channel. Of the Missouri River near my home, one hydrologist has written:

> The natural process of give-and-take . . . involves eroding banks and soil at one point and accreting silt and sediment at another, largely by the whims of nature, creating a healthy biodiversity with oxbows, sandbars and islands.[38]

Much of the work of change toward justice is also little by little, due to steady pressure, importunate questioning, and persistent conversation. Nor is it a steady progress forward; there are meanders and setbacks, bad compromises and corruptions along the way.

1 Thessalonians 4:13-18 Paul wrestles with understanding just how the resurrection is going to work—for those yet to die, for those recently dead, for those dead long before Jesus was born. The sequence of these events seems to have been problematic for the churches of Thessaloniki. With our contemporary understanding of time and eternity, these questions seem less pressing if no less intriguing. Time as we can measure it moves in only one direction; we cannot go backward through it, save in memory.

In this physical universe, at every level we can measure, time runs only one way; the broken teacup does not reassemble itself and regain its spilt contents. But in God's time and eternity, those already dead may neither precede nor follow those who will die tomorrow. The pre-existent Word of John's gospel connects for us the resurrection in time at Jesus' empty tomb and the resurrection out of time in which all the saints are lifted to life with God eternally, now and always.

Matthew 25:1-13 The wise virgins made sure they had plenty of oil to trim their lamps. In the Middle East, oil had many other uses: an unguent for wounds or sore muscles; an ingredient in medicines, charms, and potions; a rub-down for athletes about to compete (to make them supple, beautiful, shining, and hard to hold); a food staple and cooking additive; a base for perfume and cosmetics; a fragrant agent for buildings; a lubricant to reduce friction (for machinery, sex, animal harnesses, sharpening weapons); and a cleansing agent where water was scarce. Oil was used to anoint the dead, and to consecrate kings and priests. All that, plus olive oil burns with a lovely, clear, steady light. If a person had oil, flour, and some fuel, she had the essentials of life. In church we use oil for baptism, scented with the sap of balsam and called chrism. We use oil to anoint the sick, usually unscented olive oil. Are not these also the essentials of life?

❦ *Proper 28*

Zephaniah 1:7, 12-18; 1 Thessalonians 5:1-10   Labor pains with no escape may seem like an odd metaphor for the end times! New research into fetal development indicates that it is not the mother's body but the baby who starts the labor process once he or she becomes stressed by hunger for more oxygen and nourishment than the mother can provide through the placenta.[39] Any mother who has given birth can attest to the power and irresistibility of the labor process once it begins. The good news, for mothers and for the people of God, is that the pains of labor often give way to new life. And so it is for the creation, laboring to bring forth the full life of the reign of God out of the confinement and poverty of the old world. How can this become a fresh metaphor for our times?

Matthew 25:14-29   In Dhaka, Bangladesh, the Grameen Bank has been established to arrange very small loans to the poorest of individuals—often women—who can borrow nowhere else to start local businesses. Using microcredit, with an average loan of $180, women can buy the materials to manufacture products for market, buy a cart, start an inventory, or rent a sales space. *National Geographic* tells the story of one woman who used a loan to buy a telephone; she now sells calls to friends and neighbors without phones. Her loan will be repaid in three years, and her enterprise is providing enough income for her debt payments and some profit.[40] Though it is no panacea for economic injustice, microcredit reduces prostitution and begging, improves the health of women and children, and allows some women to seek education. How might microcredit programs help neighborhoods in the United States where the poorest live? Could churches begin such programs, and find them profitable to everyone, growing resources for more loans even as they seed new businesses?

❧ *Proper 29*

Ezekiel 34:11-17; Matthew 25:31-46   We do well to listen cautiously to such parables of sorting and judgment. Matthew had an agenda here. Probably he was a Jewish Christian writing to warn his former community of Jews that they had incurred God's displeasure and stood under judgment for not recognizing Christ; they are the "goats" he had in mind. It is a nice twist to drive through the British countryside and see how often sheep and goats graze together, each with their own economic value to the farmer. Goats are not thrown away! The sorting image invites us to examine our own rush to judgment of others we might like to label "goats." Here are some cautionary words about one sort of judgment:

> Half the citizens in the rich world sincerely believe that it is poor tropical farmers burning the rainforests, rather than their own fossil-fuel-burning, gas-guzzling lifestyles that are causing the greenhouse effect. Somehow the prospects of millions of Indian cars and an ozone-destroying refrigerator in every Chinese home are more terrifying to them than conspicuous Western consumption. People are not pollution—they are a massive resource. . . . Once you start treating people as a problem . . . as consumers who cannot give, as mouths to feed, as claimants, as polluters, as statistics, as incubators of disease, you are on a slippery slope . . . that leads to inhuman tower blocks, to old people "locked up in old people's homes," to ethnic cleansing and finally to the street children of the megacities who simply "disappear." This is what tends to happen to people you don't want.[41]

1 Corinthians 15:20-28   All things are put in subjection under Christ. You can almost picture the hierarchical court like those Byzantine mosaics depicting Christ the Pantocrator with legions of angels above legions of monarchs above the common saints, getting progressively smaller in descending order. It reminds me of the cartoon of the food chain that has a series of fish, each swimming just in front of the engulfing, open jaws of a slightly larger fish. In contrast to this hierarchical image that would have come so naturally to Paul—who was familiar with the Roman imperial court—come the images of Christ who indwells creation and Christians, Christ the bridegroom, Christ who is the head of the body, and Christ the vine. Christ may "trample down death by death" as the ancient troparion of Easter puts it, but Christ does not trample on and crush the creation or us; rather he raises it and us up, making all worthy and lovely before God.

ENDNOTES FOR YEAR A

❧ *Advent*

1. Martin Durrani, "Glimmer of Peace appears in the Science Wars," *Physics World* (September 1997), 9.
2. Kevin Kelley, *The Home Planet* (New York: Addison-Wesley Publishing Co., 1988), 137.
3. Thomas Hopko, *The Winter Pascha* (Crestwood, N.Y.: St.Vladimir's Seminary Press, 1984), 85.
4. Wendell Berry, *Recollected Essays 1965-1980* (New York: North Point Press, 1987), 247.

❧ *Christmas*

1. Charlotte Spretnak, *States of Grace* (San Francisco: HarperSanFrancisco, 1991), 45.
2. *The Hymnal 1982*, Hymn 204, words by John Macleod Campbell Crum.
3. *Sierra* (May-June 1999): 60.
4. Barbara Cawthorne Crafton, *Meditations on the Book of Psalms* (New York: Ballantine Books, 1996), reading for January 1.

❧ *Epiphany*

1. Stephen Hawking, *A Brief History of Time* (New York: Bantam Books, 1988),165-66, 168, 174.
2. Lydia Dotto, *Blue Planet: A Portrait of Earth* (New York: Harry N. Abrams, 1991), 6.
3. Charlene Spretnak, *States of Grace*, 25-26.
4. *Anglican World* (Trinity 1998): 27.
5. George F. MacLeod, *The Whole Earth Shall Cry Glory* (Iona: Wild Goose Publications, 1995), 12.
6. *Journal of Urology* 159 (1998): 1892.
7. Richard A. Kerr, *Science* 282 (6 November 1998): 1024.
8. Jimmy Carter, *Living Faith* (New York: Times Books/Random House, 1996), 28-29.
9. William Porcher DuBose, *Unity In the Faith* (Greenwich, Conn.: Seabury, 1957), 154, 243.

❧ *Lent and Holy Week*

1. Edwin Freedman, *Generation to Generation: Family Process In Church and Synagogue* (New York: The Guilford Press, 1985), 54.

2. Wendell Berry, *Recollected Essays 1965-1980* (New York: North Point Press, 1987), 237.

3. Ibid., 105.

4. "Sing, my tongue, the glorious battle," hymn 166 in *The Hymnal 1982* (New York: Church Pension Fund, 1985).

5. From an Orthodox liturgy for Holy Saturday.

❧ *Easter*

1. Marianne Dorman, *The Sermons of Lancelot Andrewes*, vol. 2 (Durham: The Pentland Press Ltd., 1993), 8, 152-53.

2. William Ryan and Walter Pittman, *Noah's Flood* (New York: Simon and Schuster, 1999).

3. For a thoughtful treatment of new malaria risks worldwide see Ellen Ruppel Shell's cover article, "Resurgence of a Deadly Disease," *The Atlantic Monthly* (August 1997).

4. Joshua Epstein and Robert Axtell, *Growing Artificial Societies* (New York: Brookings Institution, 1996).

5. Sallie McFague, *The Body of God* (Minneapolis: Fortress Press, 1993), 133.

6. Martin Thornton, *English Spirituality* (Cambridge, Mass.: Cowley Publications, 1986), 114.

7. Roger Lewin, "All for One, One for All," *New Scientist* (14 December 1996): 28ff.

8. Timothy Ferris, "Seeing In the Dark," *The New Yorker* (10 August 1998): 55ff.

9. Georges Lemaître, *The Primeval Atom* (New York: Van Nostrand, 1951).

10. John Jerome, *The Elements of Effort* (New York: Basic Books, 1997), 186-87.

❧ *The Season After Pentecost*

1. American Academy of Pediatrics, December 1997.

2. Peter Selby, "Embracing a Common Share in God's Mercy," *The Witness* (December 1998): 16.

3. Bill Bryson, "Britain's Hedgerows," *National Geographic* (September 1993): 94-117.

4. J. Robert Wright, ed., *Readings for the Daily Office from the Early Church* (New York: Church Hymnal Corporation, 1991), 407.

5. Don Munton, "Dispelling the Myths of the Acid Rain Story," *Environment* (July/August 1998): 4ff.

6. Ann Dunnewold and Diane G. Sanford, *Postpartum Survival Guide* (New York: New Harbinger Publications, 1994), 5-6.

7. Raghavan Iyer, *In the Beginning: The Mystical Meaning of Genesis* (New York: Concord Grove Press, 1983).

8. *Nature* (April 1998): 435.

9. Zuckerman, Kasl, and Ostfield, "Psychosocial Predictors of Mortality Among the Elderly Poor," *American Journal of Epidemiology* (July 1984): 410 ff; Graham, Kaplan, Cornoni-Hunley, et al., "Frequency of Church Attendance and Blood Pressure Elevation," *Journal of Behavioral Medicine* 1, no. 1 (1978): 37ff; D. R. Hannayv, "Religion and Health," *Society, Science and Medicine* 14A (1980): 683-685.

10. Laird Harris, Gleason J. Archer, and Bruce K. Waltke, *The Theological Wordbook of the Old Testament*, vol. 2 (Chicago: Moody, 1980), 606.

11. See also Debra Niehoff, *The Biology of Violence* (New York: The Free Press, 1999).

12. *Emu* 97 (Australia): 248.

13. From a Lansing, Michigan workshop on "The Terminally Ill Patient and the Helping Person" conducted by Amelia J. Barbus, Associate Professor of Nursing, Wayne State University, Detroit.

14. David Pimental, *BioScience* (February 1997).

15. New reading on this subject from an ID proponent: William Dembski, *The Design Inference* (Portchester, N. Y.: Cambridge University Press, 1998).

16. Martin Thornton, *English Spirituality* (Cambridge, Mass.: Cowley Publications, 1986), 112.

17. Dugald Stermer, *Vanishing Flora* (New York: Harry N. Abrams, Inc., 1995), 12.

18. From "Collecting the Elements" by Barbara Jordan in *Channel* (Boston: Beacon Press, 1990).

19. Sea Web and Natural Resources Defense Council, December 10, 1998.

20. *The Economist* (28 November–4 December 1998): 87.

21. Richard Feynman, "The Relation of Mathematics to Physics," *The Character of Physical Law* (Cambridge: The MIT Press, 1965), 55-56.

22. Mary Pipher, *Reviving Ophelia: Saving the Lives of Adolescent Girls* (New York: Ballantine Books, 1994), 169-170.

23. Statistics from *Parade Magazine* (November 1998).

24. *The Witness* (December 1998) ran a series of articles about electric power and solar energy in which some of these details appear.

25. Jim Blackburn in *Earth Letter* (March 1998).

26. Mike McCullough, *To Forgive is Human* (Westmont, Ill.: InterVarsity Press, 1997).

27. "Debt Burden on Impoverished Countries," The Episcopal Church Office of Government Relations background paper for Lambeth 1998.

28. Cheryl Silver and Ruth DeFries, eds., *One Earth, One Future* (Washington D.C. : National Academy Press, 1990), 18.

29. Matthew Fox, *The Coming of the Cosmic Christ* (San Francisco: Harper, 1988), 88.

30. *Missouri Resources* 15, no. 4, 17.

31. J. Robert Wright, ed., *Readings for the Daily Office from the Early Church* (New York: Church Hymnal Corporation, 1991), 155.

32. *Science News* 154 (17 October 1998): 248.

33. "Debt burden on Impoverished Countries," Office of Government Relations of the Episcopal Church background paper for Lambeth 1998.

34. Gro Harlem Brundtland, "Global Change and Our Common Future," *One Earth, One Future*, ed. Cheryl Silver and Ruth DeFries (Washington D.C. : National Academy Press, 1990), 148.

35. Bruce Selcraig, "Reading, 'Riting, and Ravaging," *Sierra* (May/June 1998): 60ff.

36. Peter Marzuk, *The New England Journal of Medicine* (5 December 1985): 1474-76.

37. "The Hermit and His Blackbird," *Celtic Prayers*, ed. Robert Van De Weyer (Nashville: Abingdon Press, 1997), 31.

38. Tony Fitzgerald, *Signals from the Heartland* (New York: Walker and Company, 1993), 96.

39. I. C. McMillen, *Reproduction, Fertility and Development* 7 (1995): 499.

40. Erla Zwingle, "Women and Population," *National Geographic* (October 1998): 36-55.

41. Fred Pearce quoting John Gummer, *New Scientist* (20 July 1996): 47.

YEAR B

ADVENT

1 Advent

Isaiah 64:1-9 We, like our ancestors, sometimes interpret natural disasters as signs of divine disfavor. Yet earthquakes and volcanoes are part of the creative processes of the planet itself—the lifting and folding of tectonic plates and the bubbling up of magma that form the newest ground on earth. (Remember the wonderful first chapter of James Michener's *Hawaii* describing the formation of those islands?) We connect our own sinfulness with the contrasting awesome power of God. It is easy, though not perhaps helpful, to think of nature as the agent of that judgmental power against us. Yet Ecclesiastes speaks of God sending "rain on the just and the unjust." How else might we think theologically about the power of God revealed in nature? How might we express thanks for it despite our fear?

1 Corinthians 1:1-9 Christians are "called to be saints together with all those . . . in every place." Our care for the earth as helpers in God's creative work calls us to collaborate, to look beyond local concerns to our common humanity and our common vocation as saints. Farmer and poet Wendell Berry writes:

> There is a kinship of the fields
> that gives to the living the breath
> of the dead. The earth
> opened in spring, opens
> in all springs. Nameless,
> ancient, many-lived, we reach
> through ages with the seed.[1]

Mark 13:24-37 The fig tree leafs out as a "sign of the times." On a smaller scale, what are the signs of our times with regard to the passing away of the earth? A Christian Science Reading Room display window I passed said that people of faith need not be afraid of nuclear war or massive environmental catastrophe because God would intervene. Do you believe that God will save us from the consequences of our own behavior? Or that the suffering and destruction of natural disaster means God does not care for or watch over us and creation? We have a fascination with the big bang/big crunch theories of the origin and end of the universe, asteroids colliding with earth, and other apocalyptic visions from the world of science. What is this all about?

❦ 2 Advent

Isaiah 40:1-11 Why is the coming of the Lord heralded by changing topography? Valleys and mountains are significant in scripture: valleys are places of shadow and danger and ambush, but also fertile; mountains are barriers to travel but also places of revelation and theophany. Zion is sent up to a high mountain. What might it mean for such mountains to become plains and a highway? How do we experience the outer landscape as related to the inner landscape of pilgrimage, full of holy places? How do the landscapes and cityscapes we create on an individual and a corporate scale express our sense of the holy or lack of it?

2 Peter 3:8-15, 18 God's time is not our time, says the apostle. Creationists reject the timetable of planetary and cosmic evolution as though these two kinds of time were the same. Anglicans assume that scientific knowledge about the world will help correct and deepen our interpretation of scripture and will point in new ways to the activity of God in creation. We distinguish poetic time from historic time. Apocalyptic literature warns that the earth is to be burned up on the Day of the Lord. How might the fragility of the world and our own ephemeral nature lead us to treasure these in the time we have, and to live lives of holiness? What are the varied ways we experience time in our own lives?

Mark 1:1-8 How concrete and earthy are these details of the story of John the Baptist! The wilderness setting; the Jordan River and its waters; a camel's hair coat and a leather belt; a diet of locusts and honey. All these material things sing with meaning in the context of the gospel. We might find *The Spiritual Exercises* of Ignatius of Loyola a useful starting point for prayer. He encourages the person praying to enter into a devotional scene—often a scene from scripture—with the full imagination and all the senses in order to have the heart stirred toward God. The elements are evocative: blowing dust and a hot dry wind, John's coarse clothing and the smell of sweat, the strange taste of his simple food, the way he bends down to tie a leather sandal thong at Jesus' feet. How might we be moved to pray as we enter the sensual details of this scene?

❦ 3 Advent

Isaiah 65:17-25 "I am about to create new heavens and a new earth.... Jerusalem as a joy." Creation has not ended, but is the continuing work of God. Current theologians are exploring an understanding of humanity as co-creators with God, bearing an adult responsibility for what we bring into being or remove from being. What are the feelings stirred by the notion that God might be doing new, unprecedented things that require us to change our attitudes and foster openness? The new city of the reign of God will be a place where poverty and the death of children and the elderly will not happen, where inhabitants will be able to live on what they produce. The vision of the reign of God as a "peaceable kingdom" also does away with predation. How might living into this vision transform the ways we human beings now prey upon one another? Or the ways we employ our resources?

1 Thessalonians 5:12-28 This passage offers practical advice for the Christian community. How do we value one another's labor in the world? How do we give thanks for its productiveness in our life of prayer? What would our lives and culture look like if indeed we became "sanctified wholly" (whole, hale, healthy, holy, hallow are related terms), and how is our holiness related to our health and illness? "Test everything" is an instruction that invites us to employ reason, even scientific method, to discern what prophecy is reliable and what mistaken, what activity is good and what is evil.

John 1:6-28 John the Baptist and all Christians after him are called to the work of bearing witness to the light. The dark-adapted human eye can see a single photon of light—an astonishing sensitivity. Visible and invisible light, heat, radiation, sound, microwave energy—all are on a single spectrum in the universe, forms of the original energy of creation. Why is light such a powerful image of God? There are difficulties with light/dark imagery: our culture has too often related them to white/black and good/bad in racial relations. How might we approach this problem in hearing the text and not be "blind" to our neighbors?

🌾 *4 Advent*

2 Samuel 7:4-16 In Hebrew scripture having many descendants is the sign of God's covenantal favor to Israel. The house of David is to receive a sign of God's favor in the arrival of a promised child. Modern readers wonder whether "multiplying and being fruitful" is a godly option in light of the terrible overcrowding of some parts of the earth, yet society still favors the traditional family. How do childless married and single people relate to this connection of divine favor with reproduction? How does the church favor families with children over these other households in its institutional life?

Romans 16:25-27 What is this mysterious, long-kept secret proclaimed by the prophets and now by Christ? God's great self-giving love for everything God has made! In the words of Julian of Norwich taken from *Enfolded in Love*: "I saw that God never began to love mankind...man in God's thought has always been known and loved." We, and the whole creation, are the very issue of God's love; we are woven and spun of it.

Luke 1:26-38 Here begins the Christmas story with its great ongoing theme of the incarnation—the hallowing of creation by God's entry into it in human flesh. Wonderful readings on this are available in Celtic Christian materials, in the early church writings,[2] and also in old carol texts such as Britten's *A Ceremony of Carols*. Those images of the stable beasts round the manger are not just sentiment, but a way of picturing God's entry into the humble, natural world to draw forth its gifts—the warming breath of oxen, the hay of the livestock for bedding, the manger for a cradle, the protective watch of the beasts by night over the newborn child and his parents—and to transform it with radiant holiness into the "peaceable kingdom" of Isaiah 11:6 that is to come in the fullness of God's reign.

CHRISTMAS

𝖏 *Christmas Day I*

Isaiah 9:2-7 A carol from the *Carmina Gadelica,* a collection of traditional Hebridean prayers and poems gathered in the nineteenth century, envisions how at the first Christmas as the foot of the redeemer first touched the earth, all creation glowed in response:

> This night is born to us the root of our joy...
> This night is the long night...
> Glowed to him wood and tree,
> Glowed to him mount and sea,
> Glowed to him land and plain,
> When that his foot was come to earth.[1]

Psalm 96, one of the great songs of creation in scripture, seems to capture the same resonance of the creation with its savior. Because of the incarnation, we Christians have also been given a "new song." But it is not given to us alone: "the whole earth" is to sing to the Lord. The trees shout for joy, the sea thunders, the field also rejoices. A world so firm "it shall never be moved" dances in exultation for the fulfillment of our "blessed hope." Salvation is for all. Jesus is laid in the feeding trough of the welcoming beasts. Sheep and their shepherds are startled by the heavenly hosts bursting into light and song over the hills. The angels also proclaim glory on heaven and earth. All together are needed to properly laud this great deed of God.

Titus 2:11-14 After the exuberance of the vision of Isaiah and Psalm 96, Titus seems to offer such buttoned-down instructions to an increasingly institutional

Christian community. Yet Christian ascetics in every age have reminded the church of the deep connection between self-discipline, virtue, and joy. Our joyful feasting at Christmas lacks justice if it is not extended in giving to those who do not have the means for a feast. Our feasting becomes intemperate if we gobble more than our share of creation's goods and leave others hungry. But as we practice virtuous, holy living, our joy is greatly magnified.

Luke 2:1-20   I once visited a rebuilt first-century house near Bethlehem. Up a few stone steps, one enters a single space smaller than the average American bedroom, with a floor stepped on two levels. In one part the men would have sat together, perhaps making music or sharing refreshments. In the other, women would gather around a brazier, perhaps grinding grain in a handmill and cooking the family meal. If a visiting woman arrived about to deliver a child, she might cause the whole household to become ritually unclean, and it would be an act of courtesy and kindness on her part to go into the earth-floored downstairs compartment, possibly used to secure livestock at night, to deliver her child in a bit of privacy.

Perhaps Mary gave birth in similar circumstances, not in an "inn," but in a small crowded home. We are used to so much space and privacy in our western culture that it is hard to imagine having to go outdoors, even into the wild country, to be alone, and sharing every indoor moment elbow to elbow with many others. The savior of the world brought "heaven and earth to little space," as an old carol sings. We who take up much room on earth might well remember the One who came into a crowded place and dwelled among the poor without privacy or possesions for our sake.

❦ 1 Christmas

Isaiah 61:10–62:3   The growth of shoots and seeds in fertile soil is irrepressible, a wonderful metaphor for the springing up of righteousness and praise as God's reign is fulfilled. Yet we have the power (at least temporarily) to damage the growth of the earth through our pollution, strip development, urban sprawl, and poor soil care. Euros Bowen, the great Welsh poet of the twentieth century, writes:

> Under our government
> the privy council of the stars is excommunicated.
> The brightness on the sea
> is the spittle of oils,
> slag-heaps are filth's poison,

and the gold of the heavens is lead
that fouls lungs, wings and leaves.[2]

How can we collaborate with God, the gardener of creation and justice?

Galatians 3:23-25, 4:4-7 Growing up in the gospel calls us to think for ourselves—not to be handed our instruction by a tutor, or kept on the path by a paternal disciplinarian or a set of rules about every aspect of life. How shall we conduct ourselves as adults in creation? What part of a child's conduct toward the natural world should we retain (wonder, curiosity, delight) and what part leave behind (self-centeredness, magical thinking, small vision)?

John 1:1-18 God's creativity is praised in the language of sound and light. Scientists have mapped a microwave image of the cosmos that captures the hum of creation present since its first instant. Radiation from the initial cosmic explosion of light spread out into the cosmos and is still traveling outward, detectable by radio telescopes. In the spectrum of energy, sound and light are on a single continuum. The visible light of the big bang radiation quickly cooled and was stretched by the expanding universe across space. The longer microwaves remain as a distant echo. The presence of this background microwave radiation was accepted as confirmation of the big bang origin of the universe: it showed us the universe at its first half-million-year mark when the brilliance of the initial explosion cleared.

In the east, that sound is called *Aum* (or *Om*), the "unstruck sound," also used as a name for God. It is the primal sound of the universe that we may equate with the speaking of that Word into the nothingness before creation. The Word is a hum, a song, God's *son et lumière*—and Christians know it as light, the light we call Christ.

☙ 2 Christmas

Jeremiah 31:7-14 "Their life shall become like a watered garden." The prophet gives us a vision of the restoration of exiles to a place of rootedness and nurture and plenty. These images of sheep, brooks, farming, and countryside are comfortably familiar to some rural Christians, but inaccessible to others whose only landscape is the inner city. How do we translate them for urban dwellers? Can we generate an image of clean sidewalks, green parks, flourishing city trees, window-boxes of flowers, and a block party as an urban version of the exiles' homeland?

Ephesians 1:3-19 God will give to God's children "a spirit of wisdom and revelation as you come to know him…with the eyes of your hearts enlightened." How does worldly knowledge—the gathering of facts and observable data in the sciences—relate to the spirit of wisdom? How would we see the earth and ourselves with the eyes of our hearts enlightened? What connections would we perceive?

Luke 2:41-52 Most parents of teens can identify with the parents of the adolescent Jesus. The school-age child strives for mastery over environment and self, developing a conscience and a set of social skills. Adolescence is a period of choosing among many alternatives for shaping the adult personality, and is by nature turbulent and unstable. At this age the young person wants to be treated as an adult, yet fears adult responsibility; longs for freedom and autonomy, yet feels inadequate.

If we accept the full humanity of Jesus, we may imagine that he, too, had to grow into his changing body and changing social roles. Likely this was not easy for his family or for him. How do we let our children grow up, balancing their need for care and protection with their need for freedom and separation? How can the church assist teens and parents in this threshold phase of adulthood?

EPIPHANY

🔥 *The Epiphany*

See entry in Year A, page 12.

🔥 *1 Epiphany*

Isaiah 42:1-9 Bringing forth justice is the central work of the people of God. How shall we share in this work? What is the "just and proper use of creation" described in our prayers of the people?[1] Our baptismal vows neglects to mention our relationship with creation, except insofar as we recognize God as Creator and are called to justice toward all people. What might a suitable baptismal promise be regarding our place in creation? What are the "new things" God declares? What is our obligation in return for the Spirit's "gift of joy and wonder" in all God's works?

Acts 10:34-38 "God shows no partiality": literally, God is not a respecter of faces or of personas. God sees our true selves, not the social or religious masks we put on. God is not bound by our biases and discriminations, but is "Lord of all." Human beings have used science as a rationale for making one group dominant over others: non-Caucasian races have been labeled inferior, less human, less moral, less godly, less evolved by Caucasians; certain cultures have been defined as "high" or "low," "first world" or "third world."

But science can also reveal our commonality: in prehistoric ancestry, in ancient migrations and intermixing of ethnic groups, in our blood types and DNA similarities.

We are all to some degree hybrids, sacraments of the joyful and fruitful coming together of human beings across lines of difference. Only our sin obscures this reality.

Mark 1:7-11   The Spirit descends like a dove (a pigeon, actually). What are the delights and problems with having this bird as a divine symbol? The dove in this passage is a close cousin to the pigeon (of the bird family *Columbidae*)—those despised birds of the cities. It is a pigeon that Noah sends out from the ark to seek land. Many birds have extraordinarily keen vision: the raptor, for example, can see a mouse in the grass from a great height. Sadly, pigeons have been employed to identify the spot for the release of bombs over a target, so accurately can they see from the air and locate landmarks below. Birds have the freedom of the sky, close to our symbolic heaven. Some of them—even the smallest—have remarkable stamina and migrate thousands of miles over oceans to seasonal feeding grounds. Doves, with their soft colors and soothing calls, have long been an emblem of peaceableness. What about birds moves and uplifts our spirits and speaks to us of the divine?

🌿 *2 Epiphany*

1 Samuel 3:1-20   Eli is part of a doomed generation and he knows it; his sons are given up to sin. Yet he guides and blesses the child Samuel who is to be the new generation of hope and holiness. How do we live as elders in a tarnished creation and raise children of hope with a new vision? How do we leave the world better than we found it for their sake? How do we take responsibility corporately for our children so they do not dishonor God by word or action? Neuropsychologist James Prescott, who studied 400 pre-industrial societies, holds that cultures that lavish physical affection on infants tend to be less violent. He believes that "cultures with a predisposition to violence are composed of individuals who have been deprived—during at least two critical stages in life, infancy and adolescence—of the pleasures of the body."[2]
In our time, which is hypersensitive to sexual misconduct and anxious about touch, how shall we raise children on whom healthy physical affection is lavished as an antidote to violence?

1 Corinthians 6:11-20   This passage describes sorting out what is helpful and holy from what is not. What is the Christian relationship with the physical world through our bodies? On the one hand, Peter had a vision of clean and unclean food being given to him by God to eat: the dividing line separating what he had considered holy and unholy was broken down. On the other hand, we are bidden to think carefully of *what* we join to ourselves through our bodily life because we are members of Christ.

Modern individualist thinkers may find problems with speaking of sexual relationship as literally "two people becoming one flesh." How do we glorify God in our sexual bodies? How do we speak about the separate personhood of two partners while also speaking of their unity in covenant relationship?

John 1:43-51 Jesus seems to have a prescient knowledge of Nathaniel, standing far off. In the gospels we find glimpses of a tension between miracles offered as an enticement to belief in Jesus as the Messiah, and reminders that belief should come not because of the supernatural "signs" of the reign of God, but because of who Jesus is: the human-born, dying, and resurrected one. Biblical miracles often are problematic for modern rationalism, yet much that would have been regarded historically as miraculous—heart transplants, psychotropic medication, limb reattachment, recovery from coma, and technology like the aqualung or space shuttle—we consider mundane, and therefore "nothing to do with God." What sort of signs of the reign of God do we seek in our time? What signs do we overlook?

🌿 *3 Epiphany*

Jeremiah 3:21–4:2; 1 Corinthians 7:17-23 Jeremiah exhorts against idolatrous worship. In what ways do we idolize our technology and culture? Similarly, the epistle evokes questions about ways we may be enslaved by human beings, our culture, and technology. Organizational consultants Anne Wilson Schaef and Diane Fassel developed a theory that organizations can take on addictive characteristics such as negativism, dependency, defensiveness, fear, crisis-orientation, frozen feelings, manipulation, denial, and dishonesty that foster similar unhealthy, compulsive behaviors in their employees. They define addiction as "any substance or process over which we are powerless."[3] I would define idolatry as *handing over* our power and responsibility to a substance, person, or process that we expect to act on our behalf: we exalt that being or thing while diminishing our humanity and displacing God. How are we enslaved by our work itself, making it an idol or an addiction?

Mark 1:14-20 What does it mean to be followers of Jesus in our time? Does the gospel invitation actually summon some of us to leave our livelihoods, especially if they are in conflict with gospel values? Are there exploitive, destructive employments not suitable for Christians? Can one be a Christian and still build nuclear weapons, create toxic chemicals, pollute waterways, log virgin forests, or import clothing from countries where workers earn pennies a day? How do individuals and communities practice discernment of these moral questions, and what is the role of each?

🌿 4 Epiphany

Deuteronomy 18:15-20 Are scientists the prophets of our time? How do we weigh the contradictory voices who claim to speak with authority? Scholars Robert Jay Lifton and Greg Mitchell researched the culture of atomic bomb development in the 1940s as a way to explore our changing framework for coming to terms with death:

> Hiroshima forced us to look much further into absurd death in connection with imagery of extinction. For example, when a Christian theologian calls for a nonfundamentalist "retrieval of the apocalyptic tradition," he is asking for an expression of apocalyptic imagination appropriate to our plight. . . . And concerning the larger death event, we need to explore what our own growing awareness of the mortality of the planet is. Deepening that recognition could contribute to powerful constructive energies. Western philosophy has long realized that we must imagine our own death in order to live more fully. After Hiroshima, however, our further task is to imagine the end of the world in order to take steps to maintain human existence.[4]

1 Corinthians 8:1-13 How do we use knowledge to build up or trip up others? What happens when our factual knowledge gets ahead of our wisdom and discernment in such matters as genetic engineering and testing for hereditary diseases? Genetic tests are rapidly being developed to find markers for hereditary illness or propensity for diseases such as cancer. Some researchers have been surprised that consumers are not flocking to take such tests. Aside from justified anxieties that having a genetic marker for disease might cost them eligibility for health insurance, many consumers are deciding that they simply do not want to be burdened with worrying information— no matter how factual—unless there are concrete, productive steps they can take to modify their risk. They are weighing the probability of developing illness (usually an unknown statistic) against the certainty of anxiety and unhappiness should they be found to have genetic markers associated with disease. Is knowledge always a blessing?

Mark 1:21-28 A man with an unclean spirit is healed. This may have been a contrary person out to sabotage the congregation and Jesus, or someone with what we would diagnose as a mental illness. What sort of behavior might be the equivalent in our time to "having an unclean spirit"? How do we distinguish mental illness from delinquincy, healing from exorcism, eccentricity from personal freedom? And how does a community set effective yet compassionate boundaries to contain and limit malice and disruption?

❦ 5 Epiphany

2 Kings 4:8-37 Some interpret this story of the healing of the Shunammite woman's son as an early account of cardiopulmonary resuscitation. What do we believe about God's role in such healing? And what are the roles of individual and congregational prayer, and medical practice in healing? How do we hear such stories in light of the experience of Christians who have prayed hard for the healing of their loved ones, only to see them die?

1 Corinthians 9:16-23 Many scientists believe that their worldview contradicts religious belief, that they would have to suspend reason to be Christian. Paul describes tailoring his style and message and method to fit his audience for the sake of winning lives for Christ. How might the church—all of us—do a better job of speaking the language of scientists to help incredulous ones believe? In the late 1950s, at the height of the age of science, Rudolf Bultmann wrote:

> In faith I realize that the scientific world-view does not comprehend the whole reality of the world and of human life, but faith does not offer another general world-view which corrects science in its statements on its own level. Rather faith acknowledges that the world-view given by science is a necessary means for doing our work in the world. Indeed, I need to see the worldly events as linked by cause and effect not only as a scientific observer, but also in my daily living.[5]

Does Bultmann's approach hold up as we enter the twenty-first century?

Mark 1:29-39 Epiphany is a good season for preaching an educational series on healing and faith. Is healing the work of a few (doctors, clergy, specially gifted individuals) or all of God's people? What *is* healing : care, cure, mending, transformation? Agnes Sanford, well-known practitioner of healing prayer, offers this reflection:

If we try turning on an electric iron and it does not work, we look to the wiring of the iron, the cord, or the house. We do not stand in dismay before the iron and cry, "Oh electricity, *please* come into my iron and make it work!" We realize that while the whole world is full of that mysterious power we call electricity, only the amount that flows through the wiring of the iron will make the iron work for us. The same principle is true of the creative energy of God....As soon as we learn that God does things *through* us, the matter becomes as simple as breathing....Few of us in the north would ask God to produce a full-blown rose out of doors in January. Yet He can do this very thing, if we adapt out greenhouses to His laws of heat and light, so as to provide the necessities of the rose. And He can produce a full-blown answer to prayer if we adapt our earthly tabernacles to His laws of love and faith so as to provide the necessities of an answered prayer.[6]

🌱 *6 Epiphany*

2 Kings 5:1-15   How do attitude, psychology, and soul relate to physical healing? Two of the lections this week are about leprosy, a term that referred to a whole range of skin ailments. They invite reflection upon social stigmatization, communicable diseases, and the ways our society is inclined to isolate the sick, considering them unclean. There are exemplary ministries to lift up, like that of Father Damian, or Constance and her companions, the martyrs of Memphis, who ministered to the sick in an epidemic of yellow fever in 1878 when others fled the city.

Fourth-century Bishop Gregory Nazianzus asked about our responsibilities to those who are ill: "What then shall we do, we who have received a share in a great name, who have received a new name, the name which comes to us from Christ...who has borne our ills? What will our thoughts and attitudes be toward those sick human beings?"[7]

1 Corinthians 9:24-27   Athletics—its physiology and training (asceticism)—is a provocative metaphor for the life of discipleship. In a wonderful chapter entitled "AIDS as *Memento Mori*, the reminder of our mortality," theologian John Snow touches on athletics, fear, and death in the context of AIDS. Striving; bearing pain and discomfort; showing up regularly for training; being reliable to one's team; pushing the limits and taking risks; carrying both defeat and victory with dignity; doing the hard work of healing; accepting criticism and making use of it to change; seeking wise mentors; entering into the ecstasy of effort—all of these characterize the training of the soul as well as the body.[8]

Mark 1:40-45 In some congregations, illness, addiction, or the need for surgery is felt to be a sign of weak character and an occasion of unacceptable vulnerability needing to be hidden from all but closest family. Mark raises the issue (a favorite theme of his) about secrecy and proclamation. What are the current issues around privacy versus community support and prayer in your congregation? A Quaker friend once said to me in a conversation about confidentiality that in their meeting, they strive for confidence rather than confidentiality. How might we create church environments of sufficient trust that difficult or painful information can be willingly shared, and members may pray well and care well for one another?

❦ 7 Epiphany

Isaiah 43:18-25 "Do not remember the former things" is a shocking instruction to the Hebrew people, whose whole identity is centered on remembering what God has done for them. Neuroscientists have discovered that the brain of songbirds puts memories into different types of storage depending upon their importance. Some are earmarked for long preservation, others for short. It is theorized that human brains might store memory in similar ways: to function in a complex world, the ability to sift memories—forgetting some in order to store and recall others—is a vital function.

Aiding and preserving memory—handing down the story through generations—is an important part of every religious tradition. What is the role of remembering for Christians, and what is the role of forgetting? How do we resist progress and fear change in the various spheres of our life by holding onto the past fruitlessly? What is springing forth in the world that we do not want to perceive? How do we stay open to a paradigm shift—a whole new understanding of God, creation, the church, history, and ourselves?

2 Corinthians 1:18-22 Yes and no and shades of grey! God's yes summons us to great courage in embracing the new, in trusting that God can and will speak through it. Few ethical decisions lead to quick and simple yes/no answers: sometimes we feel paralyzed by the difficult choices that face us. In the area of reproductive technology, for example, choices for an infertile couple may range from *in vitro* fertilization, egg or sperm donation, or corrective medical interventions, to adoption or even surrogate parenting. We are summoned to prayer, congregational and family discourse, pastoral counsel, wrestling with conscience, responsible choice, and then congregational support for the decision made and its consequences. God's yes gives us gracious space for our adult decision-making.

Mark 2:1-12   The lowering of the paralytic is eloquent of the role of the community in healing, and is an opportunity to discuss the relation of healing and illness to sin. The people around Jesus had a harder time believing that someone could assure them of God's forgiveness than believing that the same person could heal a paralytic. Both healings address a paralysis, after all—one of the body, and one of the soul ensnared by sin. For God, all kinds of healing are possible, and healing wherever we find it points to the presence and power of God as Jesus showed it to us. In our time, the healing of sin is regarded as a highly private matter. How might it be helpful to bring such healing into the corporate life of the church and society in fresh ways?

❦ 8 Epiphany

Hosea 2:14-23   Hosea writes of the renewing of the covenant with Noah and all creatures as a sign of the marriage between God and the people. The *shalom*—peaceful order—of God is characterized by the four major attributes of God in Hebrew scripture: righteousness (*tsedek*), justice (*mishpat*), steadfast love (*chesed*), and mercy (*rachmah*). How do our actions in creation manifest these holy attributes? We tend to concentrate on the Abrahamic covenant between God and the people, overlooking this other covenant with *all* creation as though the two could be separated. How are they, in fact, intertwined?[9]

2 Corinthians 3:4–4:2   Our sufficiency is from God. How often do we offer thanks with any detail or heartiness for all the abundance of creation that we enjoy; for what we eat, and the earth, water, weather, and human labor that produce it? Or for our fellow creatures, whose bodies we use for such a variety of products—pigs, for example, whose heart valves and vessels and tissues are used routinely for transplant surgery? Our old ways of reading Genesis 1 have led us to consume the creatures by "right." But God is the giver, and perhaps through Noah's covenant we find an understanding that leads us toward gratitude and just relationship with the whole creation.

Mark 2:18-22   Two separate ideas are here: fasting and feasting, and new versus old. Fasting is a little-observed asceticism among many religious people; we are more inclined to just "give something up for Lent." In Orthodox tradition, fasting focuses on the particular foods proper to each season: the goal is not deprivation, but a mindfulness of God through the body's experience of eating different foods at different seasons in the church year. How might we fast so as to be mindful of God? Recently, fasting has come to be used at Thanksgiving as a way to choose to be in solidarity with the poor of the earth—as through the Oxfam fast for world hunger, in which food money is donated to hunger relief. Fasting is choosing to consume less of an overabundance of resources in order that we might remember the lack suffered by others, and help remedy that poverty.

❧ Last Epiphany

1 Kings 19:9-18   For Elijah, God is not found in the great cataclysmic forces of nature, but in the "still small voice." How well do we look for God in the details? It is easy to look for God in the earthshaking experiences, yet traces of God's love and generative power lie in the minute diversity everywhere in creation. Open any insect book and notice the thousands of shapes and colors and kinds of beetles; a single wild plant may have dozens of varieties. What do we learn about God from this wealth of diversity, detail, and complexity in creation?

2 Peter 1:16-21   This text offers an opportunity to address the authority of scripture not as inerrant and literal, but as living. Its authority is grounded in history yet informed by new knowledge and experience, open to scholarly interpretation in every age within the context of the community's prayer. The era of the pastoral epistles was a time of anxiety about the freedom with which Christians were seizing upon and interpreting sacred texts and living them, and a time of consolidating hierarchies of authority and power in the church. How, then, do we hear words of prophecy from past ages in a way that informs our faith? What do we say to creationists and other literal interpreters of select parts of scripture? Is there common ground on which creationists and evolutionists can communicate out of the shared desire for a universe full of purpose?

Mark 9:2-9   Mountain, light, and cloud are the landscape where the transcendent and the immanent intersect in this text. What do each of these elements signify? How do they relate to our experience of God? Landscape designer and author Julie Meservey suggests that from an early age human beings tend to claim one of seven landscape forms as particularly holy: island, sea, mountain, cave, sky, harbor, or promontory.[10] Each of them evokes powerful memories from early life. Each of them says something about how we may experience God most powerfully: as within us, as boundlessness, as refuge, as invitation, as place of homing and departure, as transcendent, as native element, as a launching place to the unknown, or as familiar womb.

❧ LENT AND HOLY WEEK

❧ *Ash Wednesday*

See entry in Year A, page 24.

❧ *1 Lent*

Genesis 9:8-17   Why does the covenant with Noah and the creation receive so little attention compared to the one with Abraham? Notice our tendency to think that the Abraham story is more "factual" than the Noah story—why? Both come from the long oral history that preceded the first texts (with Exodus likely written before Genesis); both may contain truth rather than fact. An extensive 1999 report from the United States Geological Survey raises new concerns about the acceleration of man's impact on the earth due to urban sprawl, population growth, and demands upon our natural resources. In the southeast, almost 20 percent of the fish species are now endangered or threatened due to the creation of reservoirs.[1] What might this covenant say about the importance of maintaining the diversity of species? About God's love extending beyond the human species?

1 Peter 3:18-22   Peter offers a theology of baptism based on deliverance through water—deliverance of Noah's family, rather than Israel. Both baptism and the ark bring an inner cleansing from sin and justification according to this epistle. The Noah story suggests a recreation of the original order of the garden of Eden after sin has disrupted it. Though sin persists in the new creation of Noah, there is yet another new creation through the resurrection of Christ. Early Christians for a time believed that if one sinned after baptism, the sin could not be forgiven. This view gave way to an understanding that though baptism was a new creation of the person, sin persists—but its ultimate effects are set right by the resurrection. Sin no longer has dominion.

Mark 1:9-13   Like Noah, Jesus is cut off from the human community and in the company of beasts for forty days, and a dove serves as an intermediary and a sign of future ministry. What purpose might the presence of these creatures in the story serve? How might the story be different if, for instance, Jesus had withdrawn to an upper room to prepare for ministry instead of going out into the wilderness?

Of our own wilderness one conservationist has written:

> These deserts of ours that have a quiet majestic look are alive with creatures, playing specialized roles in the cosmic plan.... The American deserts have been put into great jeopardy by man. Mechanized vehicles, known as "dune-buggies," now roar across them, churning the fragile soil and uprooting the sparse vegetation. As population increases, these vehicles, unless restrained, will produce a Sahara-type desert of shifting sands that will eat savagely into its edges, as it moves east and north under the force of winds.[2]

We are drawn to the desert places, but our intrusive presence changes them from the very environment we seek unless we enter the country on its own terms.

🕊 2 Lent

Genesis 22:1-14   For centuries this text about Abraham's offering of Isaac has been proclaimed as a story of the utter dependence and obedience deemed necessary for relationship to God. Other interpreters argue that by providing the ram for sacrifice, God was declaring an end to human sacrifice in the name of divinity. With World Wars I and II, another interpretation gained currency. In Benjamin Britten's masterpiece *The War Requiem*, the retelling of the Isaac story ends instead with "but Abraham took and slew his son and half the seed of Europe, one by one."

War and holocaust, the epidemic of child abuse—these realities bring today's listeners to hear this "text of terror" in a new way that takes seriously our propensity for bloodshed in the name of religion, and our wasting and devastation of creation. In what ways do we delude ourselves about what we offer and what God asks of us?

Romans 8:31-39 Creation does not separate us from God. We tend to hear in this text that all the various elements named, natural and supernatural, are obstacles to the love of God. Another approach might suggest that our relationships with all these things are *changed* through Christ: they become vehicles for closer relationship with God. Seen in this light, our troubles and disasters—as well as the stuff of creation— all become revelatory of God's love once we seek for and find God in and through them.

Mark 8:31-38 What is godly self-denial? Social science rightly points to the prevalence of unwholesome self-denial, and particularly to the way in which women have been socially schooled to deny themselves in order to care for others. A number of psychologists have written about the need to develop a true self in childhood rather than a false, defensive self, in order to be capable of genuine empathy, joy, and relationship. So the sacrifice of self Jesus speaks about does not refer to being without "self" but instead to a willingness to lay down our life and interests for love of the gospel and our neighbor. Courage like this requires an authentic and healthy self, just as the self-sacrifice of good parenting does. A helpful book on this topic is Alice Miller's *Prisoners of Childhood*.[3]

❦ 3 Lent

Exodus 20:1-17 The Hebrew word for justice, *mishpat*, is derived from *mishpacha* (family or clan), and appears hundreds of times in Hebrew scripture. It is not an abstract idea, but a right ordering of relationships between people, and between God and humanity. What do the commandments say about the complex relationships between humans and animals and the whole structure of creation? How might we best honor their intent today? What does it mean to treat the earth justly? Our notion of justice between human beings has grown and evolved through history (as over the issue of slavery); we have yet to be as clear about the changes required of us in doing justice to animals, plants, and the planet itself. What would a declaration of the rights of non-human creation include today?

Romans 7:13-25 In Romans, Paul's intent is not to denigrate the "old law" but to point out that both Jewish and Gentile Christians are equally in need of and saved by God through the death and resurrection of Jesus, who puts right all laws of this world corrupted by sin. So rather than emphasize the either/or quality of Paul's spirit/flesh image, it is helpful to look at the unitive intent of his conclusion. Paul's Greek readers tended to believe in a material world at odds with a spiritual world, but this was not a Jewish concept. Paul saw creation as being transformed by (groaning in birth pains with) God through Christ, not as unsaved and hostile. How is our modern thinking about creation unitive or dualistic?

John 2:13-22   The cleansing of the temple—the expulsion of those who were using it as a place of commerce—is connected to a saying about the raising of Jesus' body in three days. Selling animals for ritual sacrifice by pilgrims in the temple precincts was an ancient practice, but perhaps prices had become extortionate, or maybe the buyers and sellers had simply forgotten the purpose of the temple as a place of prayer. From the perspective of the Johannine community such abuses were part of the pattern of corruption that led to Jesus' crucifixion by the powers and principalities of this world.

The text tempts us to draw a line between the sacred and the profane, the clean and the unclean. Reading this gospel in light of the other lectionary texts suggests instead a focus on justice, on the right ordering of relationships and transactions in the world in order to honor God and God's role as originator and hallower of all. How do we participate in commerce—as buyers and sellers—so as to honor God and be just? If the division between sacred and profane is not the division between the material and spiritual, then what is profanation and what is hallowing, and how do we engage in each activity?

❦ *4 Lent*

2 Chronicles 36:14-23   Chronicles offers a startling view of *sabbath*. The destroyed city and empty agricultural land lie desolate for seventy years after the conquest of Cyrus, whom the prophets saw as a messianic force sent by God to correct the idolaters and the unfaithful people "until the land enjoyed its sabbaths." Wise farmers rotate crops with plantings of winter wheat or nitrogen-fixing plants to rejuvenate tired soil. The failure to care for the soil—to let it rest—through overcultivation, monocropping, and heavy chemical fertilizing leads to its loss through erosion and desertification. Careless irrigation of dry lands consumes irreplaceable water and leaves the ground poisoned with salt. Images of modern warfare—forests decimated by Agent Orange in southeast Asia, or oil-smoke polluted skies and sands in the Middle East—suggest that we are far from allowing the land its sabbath rest. How might we witness to the land's need for sabbath?

Ephesians 2:4-10   We are of God's workmanship. As we are made, so we are also makers, after God's image. What things are good and godly for us to make, and what not? Scientists now breed laboratory animals with oncogenes (or cancer genes) so that they will develop tumors for treatment research. Livestock are bred and raised to be so fat they can hardly move for maximum profitability at slaughter. Anthrax and other diseases are cultured in military laboratories for germ warfare. Plants and insects genetically engineered for traits considered desirable are released into the environment where they will interact with other organisms with unknown consequences. How does the Christian community weigh difficult moral choices affecting the creatures around us? How do we decide what we *could* make but *should* not make? How do we repent from our choices when history shows them to have been disastrous?

John 6:4-15   A question for the well-to-do of the world: "Where are we to buy bread for these people to eat?" What is our responsibility for feeding the hungry of our own neighborhoods and of the poor nations far off? When we consider global neediness, we may be as overwhelmed as the handful of disciples facing the five thousand with five loaves and two fish. The story warns us wonderfully against despair. One disciple notices a little boy with a lunch basket, and from that tiny start, all are fed.

Jesus instructs the disciples, "Gather up the fragments left over, so that nothing may be lost" (a favorite theme of John's). In the economy of God's reign every fragment is precious, none shall be overlooked or wasted or disregarded. How do we live out this ethic of conservation?

❧ 5 Lent

Jeremiah 31:31-34   A prophecy of the new covenant to be written on the hearts of the people. Christian scripture speaks at length of the way that the new covenant in Christ does not demolish the previous covenant relationship of God with the people, but fulfills it. So the covenants of Abraham and Noah that required a just ordering of people's lives and actions are not obliterated by the new freedom; rather, justice is to be taken even more deeply into our hearts, along with righteousness and compassion, as we inwardly "know God." Of old, God led the people across a new frontier into a land of promise. Now we find ourselves on a planet with few frontiers left, and instead of expansion, conquest, and outward movement, our sense of call is to be careful stewards of our settled lands; to cherish the resources we enjoy; to deepen wisdom and maturity; and to live peaceably among competing neighbor nations. In America, many of our myths and images of expansion seem bankrupt (the new frontier, the golden door, the wild west, even the space race). What new sacred myths and images might we need for the next millennium?

Hebrews 5:1-10 A text about the priestliness of Jesus invites us all to claim our role as priests in "a kingdom of priests," and, as the words of the hymn exhort, "to daily lift life heavenward."[4] Priestly work is the labor of blessing and offering. How do we hallow life and offer it back to God? The offertory at the eucharist is the sign and model for this activity. All our life and labor and the whole creation is brought forward by the people and laid on the corporal as the "body" of the sacrament in bread and wine. Its holiness is established through the Spirit, and it is given back to us and incorporated into us for our new labor and transformation. How do we "lift life heavenward?" How do we claim our priestly calling?

John 12:20-33 A grain of wheat dies in the earth to become fruitful: an ancient image of resurrection. Modern biology looks askance at the idea of wheat dying in the ground in order to grow. We know about the structure of the seed: the cells of the new plant begin to multiply and diversify from its apical meristem as water and nutrients pass through the semipermeable cell membranes from the ground. The seed's husk then breaks and rots away, returning its elements to the soil to nourish other plants. So the old metaphor seems a little crude. And yet we also know about the marvelous complexity of living organisms, how they are made up of cells that are constantly dying and being replaced in the processes of growth. Our new metaphors of death and resurrection may be more complex and intriguing—how might we explore them? How else do you see death fostering new life in the world?

🔥 *Palm Sunday*

Isaiah 45:21-25 God is the salvation of the whole earth from end to end. The creative word of God has gone forth and will not return. These images moved theologians like Teilhard de Chardin to reflect on the evolution of the universe and to conclude that it is moving upward toward the perfection of God's plan. Historians and scientists have a more difficult time embracing this historical positivism. Some cosmologists still argue for an eternally expanding universe; some for a steady state universe; others for a rhythm of expansion and contraction, beginning and ending. How do these theories about the origin and destiny of the universe affect our thinking about God's plan in creation? How does our optimism or pessimism about the future of the world, human and natural, affect our sense of responsibility? Can we fathom that our choices may affect the destiny of creation? How do we weigh freedom and determinism in light of the new science?

Philippians 2:5-11 Paul describes the self-emptying of the servant of God. How do we envision servanthood and humility in an era and a culture that stress pride and individualism? The word "servant," like the word "steward," is problematic for modern hearers. We miss the complexity of relationship that Paul's contemporaries would have understood—how those who were under authority were also authorized to offer care and hospitality on behalf of the host—because the images of slavery and oppression, of groveling and the denigration of persons, corrupt the useful sense of the words. Is there new language to help us retrieve the original meaning and better understand our relationships with God and each other?

The service of Jesus on the cross opens reflection on all the rich meaning of the incarnation, the hallowing and glorifying of humanity and creation. As Eucharistic Prayer 1 in *The Supplemental Liturgical Materials* says of Jesus Christ, "dwelling among us, he revealed our glory."

Mark 14:32–15:47 Mark's passion narrative is full of the frailty of flesh, human fearfulness, and the darkness that came "over the whole land" with the death of Jesus. It is from the mystery of this fragility—Jesus praying in distress in the garden, the slave's cut-off ear, a young man fleeing away naked, the broken flesh, Peter cold and weak beside the fire, the scorned savior, Jesus' body wrapped in a linen shroud—that the shocking mystery of resurrection is to break forth.

❦ *Maundy Thursday*

Exodus 12:1-14; 1 Corinthians 11:23-26; John 13:1-15 The lessons are full of the most concrete and bodily imagery: lambs slain and eaten in haste; blood smeared on doorposts; bread and wine as the body and the blood of Jesus eaten and drunk; Jesus kneeling and washing feet. God comes to us through our senses: we learn God in our bodies by eating and drinking, by being washed and washing. We are formed by our *doing*, not just our thinking, in order to be transformed more and more into the likeness of Christ. These sensual actions—taking, blessing, breaking, sharing—hallow us and the stuff of creation by illuminating the way all has already been made holy through the incarnation.

❧ *Good Friday*

Isaiah 52:13–53:12; Hebrews 10:1-25; John 18:1–19:37   The King comes as suffering servant. When we are tempted to sit back and hope that God will magically intervene to save us from our own destructive power by arriving in glory to overturn the powers of this world, we find instead the human one hanging on the cross in scandalous forgiveness. "He shall startle many nations; kings shall shut their mouths because of him"—not what we expect. Not what we want, this ruler who opens his arms in powerlessness to call us to repentance and embrace us in love. Not what we want, this God who will allow our nuclear bombs to detonate and our farming to poison the ground, who does not stay our hands from evil, but calls us to live as though evil will not have the last word or the ultimate power. God does not keep us from crucifying God, but simply brings resurrection.

❧ *Holy Saturday*

See entry in Year A, page 33.

EASTER

❧ *The Great Vigil of Easter*

See entry in Year A, page 34.

❧ *Easter Day*

Isaiah 25:6-9   The prophet looks forward to the coming of God's reign as a banquet for all people. On Easter Day, I always think of the fanciful tale of Mary Magdalene at Caesar's feast. Legend has it that she was a woman of considerable means and status and, after Jesus had been resurrected, procured an invitation to a great banquet at the royal court. Boldly, she approached the emperor to complain about Pilate's miscarriage of justice and announce the good news that Jesus had been raised from the dead. It is said that Caesar was about to peel a hard-boiled egg. When he heard her words he held the egg up and said dismissively, "He can no more be raised from the dead by God than this egg can turn red." There in his hand, it became as red as a ruby.

This tale may not be historical, but it accounts for the many Eastern icons that show Mary Magdalene holding a red egg, the color that many Orthodox Christians dye their eggs at Easter, and reminds us that beyond all our expectations, "God is able."

Colossians 3:1-4   This tiny fragment of Colossians comes from a larger argument urging Christians not to disregard their surroundings, but to live with virtue and integrity in the community, as befits those raised with Christ. Christians must treat each other kindly, avoiding malice and anger, abusive talk and lying, and give up the illusion of status based on ethnicity, religious practice, or social standing. To do so is to be renewed in knowledge according to the image of God. The mystery of this resurrection feast, our new baptismal life hidden with Christ in God, always turns us back at once to the most pragmatic aspects of our life in this world: we are to live justly, kindly, bravely, and prudently. We are to deal with the world as it is—not dwell in our illusions about it—and thus honor its maker.

Mark 16:1-8   The empty tomb and eggs and bunnies collide on Easter morning— another good reason for having the primary feast on the evening before! On Easter morning, the children (of all ages) come back to the font to see in the light of day where the fearful mystery happened. This can be a day for interpreting Easter to the little ones, even a day for an Easter egg hunt in the nave when the preacher brings out an icon of Mary Magdalene with her egg and tells the Eastern story of Tiberius Caesar and the red egg (see Isaiah above).

The sentimental creation images of Easter—bunnies, lambs and chicks, flowers and the like—are all childlike ways of wondering at new life. Just as the grown chicken is by no means as charming as the chick, the grown Christian is more gawky, complex, and grubby than the newly-baptized. Yet that wondrous new life continues on in us—adult, sin-befuddled creatures that we are—and this day, we feel it stir in witness of the risen One.

🌿 2 Easter

Acts 3:12-26   It is curious that Christ is called "the Author of life," a title we would be more likely to attach to God. Yet Jesus as pioneer and first fruit of resurrection did "write the book," maybe the guide book, on our resurrection destiny. Films like *Jurassic Park* underscore the ways in which we as a species may more and more see ourselves as authors of new life, bringing genetically engineered species into being (an extension of our long-time hybridizing work), working with in-vitro fertilization technology, altering fetal genes to prevent inherited disease or change characteristics, and the like. We also usher species that God has "authored" out of existence. In what way has our understanding of God's authorship shifted, or may it need to shift? How does God's authorship relate to ours? How do we make moral decisions as authors?

1 John 5:1-6   Loving God is to be extremely concrete, not just a state of mind and heart, but a rule of life. The first letter of John ends (and this was probably the actual ending to which the last ten verses were appended) with a curious triad of "Spirit, water, and blood"; together they serve as "witnesses." At once, we are reminded of the two sacraments of baptism and eucharist, washing and feeding, that root the community of faith in Christ—two actions that are powerful both at the literal and the metaphoric level. How do these function as "witnesses"?

John 20:19-31 An interesting alternate translation of the Greek for the familiar verses about forgiveness and sin is: "If you forgive the sins of any they are forgiven them; if you seize (constrain, lay hold of) anyone's they are subdued." There is a distinction made between those sorts of sin that a community can easily move past—with confession and apology and some setting right—and the kind of sin that requires constraint. A counselor working in an adolescent mental health unit described to me the strategy used when a patient becomes explosively violent and self-destructive: in the same way that infants are swaddled with blankets to give them a sense of safety, the workers simply hold the patient down firmly until the emotional storm quiets. Some sin cannot be allowed to rampage, but must be seized and subdued. How do communities make distinctions between the gravity of various sins among their members? Which of our societal sins need gentle forgiveness and a fresh start, and which require firm and forceful intervention?

❦ 3 Easter

Micah 4:1-5 The image of swords beaten into ploughshares challenges us to consider the need to convert technologies and economies of war into those of peace. The hot-burning propulsion systems of rockets and missiles are now capable of being used to incinerate hazardous wastes safely: one modern instance of transformation. A common microbe found in wastewater is capable of breaking down explosives. A few years back, a huge storage container of Cold War mortar rounds and rocket shells was uncovered in East Germany and scientists were faced with the need to dispose cleanly of 20,000 tons of explosives. The chemicals were treated with other chemicals and then fed to bacteria; these harmlessly broke down the toxic molecules, leaving a sediment of ammonium nitrate that can be used for agricultural fertilizer. Can you think of other ways swords have become plowshares?

1 John 1:1–2:2 God is light and in God there is no darkness at all: through the blackness of deep space light is traveling toward our eyes from unimaginably distant stars, and the microwaves from the founding of the universe hum and glow as a background light beneath our range of seeing. John chose the polarity of dark and light to amplify God's unequaled brilliance and goodness to say, "God is all goodness." Yet the God of Isaiah's prophecy states, "I make peace and I create evil." This reveals a God who contains not less than everything. In God there is both darkness and light; the dark and the light in God are made one. Even the dark night of our world hums with the creative energy of the Holy One.

Luke 24:36-48   Jesus proves he is not a ghost by eating some broiled fish. There are scholars who suggest that some early Christian communities had a eucharistic ritual meal that included fish. Fishing is one of the basic ways human beings have fed themselves for millennia, yet the current generation is the first to grow up with the possibility that there will be few or no fish left to eat in the oceans because of centuries of overfishing, and far fewer freshwater fish because inland waterways are polluted by acid rain and agricultural and industrial run-off. In coastal areas of the North Atlantic, fishing towns are faced with the hard reality of choosing to forego their livelihoods or face fishing grounds empty of fish. How might Christians weigh the pressing needs of people to make a living and those of marine (or other) environments to be protected? In gospel stories, Jesus fills the nets of fishers. What might a new gospel story be for the empty-netted fishers of today?

❧ 4 Easter

Acts 4:23-37   This text, describing the early Christian economy of sharing goods, is not among those usually quoted to justify the reordering of American society. Is this the economy that develops because disciples are "of one heart and soul," or the means whereby they become so united? Is the radical redistribution of wealth essential to a Christian society, or a hopelessly utopian ideal? And how might the claim of this text upon our one-third of the world—with the large majority of the world's wealth—differ from its claim upon the other two-thirds, the developing world?

1 John 3:1-8   "We do not know what we will become," even in our age of hyper-awareness of biological processes. We know that our bodies will decay in the earth; we can detail the chemical and organic processes by which they break down. We will, sooner or later, be buried or cremated and thus become compost for the ground. Even this physical destruction is not wasted in God's provenance, but contributes to the good of the soil. But we are not captives to the processes of disease or decay because God has made us and we are God's; we will be like God, all our sin and corruptibility stripped away, finally transformed in our shining resurrection bodies.

John 10:11-16 Jesus speaks of "other sheep that do not belong to this fold," a phrase that has intrigued Christians through the centuries. Some hear him speaking of devotees of other religions. It is fun to speculate that if extraterrestrial intelligent life were discovered—and many astronomers think that given the vastness of the universe, it is likely to exist somewhere!—God would prove to be its creator also. "Creationism" tends to have a very small vision of one planet, fully formed and non-evolving, a few millennia of history, and one chosen people—with a messiah and a cosmic destiny just for the few faithful. Yet creation may be unimaginably larger and more complex an enterprise than we expect, and everywhere we explore we may bump into God's creativity, shepherding, and fearless love extending even there. How might "other sheep," whoever they may be, invite us to a little humility, a little wonder and curiosity, a bigger vision?

❦ 5 Easter

Acts 8:26-40 The Ethiopian eunuch is reading a passage of scripture that must have cried out to him about his own social condition of ironic, limited privilege based on sexual mutilation. Because he is a eunuch he lives outside the bounds of power, normalcy, and generative expectations; he thus shares, alongside Jesus, the humiliation of "life taken away." There must have been more than a little fear in his question, "What is to prevent me being baptized?" Socially, everything about this man made him unclean and unacceptable, even unholy. Yet Philip, in the fire and courage of the Spirit, saw no obstacle to even this man being joined into the Body of Christ.

Who in our time perceive themselves as unholy and unclean, or too damaged to claim full membership in Christ's Body? Psychologists are quick to remind us that those who have suffered physical, emotional, and sexual abuse often have learned to think of themselves as unclean and unfit. They would add gay, lesbian, and bisexual people—especially teenagers—to the list of those who may be shunned by the church or feel unfit to seek membership. When it comes to human sexuality, our science is still in its infancy; we have little idea what roles biology, chemistry, sociology, individual character, and choice play in our sexual development and behavior.

1 John 3:14-24; John 14:15-21 The fruits of resurrection love are an open heart toward our sisters and brothers, the keeping of the commandments, and the sharing of the world's goods with those in need. In 1995 for the first time in 23 years world-wide grain production fell below 300 kilograms a person. That same year brought a better harvest and increased reserves, challenging those scientists who forecast increasing famine. Even so, improved food production has not brought an end to hunger. The real problem is getting food to the people who actually need it: the 800 million chronically undernourished—200 million under age five—many of whom do not have money to buy food or the means of producing it.

The Holy Spirit traditionally bears the name "Comforter." If the eucharist is our real "comfort food," not chocolate and ice cream, then how will we work to provide the comfort of bread (grain, beans, basic protein) to all who hunger?

🌿 6 Easter

Acts 11:19-30; 1 John 4:7-21   The earliest Christian communities organized for famine relief. The 1996 United Nations World Food Summit heard that aggressive patenting of biotechnology by the well-fed west may create a "scientific apartheid" by keeping information about new developments from the 80 percent less prosperous and developed portions of the globe. Single companies in the west can obtain blanket patents to entire areas of new technology. Agracetus, a Wisconsin corporation, developed a method for creating transgenic soya bean plants and was granted a European patent that includes *all* methods of creating transgenic soybeans. For the next millennium, food production and sharing to prevent and relieve famine will involve not just the means of production, but issues of intellectual property rights and the free flow of knowledge between nations.

It is difficult to maintain compassion for the sisters and brothers we do not in fact see, who may be in need both in remote lands and in the forgotten corners of our own cities. Christians are challenged to see "with the eyes of our hearts enlightened" and extend compassion with the kind of generosity and universality characteristic of God's lovingkindness. How might we keep our own eyes of compassion open to the world?

John 15:9-17   Exploring the same theme, the gospel speaks of the fruits of love that abide, epitomized by laying down our lives for others. Can it be that many a good person who might be willing to lay down life for another, especially in a local emergency—running into a burning building to save a child, for example—has a much harder time laying down a few luxuries and comforts of life for the many who are in need every day? There is a gap between an act of heroism and a life of discipleship that challenges us to ponder our choices.

❧ 7 Easter

Acts 1:15-26 In this passage, we hear one of several colorful tales of the death of Judas resulting from his guilt for betraying Jesus, and the preacher usually moves right on to the theme of call and leadership among the remaining disciples. But consider: where might we find our modern "fields of blood," purchased at the expense of life? Brazil contains sections as wealthy as the most privileged communities of America, and drought-plagued areas as poor as any part of Asia or Africa. It produces a huge number of food crops and is an exporter of fruit, coffee, sugar, and soya, yet an estimated 15 million landless Brazilians (10 percent of the population) live on the edge of starvation. The government has promised land reform but faces massive opposition from landowners. Where landless workers have attempted to squat on the ground they work in order to claim it, violence has erupted; forty-seven people died in such conflicts in 1996, and church leaders claim that some killings were in cold blood, though there have been no arrests.

How can communities find just solutions to the conflicting claims of the wealthy and their poorest migrant workers for land and food? What is a suitable role for Christians and for the church in seeking land reform?

1 John 5:9-15; John 17:11-19 How fascinating and provocative are these reminders that if we ask anything according to God's will, God will hear and grant our requests. When I was a small child, I remember praying as Christmas approached for a particular doll in a department store window harder than I had ever prayed for anything, night after night. It was far too expensive for my family, though I knew little about such things. When it did not appear under the tree, I was thrown into a long period of confusion about prayer.

From the reported saying of Jesus in the synoptic gospels to this later instruction of 1 John, the caveat bidding us to ask "in accordance to God's will" gains emphasis. As individuals and a community at prayer, it is our responsibility to inquire into the will of God. It is only insofar as we are "not of the world"(that is, free of its cravings and hollow desires) that we become sanctified by truth and able to ask for the right things. Folk tales are full of disasters brought about by frivolous and selfish wishes magically fulfilled. Asking out of a spirit of holiness and within the frame of community steers us toward careful petitions and even more careful discernment. Our prayers for ourselves become requests for increased holiness and wisdom. Our prayers for others require us to listen carefully for their genuine needs, and to realize our own obligation to help fulfill those that accord with God's will. What is it suitable for us to ask for in prayer? Is it acceptable to pose our desires and wishes to God in a childlike way? How do we balance truthfulness in presenting ourselves to God with being responsible in our asking?

❧ *The Day of Pentecost*

Acts 2:1-11; 1 Corinthians 12:4-13 "All began to speak in other languages, as the Spirit gave them the ability." Physicist Freeman Dyson theorizes that linguistic diversity was not a historical accident, but evolution's way of making humankind evolve quickly. He writes: "Just as speciation gave life freedom to experiment with a diversity of form and function, the differentiation of languages gave humanity freedom to experiment with a diversity of social and cultural traditions."[1] Does diversity contribute to the stability of global society? Evolutionary biologists might argue so, finding that habitats with a multitude of species withstand critical events such as floods, droughts, fires, and the like better than systems with few species. So in evolutionary terms, the fall of the tower of Babel may have been inherent in its origins: "one single language" that claimed to have a godlike corner on truth.

John 20:19-23 Diversity in the human community, in this case the city of Jerusalem, has produced fear—the text speaks of "fear of the Jews." We need to remember that those Jewish leaders with the authority to persecute others had it *only* insofar as it met the goals of the Roman occupying government. Conflicts between Christians and Jews in the time this gospel was written globalized blame and suspicion: the collaboration of a few leaders has been writ large, while the resistance of many Jews (of whom Jesus was one) has been downplayed in our texts. Over and against fear, Jesus, resurrected, brings peace. Diversity and conflict need no longer frighten and isolate the disciples. They are sent back out into the city and the world in courage, to meet others and share their good news.

Can fear of difference be taught, or is it inherent? Some behavioral research suggests that certain infants are more fearful and anxious of change and novelty in their environment than others, yet good parenting does much to help a child sort through and face fears, separate the rational from the irrational, and act appropriately. Of what—of whom—are we irrationally afraid or anxious? In what ways can the media contribute to such a climate of anxiety? How does political language in our own time magnify our fears and consequent hatreds?

❦ Trinity Sunday

Exodus 3:1-6 In a moment of revelation, Moses sees God in a bush aflame and hears that the ground on which he is standing is holy. How many bushes did God have to set on fire before Moses finally noticed? Once we have looked as long and as reverently as Moses, perhaps we will discover that we too are standing on holy ground, and that *all* the ground is holy.

Under our feet are wonders we have barely begun to notice that whisper to us of God's imagination. For example, one fungus in a forest in Montana—a single genetic unit—stretches underground for 15 hectares, is over 1000 years old, and weighs more than 100 tons. Fungi are not individual fruiting bodies like mushrooms, but are a decentralized network of underground threads that express various genes depending on their environment. They have twice the biomass of all animals on earth, and are an immensely important life form. Fungi remind us that environment may control DNA expression, and not vice versa, and that evolution is far more complex than we once realized.

Romans 8:12-17 We are "children of God" and "joint-heirs with Christ"—what about those who are heirs to us? Recent studies in the heavily polluted cities of eastern Europe demonstrate that air pollution can stunt the growth of fetuses in the womb. Polish babies whose mothers are exposed to very small pollution particles of sulfurous urban smog are born with smaller heads and bodies, and it is feared that stunted babies may suffer learning deficits and run higher risks of childhood illness. Possibly embryos are especially vulnerable to pollutants carried through the blood because they are less able than adults to repair damaged DNA. Our concern for the cleanliness of our air is a way of honoring the Holy Spirit who "brooded over the face of the waters" in creation, and which God breathed into the lungs of Adam in the second creation story (Genesis 3).

John 3:1-16 The wind is one of the most venerable metaphors for the Holy Spirit. While North Americans are squandering oil in their ever-larger and less efficient vehicles, Europeans are developing wind power as a major energy source. Denmark, Spain, Britain, and the Netherlands each will generate more wind power than the United States before the millennium. Many parts of the United States experience winds of a frequency and strength to generate masses of power. It is estimated that the state of North Dakota alone contains enough suitable wind farm locations to supply the other forty-eight continental states with one-third of the power they currently consume. California has had success in developing efficient and long-lived turbines: they now generate nearly 2 percent of that state's energy. There are some environmental concerns—wind farms are large and noisy—but if properly situated they are less damaging than other types of power stations, and even have a certain beauty.[2]

THE SEASON AFTER PENTECOST

🌿 *Proper 1*

2 Kings 5:1-15; Mark 1:40-45 Leprosy in the Bible probably represents a whole host of skin symptoms and disorders. In our own time, Hansen's disease is the name given to what was in the last century called leprosy, an infection by the bacterium *Microbacterium leprae,* which causes nodules, ulcers, white patches without feeling, and, if untreated, eventual deformity or even loss of body parts. It is contagious, though not highly so. Nowadays sufferers can be treated with a long course of medications that can cure the disease; formerly they had to be isolated lifelong in colonies like the one on the Hawaiian island of Molokai where Damon, revered as a saint for his selfless care of lepers, lived and died of the disease.

The World Health Organization has been campaigning to eliminate Hansen's disease from the globe by the end of the century, a tough task since it affects some of the remotest areas of the poorest nations. An estimated 1.3 million sufferers are found in sixty countries, many of them in southeast Asia, where it is difficult to fund and administer drug treatment. How might we widen our embrace to include our brothers and sisters who cope with disfiguring diseases?

1 Corinthians 9:24-27 "Athletes exercise self-control in all things." As Paul makes clear, this is not a pleasant or easy process. He uses the terms "punish" and "enslave" to describe the arduous training that focuses all one's energies toward a single goal. The runner in the stadium and the pugilist in the boxing ring share this conditioning that makes right action second nature. Behavioral psychologists have observed the way that animals can be conditioned to a certain behavior by giving them either a reward or a punishment, until the desired behavior becomes automatic. Conditioning a person to behave as a disciple of Jesus—otherwise known as "formation"—is the goal of baptismal catechesis and should shape our whole Christian lives. How might Christ's first nature become our "second nature"?

𖥸 *Proper 2*

Isaiah 43:18-25   In ancient times, making a "river in the desert" was so unimaginable that it was considered a sign of God doing an unprecedented new thing. Nowadays we turn the desert green with irrigation pipes and think it a modern miracle. But our miracle has a cost, for we are not just doing a "new thing" (though irrigation systems go back millennia in history), we are using and using up some of our oldest non-renewable water sources. The Ogallala aquifer, the largest underground body of fresh water in the world, underlies eight northern and midwestern states and was formed in the Pleistocene and Pliocene epochs. If we continue to draw from it at the current rate of 14 million acre-feet of water a year in the Texas and Oklahoma area alone (one year's flow of the whole Colorado river), we will soon use it up. We are mining this water far faster than it can be replenished from snowmelt and rainfall.

2 Corinthians 1:18-22   God's word to us is always yes. God's Spirit within us urges us forward toward the future. It is no accident that monastics and theologians through the centuries have often been scientists, burning to understand just how God is operating in creation. The medieval monk Gregor Mendel spent countless hours in a monastery garden breeding, cultivating, and observing pea plants to understand how their particular characteristics were passed down from parent to offspring plant, how they combined, and how some qualities dominated. With no microscope, no awareness of DNA, he was able to deduce the basic rules of genetic inheritance. For the person of faith, new knowledge need not shake one's spiritual foundations, but may simply bring one to greater awe and delight and further curiosity—which can be a spiritual virtue for the strengthening of the community.

Mark 2:1-12   The paralytic is healed, thanks to the creative intervention of his friends. When I think of this paralytic and his friends, I remember a woman I met in hospital in the late stages of Amyotrophic Lateral Sclerosis (Lou Gehrig's disease). She had progressively lost the use of nearly all her muscles and finally lay paralyzed in her bed, unable to speak. I sat by her bedside as a chaplain, often wondering what was going on in her active, highly intelligent mind, for I knew she had been a scholar and teacher. One day the biomedical engineer at the hospital came through the door carrying a large sheet of Plexiglas on which he had painted the letters of the alphabet in a circle, the numbers 0 to 9, and the words yes, no, thanks. He handed me the plastic and I held it up like a window between me and Margaret in the bed. He said to her, "Now look at the letter you want to say," and to me, "Move the sheet until your eyes line up with hers and you will see which letter she intends." "Thanks," she signaled with her eyes, the only muscles of her body she could control. Her imprisonment was broken, at least for a time, thanks to the resourcefulness of a friend.

❦ *Proper 3*

Hosea 2:14-23 Hosea mentions a covenant made by God with "the wild animals, the birds of the air, and the creeping things of the ground" just like that in the story of Noah (Genesis 9). There will be peace between the creatures and humankind, and harmony between heaven and the fruitful earth. Radical pacifists are often vegetarians on principle. How might Christians think about our relationship to the livestock that feeds us? Does it matter how food creatures are treated? What are the parameters of our covenant with the animals? Breton poet Anjela Duval considers our heavy-footed presence among them:

> Ah. How heedful I am at each step
> Heedful of crushing, of smashing
> Along the path or through the field
> Tiny humble creatures beneath my foot:
> The green beetle crouched in the moss,
> The minute ant carrying
> With great effort and ingenuity
> The short-straw to her anthill.
> . . . .
> It seems to me I hear their lament:
> —"Why then, Lord, did you not give
> Wings to man?
> Ah! How heavy is the weight of his foot on us!"[1]

2 Corinthians 3:4–4:2　"Not that we are competent of ourselves to claim anything as coming from us" is Paul's disclaimer. With the wonders of science and technology in our time, there is much that we "claim" as our own doing. People of conscience worry that cloned or genetically engineered plants and animals may be dangerous new creations that have nothing to do with God's intention. Yet God's sovereignty is over the whole of creation, including those changes that humankind ushers in, and nothing we bring into being exists outside relationship to God. The question for Christians is how our actions toward other creatures affect our relationship with our Maker. Should we arrive at the day when a human being is cloned, the question for us will not be "Has it a soul?" but "How shall we love and form this new being in order to give honor to God, to diminish its suffering, to recognize its holiness and value?"

Mark 2:18-22　"New wine into fresh wineskins": it is difficult to change our patterns of thinking, to adopt "new paradigms," as popular jargon puts it. Those of us now in midlife may be painfully aware of how ideas about the material world we learned in school have been supplanted by new understandings. The Newtonian world has been challenged by superstring theory and chaos theory and the quantum universe. This requires that we be lifelong learners, always stretching our minds to fit new knowledge. In the same way, our lives of faith, though rooted in tradition, call us into fresh ways of understanding. We need never fear that our knowledge will make God obsolete, for God is the source of our wisdom and the one who blesses inquiry. From this mind-set, even scientific research can become an avenue of prayer. Everything fresh we learn will bring us to greater awe of God's marvelous imagination.

🌿 *Proper 4*

Deuteronomy 5:6-21; Mark 2:23-28　The sabbath was made for humankind. The sabbath, if it is well observed, teaches us our finitude. We rest from labor and the globe continues to rotate and revolve; the creatures pursue their lives as beings largely independent of us. As we taste our own humility it may bring both pangs of discomfort and great relief. We do not control everything; we cannot fix everything. God is in charge of the universe, thank God.

2 Corinthians 4:5-12　"We have this treasure in clay jars," in mortal bodies. We are, as a society, riveted by forensic science. Our bookshelves are full of mysteries about the work of medical examiners. There is even a book that details the processes of dying from dozens of diseases and traumas, blow by blow. At best we confront our fear of dying; at worst we use it to titillate ourselves. We are not the first generation to do so. In the high Middle Ages, a time of pandemic infant mortality, artists were fond of depicting skeletons and decomposing bodies as religious art. The scenes reminded people to prepare for their death and judgment and get their souls in shape, expressed some of their powerlessness over disease and death, and poked satiric fun at the high and mighty who seemed to forget their own inevitable mortality. What scenes would a like-minded artist paint today?

🔥 *Proper 5*

Genesis 3:1-21   In this reading, we glimpse the garden of Eden. I once saw a parish banner of Eve, the mother of all living, depicting her in a fleshed-out image of "Lucy"—that early hominid skeleton marking one of the bridges between apes and modern *Homo sapiens*. This caused some stir in the parish. Was it irreverent to depict Eve with apelike features? Must we think of God creating human beings much like ourselves? How do we see God at work in the evolutionary processes of humanity?

2 Corinthians 4:13-18   "What can be seen is temporary, but what cannot be seen is eternal." Our wasting away from aging and disease brings moments of challenge to faith but also the opportunity to invest ourselves in an eternal hope. Our bodies are part of the gracious cycle of death, decay, and new life of the earth, while our souls—our spiritual bodies—are on a trajectory toward eternal glory. The community *together* is able to remember the wholeness of this hope, even while its individual members may be in the midst of grieving the end of their own particular lives and hopes. Not every Christian can always be hopeful and faithful, but the Body of Christ together holds onto its identity and promise and carries those who lose sight of the eternal.

Mark 3:20-35   "Who are my mother and my brothers?" How small our circle of concern can become when we are overwhelmed with trouble. We tend to look first to our nuclear families, our closest kin, and then our friends. But the gospel stretches us to see a much broader circle of family in the Body of Christ. Even people who did not see the movie were intrigued by the notion that there are only *Six Degrees of Separation* between any two people. How shall we steward the earth's resources if the whole human race are our sisters and brothers? How shall we maintain our compassion and concern in the midst of needs that seem so global and continual while our energies are small and short-lived?

❧ *Proper 6*

Ezekiel 31:1-14   The cedar of Lebanon flourishing, and then broken: a powerful image of old-growth forest! Who has not visited or seen photographs of the great red-woods and bristlecone pines of California or the Joshua trees of the southwest? Sequoias live as long as 2500 years, and a bristlecone pine has been measured at 4950 years old. Our need for timber products and employment in forested regions must be weighed against the value of pristine forests and their inhabitants. Such equations are not simple and deserve more than reflex responses. Here, even the fallen tree becomes habitat for the animals and makes way for new tree life, offering a lesson to us about all that passes away, and that which can be sustained nonetheless.

2 Corinthians 5:1-10   We long to be "clothed with our heavenly dwelling." Paul reminds us both of our responsibility to keep our physical selves healthy in body and habit, and of the reality that we can expect at times to groan under the burden of our flesh and finally to surrender it in death. In our youth-oriented culture of beauty and self-improvement, compulsive exercising, and the extremes of overeating and diet-ing, this spiritual balance is hard-won. The old name for the virtue of consuming our just share of the world's resources and no more so that there may be enough for all was *temperance*. What might a spiritually balanced life look like today? How might the Benedictine rule of life that balances prayer, physical labor, and rest offer us a useful model?

Mark 4:26-34   Two parables describe sowing, then sleeping, and the mustard seed. The first parable invites us to consider timeliness—how to work at sowing and then to wait patiently but alertly for the moment of harvest, avoiding compulsiveness or sloth in our labors. The second describes God's miraculous provision for the diversi-ty of creation in a small seed that becomes a great hospitable tree for all the birds of the air. It is a parable about faith, but is it not also a reminder of the great importance of tiny, seemingly insignificant things? A few microbes may bring disease or a minute dose of drug, healing. A few particles of pollutant may poison drinking water; anoth-er chemical may precipitate a toxic substance out, rendering water potable. God works in the small as well as the great and we do well to pay attention.

⚘ Proper 7

Job 38:1-18 "Where were you when I laid the foundation of the earth?" We were not there, so we generate theories. One of the hottest new theories about the origin of the universe, "inflation," is offered by American physicist Alan Guth. He suggests that in a supercooled negative pressure state during the earliest moments of the big bang, a tremendous pressure caused gravity to push out instead of drawing in. This prompted the newborn universe to inflate like a balloon and draw virtually limitless energy out of the vacuum-like void.[2] Though the theory explains some mysteries about the measurable universe and contradicts others, it cannot be put to any experimental test. We may never know just how God pulled off the creation of the universe.

2 Corinthians 5:14-21 "In Christ there is a new creation." In the words of an old Celtic poem:

> All around me the most beautiful music plays: the songs of the birds, the lowing of cattle, the leaves rustling in the wind, the cascade of the river. No king could hire such music with gold; it is the music of Christ himself, given freely.[3]

When we are tempted to take the familiar world for granted, then baptism reminds us that we are called to live as those who see the cosmos with renewed vision, as showing forth Christ everywhere. Even in the city we may hear the birds, the wind, the cracking of ice, the music of Christ given freely to us, calling us to praise our Maker while we have breath.

Mark 4:35-41 The storm at sea. There are elemental powers on earth we cannot control—weather, tide, volcanoes, and the like. It is sobering to think that we could commit to cleaning our air by every possible means in the human community, and one volcano could emit enough particulate matter into the atmosphere to change it catastrophically. While some throw up their hands and feel powerless at such a thought, Christians are reminded of Christ's companionship with us through the tumult of the storm. We need not lose heart over what we cannot control, but are called to remain faithful for our small part. At the same time, our illusions of control often make us arrogant about challenging the forces of nature: we build houses and businesses on the flood plains of great rivers, on the muddy hillsides of California, and on the outer sandbanks of our coasts, driven by our appetite for lovely locations. Should there be religious voices raised in our communities that oppose such development on theological grounds?

❦ *Proper 8*

Deuteronomy 15:7-11; 2 Corinthians 8:1-15   Open your hand to the poor and needy neighbor in your land. A youth group embarked on a mission project in the rural south, where they helped clean up a little community in the Appalachian mountains after a hurricane had passed through. There, not thirty miles from a big prosperous city, they were invited into a woman's home (shack) with no running water or insulation and no electricity, and served tea. In our land of plenty, needy neighbors are near at hand. How might this image of lending invite us beyond charitable giving to consider ways to invest in and support self-sustenance among neighbors without such resources? Not being able to "fix" poverty is no excuse for throwing up our hands in despair. For the Deuteronomist, on the contrary, God offers us a continual invitation to open our hands and hearts to one another and in doing so, be blessed.

Mark 5:22-43   Jairus's daughter is raised from death to life and health. In this story, the despairing get a lot of attention. As Jesus approaches the house of Jairus, the people of the village are wailing and lamenting, assuming the worst. Jesus puts all these onlookers outside in order to devote healing power to the child. Where do we focus our own hope in times of illness? When do our worry and pessimism get in the way of healing, both physical and spiritual? How can we get our own anxiety and despair out of the way of Christ's healing energy and instead facilitate healing?

❦ *Proper 9*

Ezekiel 2:1-7; Mark 6:1-6   The lessons speak of prophets without honor in their own houses. It is amazing how we overlook the powerful acts of God in creation while constantly looking for miracles to surprise us. Think of the popular joke about a man in a flood-surrounded house who turned down two boats and a helicopter while waiting for God to miraculously save him—only to find out in heaven that the vehicles were all sent from God! We hardly notice organ transplantation, bypass surgery, antibiotics, and the like as God's healing acts for us because they have become so familiar and ordinary. As any asthmatic can testify, just drawing a comfortable breath can be the greatest miracle imaginable. It might be provocative to ask the congregation to keep holding its breath for as long as possible—until it becomes uncomfortable—as a reminder of how precious breath is. How might we become people thankful for God's "ordinary" blessings?

2 Corinthians 12:2-10 Paul writes of being "caught up to the third heaven." In medical lore, people resuscitated from near-death circumstances speak of encountering God, light, judgment, and their deceased loved ones.[4] Though Paul suggests a stoical acceptance of the pains and miseries of mortal life, these stories from many cultures and individuals comfort us with the marvelous possibilities of life beyond the one we know on earth. Though, like Paul, we may not know just what to make of them, and scientists may try to rationalize them away as part of the neurological phenomena of trauma, we need not dismiss such exceptional revelations. Should we not ask instead if they are consistent with the God known to us through scripture, tradition, and human reason?

❦ *Proper 10*

Amos 7:7-15 The prophet, this herdsman and dresser of sycamore trees, does not feel adequate to call his society to account. After all, his perspective is only small and local—why should anyone listen to him? God is not satisfied with this disclaimer, but sends Amos to prophesy anyway. We may also feel we can do little to mend big social and environmental problems. Yet a single child's activism mobilized a school and then a town to imagine its local ravine and creek as a place of natural wonder and value. Together they developed the political will and gathered the resources needed to stop the pollution and pick up the trash, and became knowledgeable about the animals and plants the environment sustains. If every town tended to its ravine, if every business adopted a mile of roadside to clean of litter, the landscape would be transformed little by little. One voice begins a movement.

Ephesians 1:1-14 All of creation is destined for adoption. All things are to be gathered up in Christ. We must absorb the humbling fact that God's concern is not just for people. St. Francis taught that when we regard the creatures as sisters and brothers, we learn of the wideness of God's love. His great prayer from *The Mirror of Perfection*—a hymn to the creation as family—can help us with this. Here is an excerpt:

Be Thou praised, my Lord, with all Thy creatures,
above all Brother Sun,
who gives the day and lightens us therewith....

Be Thou praised, my Lord, of Sister Moon and stars,
in the heaven Thou hast formed them, clear and precious

and comely.

Be Thou praised, my Lord, of Brother Wind,
and of the air, and the cloud, and of fair and of all weather,
by which Thou givest to Thy creatures sustenance.
Be Thou praised, my Lord, of Sister Water,
which is much useful and humble and precious and pure.

Be Thou praised, my Lord, of Brother Fire,
by which Thou has lightened the night,
and he is beautiful and joyful and robust and strong.

Be Thou praised, my Lord, of our Sister Mother Earth,
which sustains and hath us in rule,
and produces divers fruits with coloured flowers and herbs.

Mark 6:7-13 As Jesus sends the disciples out two by two he commands them to travel lightly and take nothing but a staff for the journey. So too, scuba divers are taught how to visit coral reefs, taking away only their photographs and memories and leaving behind nothing but bubbles in their wake. Campers are taught to pack out their trash. These are all ways of traveling lightly on the earth—bringing only what we need for the journey, consuming no more than our share of creation, and never leaving devastation behind us. The ancient virtue of temperance is a wise guide along the way. What are some other ways we might learn to "travel lightly" on the earth?

❧ *Proper 11*

Isaiah 57:14-21 "The wicked are like the tossing sea that cannot keep still." Learning to be still—to hush the busyness of our minds, sit, listen, and wait for God—allows a clarity out of which right action may proceed. In order to build up the reign of God with care for the earth and the human community, we need the discipline to be still and silent. We need to dwell in inner peace and calm, and let our swirling sediments settle. Only then will we be equipped for wise action.

Ephesians 2:11-22 In Christ "the whole structure is joined together and grows into a holy temple." This image of the communion of saints invites us to take the long view of our efforts to build God's reign. Some changes can only be effected over generations. Small local efforts slowly coalesce into wider processes of change. In the Body of Christ we are joined together, co-laborers in creation with God for the future God desires. We need not grow discouraged that the process is slow and that we may not see its completion in our lifetime. Can we learn to see that our part is a piece of a whole and holy structure in the making?

Mark 6:30-44 The disciples feed the five thousand with five loaves and two fish. The green grass on which the hungry are told to sit down reminds us of the green pastures of the psalms, the place where God feeds and looks after the flock. In this little oasis they discover that there is more food at hand than anyone had thought—enough to share and some left over. For us, too, in our frantic, anxious lives, going to a green and beautiful place for vacation and retreat may allow us to take stock of the resources God has provided us, be grateful, be fed, and find we have more than we thought, even food to share. Into what oases has God led us lately?

❦ *Proper 12*

2 Kings 2:1-15 In this story we celebrate the turning of generations, and the handing on of the work of ministry like the baton in a relay passing from a tiring hand to a fresh, energetic one. The mantle of old Elijah is passed to young Elisha and the Jordan parts to reveal the continuity of power between the prophets. Yet there is much in us that resists our own aging and dying, our being supplanted—as it sometimes feels—by younger people. There is a business in California that will (for a substantial fee) freeze your body at the moment of death in liquid nitrogen in the hope that decades from now a cure will be available for the disease or trauma that killed you, and one day you will be unfrozen and revived. Whether this is a reliable scientific practice is debatable.

More importantly, our fascination with even the possibility of thawing back into life invites us to consider the spiritual discipline of being intentional about accepting aging, relinquishing parts of our work as we find we must. How might we celebrate the arrival of our successors and leave them the legacy of an earth well-tended and replete with the resources God created?

Ephesians 4:1-16 A healthy body knit together by ligaments is Paul's metaphor for the community of Christ. How marvelously we are made, as modern medicine confirms. Theologian John Snow describes sculling on the river on a stunning summer day and then coming into the boathouse where dozens of young athletes are rowing fit to bust in a closed room on "Ergs"—machines that offer perfectly symmetrical stress for conditioning. He goes on to suggest that our mortality, and the way our bodies and souls are all of a piece, give urgency and poignancy to our choice to live faithfully.[5] We are those whose deaths are never trivial, whose flesh God has hallowed in Christ. Our lives are not about winning and perfection but about living as those who are raised from the dead.

Mark 6:45-52 Jesus walks on the water as his disciples row in an adverse wind. The unpredictability of weather is the hallmark of chaos at work in the systems of the universe. Try as we might, we cannot control it. The closest we get is seeding clouds with chemicals to inveigle them to drop their load of rain sooner rather than later. Chaos theory teaches us that what appears utterly random has forms and patterns and rhythms; there is unpredictability, but there is also an order even within chaotic events. As people of faith we struggle to see God's grand design unfolding both in the chaotic movements of creation—wildfires, hurricanes—and in the chaos of our own lives. Though we struggle and are tossed about, God is not. Jesus walks toward us through the worst of wind and waves, even when we cannot see him for spray.

🌿 Proper 13

Exodus 16:2-15 God gives manna from heaven to the grumbling Israelites and then waits to see whether they will follow directions. Genetic technology has improved strains of food plants for drought-resistance, pest-resistance, size, and timed harvesting. These new products are not without controversy. A strain of maize genetically engineered to resist weed-killers and insect pests also contains a gene that confers resistance to a widely used antibiotic, ampicillin. Developers argue that this is no threat; opponents fear that when animals eat the feed corn, the gene might move into bacteria in their digestive tract, and spread resistance to antibiotic animal medicine. Eventually it may be passed on to humans.

As we develop new technologies, it is reasonable and necessary for Christians to ask continually, What are God's directions to us about the use of creation? Of all the things we *can* do, which should we do and not do? Our reflections require of us great care, prudence, patience, and wisdom—not always the virtues that drive our economy.

Ephesians 4:17-25 Here is a summons to mutual correction: "Let us speak the truth to our neighbors, for we are members of one another." Listening to the truth spoken by some of the smallest and poorest of our international neighbors can be painful. At the Kyoto environmental talks of 1998, officials of little island nations in the South Pacific—Fiji, Tuvalu, and Kiribatu among them—described how global warming is already affecting their vulnerable countries. When the highest point of an island is 6 feet above sea level, and the ocean has already risen 15 centimeters in a few decades, high waters threaten to eat away islands that may be only a city block or two in diameter. A rise in ocean temperature of just a few degrees causes algae to leave its calcium structure, killing the coral and ruining the spawning ground for juvenile fish—a staple of the island diet. As the largest generator of greenhouse gases, how can we reckon with the consequences of global warming upon our most vulnerable neighbors? They will tell us if we have ears to hear.

John 6:24-35 Jesus calls himself the true bread, the staple of life. Some scientists labor to develop elaborate new technologies to produce hardier and more fruitful grains; they argue that most of the world's people who lack food are hungry because they are poor, not because they have insufficient technology. Other scientists caution that technology is not a panacea. They argue that basic research into indigenous plant food sources, simple pest controls, and low-tech beneficial farming practices is a more responsible and realistic use of funds. As Christians are fed and feed others in turn, how might we celebrate the simple reality that Jesus is as necessary as bread?

❦ *Proper 14*

Deuteronomy 8:1-10 The Israelites look forward to coming into a land of promise. At the time of their misery in the wilderness, they were not always sure that God was with them, but from the perceptive of hindsight, as the Deuteronomist points out, they can see God at work even in that wasteland journey.

Some claim that California is the most beautiful state, with its dramatic contrasts of desert, mountains, plains, and sea; others point out that the huge San Andreas fault brings the "goodness" of its coastal lands into question. Seismologist Allan Lindh sees things differently:

> Earthquakes are not an optional add-on sent by the devil to make life more difficult in California, [but] an integral part of the system. . . . The same thing that

brings the quakes also creates the beauty, the wealth, and everything else that makes California unique.[6]

The movement of tectonic plates along that fault also creates the spectacular beaches, streams, and hills that are characteristic of abrasion and folding along a fault. The high lands provide the water as run-off and as captured moisture scraped from the clouds that makes the valleys fertile. The bay itself is a tectonically created superb natural harbor. The microclimates of the hills and ocean make splendid wine country. We all might do well to bless God for the land we inhabit, and see its liabilities as integral to its gifts.

Ephesians 4:25–5:2   Honest labor, honest talk is enjoined of the Christian community: practical advice for holy living. I once visited a Hindu Ashram (community dwelling) where, in the ladies' room, I saw a sign over each stall that read: "Treat the Ashram as an extension of your spiritual body." Sure enough, worshippers took pains to wipe the sink after they had used it, and even polished the top of the waste can with a paper towel on their way out. This practice has always been exemplary for me of how spiritual devotion can spill over into the labor of everyday life. How might we treat our churches and our neighborhoods as an extension of our spiritual bodies?

John 6:37-51   "Is this not Jesus, the son of Joseph, whose father and mother we know?" asks Jesus' hometown crowd dismissively. For them, clearly, biology (and sociology) is destiny. If you know a man's parents, you know everything important about him. In most matters of human character and conduct, nature, nurture, and free will combine in complex patterns to make us who we are. It is hardly helpful to try to argue that "biology made us do it." For all the powerful urges of our hormones and neurons, and the conditioning of family and society, we are God's children by adoption and grace, called to live and act accordingly. Knowledge of the natural forces that help shape us may usefully supply a compassionate and cautionary perspective, but they do not determine who we shall be. Children abused and neglected may turn out to be kind and healthy; children gently nurtured may choose an evil path. Christian scriptures urge us to be responsible moral agents, choosing not just for our own good but for building up the human community.

❦ *Proper 15*

Proverbs 9:1-6 "Wisdom has built her house"—and what sort of house does wisdom build? New statistical research in Britain predicts that of 4.4 million new households that will come into being by 2016, 80 percent will be occupied by only one person. Longer lifespans (with more widowed persons surviving many years after the death of a spouse), more divorces and separations, more young adults living separately from their parents, and a later average age of marriage are among the causes for this phenomenon. Socially, these solo households may result in more widespread loneliness and isolation. Environmentally, larger and larger amounts of land may be consumed for housing development—possibly 169,000 extra hectares by 2016.[7] How might our own building and zoning practices witness to the fact that "more" is not always the solution? What kind of houses might wisdom best build in our neighborhood?

Ephesians 5:15-20; John 6:53-59 While Paul warns against drunkeness, Jesus tells us that to eat his flesh and drink his blood is life indeed. We know considerably more about addictive illness than our ancestors did, and that affects how we hear these texts. There are an estimated 10 million persons with the progressive treatable illness of alcoholism in the United States, representing between 10 and 20 percent of all those who use alcohol. Evidence suggests that heredity may contribute to development of alcoholism, and that it may often combine with other psychological ailments such as depression. Where nonalcoholics may drink to try to feel high, alcoholics tend to drink just to try to feel "normal," or to numb themselves from feeling.

Alcoholism is an illness needing active intervention by loved ones and colleagues, not passive waiting. This accomplished, detoxification followed by a treatment program are the ingredients for healing. Alcoholics Anonymous and Alanon. for family members affected by the alcoholic are the best resources for recovery. An alcoholic is not cured, but becomes a person in the lifelong process of recovery, recognizing his or her powerlessness over alcohol. This might be an ideal Sunday to invite some persons in recovery to testify about their own spiritual and physical healing.

❦ *Proper 16*

Joshua 24:1-2, 14-25 Choose whom you will serve. The way we spend our time is a good indicator of whom or what we are serving. Is television, then, our master? It might be a profitable spiritual exercise to challenge the congregation to keep a week's journal of the way they spend time, pray about the results, then reflect on whether they are serving God or mammon, Baal, the office, or the television.

Ephesians 5:21-33   Apologists for this text about marriage argue that the hierarchy presented is one of mutual love and respect. But the words are troubling to our modern ears, attuned to a history in which women have been denied full personhood, voice, vote, and moral autonomy. Even more problematic is the language of a husband purifying the wife as Christ the church to present her "holy and unblemished" (the Greek refers to the condition of a sacrificial animal) and free of "spot or wrinkle." For many Christian women this is a "text of terror" that diminishes rather than builds up. What adolescent girl or boy struggling with teenage acne will feel that he or she is a precious and holy child of God in hearing holiness equated with being unblemished and without spot? The good news is that God loves us as we are, in our own incarnation—which is by definition imperfect and mortal, yet through Jesus Christ made holy. As Paul more helpfully suggests: "Present your bodies as a living sacrifice, holy and acceptable to God" (Romans 12:1).

John 6:60-69   "The flesh is without usefulness" is an ironic remark from the one who speaks often of his own flesh and blood as the gifts of life. In my years as a chaplain I often sat with families as they were asked whether they and their dying relative would consider donating organs for transplant. There is a desperate shortage of such organs that may indeed bring life, vision, mobility, or health to others. Unless the decision to donate is made in advance of an accident or illness with the knowledge and consent of nearest relatives, and is communicated by a donor card, it is unlikely to be carried out at the moment of death. It is good stewardship of our flesh, when we shall no longer find it useful to us, that if another can use it, we give it.

❄ *Proper 17*

Deuteronomy 4:1-9   Many of the levitical rules and regulations may seem odd to us, but as biblical scholars point out—and our neighbor observant Jews teach us—most of them have highly useful and practical aspects. Some protected the people from foods likely to be contaminated and make them ill. Others set up rules for the segregation of people who might have contagious diseases, or governed relationships so that there would be social order and harmony. Underlying the rules and regulations was the awareness that behaviors have consequences not just for individuals but for the whole community.

So it is with many of the regulations we modern folk set up for health reasons. Vaccination of schoolchildren not only protects an individual child, but also the school, playmates, neighbors, and family. Quarantine in the case of active tuberculosis protects everyone who might come in contact with that person from infection. Jesus takes pains in the gospels not to be identified as a rule-giver, but as one who liberates from lifeless and distorted rule-keeping. Yet as the letters of the early churches make clear, some rules and regulations for the ordering of the community are in everyone's best interest. The freedom we have in Christ we have only for the commonweal.

Ephesians 6:10-20 "Put on the whole armor of God." The latest body armor under development may utilize the genes of spiders, which spin ultra-strong threads more durable than kevlar to absorb and diffuse impact without breaking. The armor of God may not look or feel like much protection, yet it makes us strong to withstand evil.

Mark 7:1-23 In declaring all foods clean, Jesus speaks graphically of the way food passes through the gut and is excreted into the sewer. Translations bowdlerize this plain—even vulgar—language. Yes, it is clear that Jesus is interested in our conduct with one another, our social and spiritual hygiene. Still, on a down-to-earth note, here is a piece of good environmental news about dealing with what comes out of us: Australian journalist Ian Melbourne reports that a new portable toilet has been designed that stores and treats sewage instead of releasing it into the ground, and successfully destroys nearly all bacteria, without using water.[8] Lack of running water has been a major obstacle to providing safe toilets for refugee camps and poor urban areas. Privies in such places are major sources of typhoid, cholera, and other diseases spread in contaminated groundwater. With the new design, waste is broken down by anaerobic and aerobic bacteria sealed into the system, and stored until safe to dump into gravel pits. The device should be low-cost and easy to transport and assemble.

❧ *Proper 18*

Isaiah 35:4-7; Mark 7:31-37 Two passages address the healing of disabilities as a sign of God's power and goodwill. In a survey taken among 87 deaf people at a 1997 Deaf Nation conference in Britain, over half were concerned that genetic testing for deafness might bring more trouble than benefit; 16 percent indicated they might make use of such testing, but one third of this group said they would prefer to bear deaf children. A very small proportion said that they might abort a fetus who could hear.[9]

Thus what one group may regard as a disability another may regard as a gift—be it dwarfism, bipolar disorder, or loss of mobility. Where a group of people share characteristics and relate intensely, a culture develops—as in the deaf community—and comes to be of great significance. Human difference itself offers value to the wider society. Our attitudes affect our understanding of suffering and well-being: we must be cautious about the way we think about other people's circumstances when we have not walked a mile in their shoes or rolled a day on their wheels.

James 1:17-27   James offers a quick analysis of anger: it does not bring forth the righteousness of God. Yet biologists tell us the neurological rousing to anger and fear are part of our "fight-flight" wiring; it helps us and other animals rally physical and psychological resources to meet danger in a way that is likely to preserve our lives. Modern psychological insight also suggests that anger can function as a healthy defense against attack or as a dysfunctional response that leads us into unhelpful conflict. Clearly, we are called into careful discernment about how, where, and why we should apply our anger. We may not be able to control what we feel, but we can decide how to act so that anger does not demolish another, tear apart the community, or cause irreparable damage to relationships. This may be what James has in mind when he speaks of "bridling the tongue": the self-discipline that enables us to temper our emotions in order to build up the Body of Christ.

🌿 *Proper 19*

Isaiah 50:4-9   God has given the prophet the tongue of a teacher. In Hebrew, the word for *teacher* and *learner* is the same: a teacher is a specialist in learning, and learning takes place in order that one may, in turn, become capable of teaching. Creation, too, is a teacher. Teilhard de Chardin, the twentieth-century Roman Catholic creation mystic, recounts a friend's experience of gazing at a Sacred Heart of Jesus icon. He saw the edges blur and the lines dissolve until the outline of Christ and its vibrant atmosphere spread outward to infinity,

> delineating a sort of blood stream or nervous system running through the totality of life. *The entire universe was vibrant.* And yet, when I directed my gaze to particular objects, one by one, I found them still as clearly defined as ever in

their undiminished individuality. All this movement seemed to emanate from Christ, and above all from his heart.[10]

What might this vision teach us about being students of God's creation?

James 2:1-18 Faith without works is dead, preaches James. In the words of Meister Eckhart:

> There is no such thing as "my" bread. All bread is *ours* and is given to me, to others through me and to me through others. For not only bread but all things necessary for sustenance in this life are given on loan to us with others, and because of others and for others and to others through us.

Recognizing the whole creation as pure gift and blessing is the start of justice. When we are humble, we see it just as much as a gift to the next person as it is a gift to us.

Mark 8:27-38 What does it profit us to gain the world and forfeit our life? Julian of Norwich wrote in the thirteenth century:

> Our sensuality is grounded in Nature, in Compassion and in Grace. In our sensuality, God is. God is the means whereby our Substance and our Sensuality are kept together so as never to be apart.

Only through this connectedness of sense, appetite, and flesh with nature, compassion, and God's grace do we live in the material world without losing our souls. How do we feel about our senses, our bodies, and their relationship to God? Are we comfortable linking sensuality and prayer? How might we move toward a greater awareness of the sacredness of our physical selves?

❧ *Proper 20*

Wisdom 1:16–2:1, 6-22 Come, let us make use of the creation, say those who see the shortness of life as a blow dealt them by an unkind universe. They harden their own hearts in response. But to those who are pure of heart, God is visible in all the creation as good giver, and the loveliness of the gift of life, brief as it is, breaks open their hearts to compassion and praise. How do we determine what is "right use" of creation? If we believe that plants, animals, and elements have "rights," how do those intersect with our call to steward the creation? Should we encounter the creatures around us as object or subject? How do we incarnate our beliefs in our behavior? How do our feelings of deprivation or disappointment fuel our tendency to exploit and grasp the material world? How might we counteract this tendency?

James 3:16–4:6   A harvest of righteousness for the peacemakers similarly comes to those who find contentment in what they have been given, and are not tossed about by the waves of appetite. The old table grace asked God to give us grateful hearts— for not all our hearts lean toward spontaneous gratitude. How might we incorporate the desire to be and feel grateful into the prayer of our communities?

Mark 9:30-37   Welcoming the child as the ambassador of Christ who comes in vulnerability is the task of the community that would welcome Jesus. In his research, author Jonathan Kozol discovered that child poverty in 1986 was one-third higher than ten years before, and has increased 50 percent since 1969. As we enter the twenty-first century, the plight of these children is not much changed. Kozol writes:

> A federal study finds that children are "routinely excluded from a fourth of rental housing." [Homeless children] offend us not by doing but by being.... They take some of our taxes for their food and concentrated formula, their clothing, and their hurried clinic visits and their miserable shelter. When they sicken as a consequence of the unwholesome housing we provide, they cost a little more; and if they fail utterly to thrive, they take some money from the public treasury for burial.[11]

How, then, are we in our locality welcoming the children, especially these poorest children, as we would welcome Christ? And if we are doing no better job than Kozol describes, what will we have to say when Jesus asks how we have cared for him?

Proper 21

Numbers 11:4-29   The Israelites are remembering how they ate cucumbers in Egypt, longing for meat, and grumbling about manna. Increasing prosperity in some parts of the developing world is leading to an increase in the consumption of meat in societies that were once primarily vegetarian. Chinese people today eat almost as much pork as Americans. While it may be arrogant of western meat-eaters to complain about meat consumption elsewhere, the trend has consequences. To reach slaughter weight, a pig in the United States is fed 700 pounds of corn and soy; the pig's meat will keep an individual at the recommended caloric daily intake for

49 days. If a person ate that soy and corn directly, they would be nourished for some 500 days. Food for thought!

James 4:7–5:6   Do we become bored with so many scriptural passages that warn about living in luxury at the expense of others? It is a constant theme. The good news is that small changes in behavior by many people produce a cumulative effect, and there are numerous ways we can move toward greater economic justice. Eating lower on the food chain (less meat, more vegetables, fruits, and grains) is one way. Working for just benefits for agricultural workers is another. Choosing goods that have a longer life and are less disposable is a third. Caring for the patch of earth we may own or live on and reducing our pollution of it is still another way. What are some small, concrete steps you can make to save the earth and care for its inhabitants so that change will come?

Mark 9:38-48   Whoever gives you a cup of water to drink in the name of Christ will be rewarded. A cup of water is an archetypal image of the gift that gives life. Most of us have more than enough water to drink, but a 1997 United Nations Environmental Program report on drinking water suggests that even in our relatively water-rich nation, 5.6 million people are drinking water that does not meet safety standards. As many as one in five Americans drinks from a water treatment plant that violates safety standards. Water with dangerous levels of fecal coliform bacteria that can cause disease is produced by 8 percent of these plants. In the next century, safe water supply will become one of the major health issues for our nation—though many of us still take clean tap water for granted.

❧ *Proper 22*

Genesis 2:18-24   "Bone of my bones" is a wonderful metaphor of connectedness. It has become clear in today's society that we must also recognize the distinctiveness of men and women within relationships, and not sanction one person speaking for both. Historian Londa Schiebinger has written an astonishing analysis of the ways that supposedly objective science has been derailed by racial and gender prejudice: "Only recently have we begun to appreciate that who does science affects the kind of science that gets done."

For example, Africans were often described and depicted as ape-like; anatomical measurements were bent into "evidence" to support such claims, and to justify the institution of slavery. Plant taxonomist Carl Linnaeus made analogies between flowers and human sexual anatomy, and "imported into botany traditional notions about sexual hierarchy." Some of his followers went on to call, for example, flower stamens identified as the male part "most noble."[12] Such scientists were slow to recognize that most flowers are hermaphroditic—having both male and female characteristics.

Hebrews 2:1-18 God left nothing outside our control. This is a daunting proclamation about our power in creation. Do we use it well or unwisely? A scientist in Japan has been collaborating with colleagues in New Zealand on a project to isolate genes from the leg bone of an extinct giant bird of New Zealand called a moa. He hopes to put these genes into chicken embryos to see if characteristics of the ancient bird can be produced. At present, little is known about the moa's color or behavior—just that it was around three meters tall. A spokesperson of the Auckland Friends of the Earth organization expressed grave doubts about the ethics of such an experiment. God does not expect us to behave like angels, but as followers of the risen One. How does our discipleship lead us in our ethical quandaries? Where does our curiosity, our hunger for knowledge, overstep its bounds?

Mark 10:2-9 "What God has joined together, let no one separate." The church continues to wrestle with Jesus' disapproval of divorce, and the realities of human brokenness in relationship. However we read the text, we are faced with a world in which spousal abuse (of which 95 percent is male against female) results in maiming and murder with shocking frequency. Abuse of wives is frequently accompanied by battering of children. Police studies confirm that battering escalates over time. Battery is about control, and often begins with one spouse telling the other, for example, who she may see or where and when she may go out. In this country an estimated 2 to 4 million women are beaten in their homes each year, and on average four women a day are murdered by husbands or boyfriends.[13]

Domestic violence is an offense against God, creation, and another human being. Preaching about it allows those trapped in violent households to know there is help available. Where violence is enacted in a family, the covenant of marriage has already been broken by the abuser, who no longer treats the spouse as "bone of my bone." How does this metaphor help us to think theologically about the covenant of marriage?

◈ *Proper 23*

Amos 5:6-15 "You take from the poor levies of grain," cries the prophet. What drives us to consume far more than our share of the world's goods? Behavioral scientists are studying why some people become "shopaholics"—compulsive buyers whose urges interfere with family life and work, and lead to floods of remorse and depression. Some psychologists suspect this behavior may be a psychiatric disorder, and link it to depression. Some blame the all-out effort of merchandisers to lure shoppers with smells, colors, and sounds that are overwhelming, even sexually exciting, according to some compulsive shoppers. Home-shopping networks and catalogs also lure shoppers to buy things on impulse.

Skeptics argue there are likely few compulsive shoppers among poorest cultures, and that these behaviors stem from plain old greed and lack of self-control. Whatever the cause, the gospel and the prophets urge us to consider justice, practice temperance, and act in our individual lives with the constant awareness that we are members of a body: our choices and our sins affect other members. It is spiritual discipline to wrestle with our compulsions, fears, and desires—for the common good and in service to God.

Hebrews 3:1-6   "The builder of all things is God," sums up the author of Hebrews. The evidence of the handiwork of the divine architect has been sought in creation as long as human beings have been religious. It is by no means contradictory for a person to be a scientist and a religious believer. As physicist John Polkinghorne writes, "The science of physics discerns a physical world shot through with signs of mind, and it is a coherent possibility that it is the rational mind of the Creator that is being discerned in this way."[14]

Mark 10:17-31   The rich man asks Jesus, "What must I do to inherit eternal life?" Jesus tells him to keep the commandments and to give all he has to the poor. Writer Arian Hough comments:

> There are three characteristics of the western lifestyle which can be shown to be contrary to the teaching of Christian theology. . . . These characteristics are busyness, usefulness and an unrelenting belief in success.[15]

Over and against these "false" teachings Hough considers the virtues of godly waiting, play, and the paradoxical failure of Jesus' ministry.

🌿 *Proper 24*

Isaiah 53:4-12   What are the roots of human suffering and evil? The roots of evil are given considerable attention in the pages of Jewish and Christian scripture. The gospel is unequivocal about sin and evil's remedy: Christ. In his book *Evil*, Roy Baumeister argues that people become evil bit by bit. When they see others acting badly, some will behave similarly in order to merit membership and stature in the group. He identifies four principal motives for evil behavior: revenge, sadism, greed, and egotism. Baumeister challenges psychologists who argue that much bad behavior comes from individuals with too little sense of self or self-esteem. He suggests that most violent offenders have little respect for others and will not tolerate being challenged.[16] Other behavioral scientists connect over-blown self-centeredness with failures in nurture, but bad beginnings do not always lead to evil behavior. What are your beliefs about the origins of human evil? In what ways might we best respond to evil in a Christian community?

Hebrews 4:12-16 Before him no creature is hidden but all are naked. An image comes to mind from a film that made me roar with laughter as a child: Joey Brown looking at himself in an X-ray machine, horrified at his own twitching skeleton displayed for all to see. Our technology has progressed in leaps and bounds: CT-scans, MRIs, scanning electron microscopes, and ultrasounds can show us our bodies slice by slice or cell by cell. Such scrutiny enables diagnosis and healing beyond our forbears' dreams. We may be quite afraid of God's ability to "see through us," to know our inmost thoughts and workings—some of them pretty unlovable. But scripture attests that God scrutinizes us out of love and for the diagnosis and healing of our souls, and we are invited to self-examination toward the same end.

Mark 10:35-45 The consequences of our arrogance, of "lording it over" one another, can be terrible. Science is not politically neutral and can wield enormous political power with far-reaching consequences. Some portion of responsibility for the terrible ethnic bloodshed between Hutus and Tutsis in Rwanda may be laid at the door of European anthropologists who magnified purported differences between two people who share the same ethnicity, language, and religion—and then taught their prejudices to others. Canadian mathematician Arturo Sangalli suggests that anthropologists compared Hutu peasants with Tutsi royalty (a select, well-fed, healthy subset) and came up with false "ethnic differences" in height, bone structure, and physiognomy that decades later became fuel for their mutual distrust. Since there was no written history in Rwanda, these "scientific" texts created a false history of difference where none existed.

Proper 25

Isaiah 59:1-19   We all growl like bears: a wonderful image of complaint. An endangered population of brown bears in Spain have something to complain about. The building of a railroad line, several roads, and a resort separated two groups of *Ursus arctos* from one another; for over 50 years they have had no contact. Now the population of brown bears in Spain is less than 100, and the smaller of the two groups is showing signs of dangerous genetic inbreeding and continuing to decline. The best chance for saving these bears from extinction is to create a way for bears to cross the man-made obstacles and reunite with one another.

Hebrews 5:12–6:1, 9-12   The author of Hebrews scolds the community for needing milk, not solid food, for being immature in discerning good from evil. In the press, environmental issues are often sketched in simplistic generalizations. On both sides of an issue, opponents offer sweeping statements that deny the subtlety of discernment needed for mature decision making. Environmental solutions are often more complex than they first appear. For example, it was hoped that creating more efficient appliances and buildings would save energy; instead, these improvements may allow more people to buy and use appliances who cannot currently afford them at all. If it becomes cheaper to run the air conditioning, people are tempted to turn down the thermostat and run it for more hours. Since the cost of oil fell, vehicles in the United States have become larger and more fuel-demanding; Americans are also driving more miles per capita, thus creating more overall pollution.

Some economists are calling for carbon taxes that, though they might not change the energy use of wealthy people, might at least generate revenue for green investments such as alternate energy sources. Ultimately, the most effective means for changing energy consumption may be educating citizens to intentionally seek to use less energy in every way possible, a spiritual task that involves changing our hearts and habits.

Mark 10:46-52   The healing of blind Bartimaeus is one of many miracle stories in the gospels. What, then, is a miracle? Is it impossible for a person of a scientific mindset to accept miracles? Physicist John Polkinghorne is also an Anglican priest. He uses the example of heating water:

> As the water heats, the thermometer goes up steadily, bit by bit...until the thermometer comes to 100 degrees Centigrade. Then something happens that, had you not seen it happen several times every day of your life, would totally astonish you. The totally regular behavior suddenly stops, and some-

thing entirely different happens. The thermometer remains steady, and a small quantity of water turns into a very large quantity of steam. This is what physicists call a phase change. . . . My point is this: the laws of nature do not change at 100 degrees Centigrade. They are utterly consistent, but the *consequences* of the laws of nature may change quite drastically when a situation changes. That to me is a model of how we are to think of miracle. God does not change, but in new circumstances new things are compatible with continuing divine consistency.[17]

❦ *Proper 26*

Deuteronomy 6:1-9   Multiply greatly in the land flowing with milk and honey—this was God's message to the ancient Israelites. Yet today we need to think differently about reproducing ourselves if we are to be wise stewards of creation. Earth's population passed 6 billion in 1999. Though birthrates have lowered in many developing nations—including China and India, which have been assertive in promoting birth control—other nations are burgeoning. Changes in health care, contraception, and cultural attitudes toward population control, along with the education of women, are key factors in reducing growth rates. How can we hold this notion of stewardship in tension with God's promise to the chosen people?

Hebrews 7:23-28   "The former priests were many in number, because they were prevented by death from continuing in office." What a curious observation! (Aren't we all?) The good news is that we are tending to live longer on average than our ancestors. Our health is generally better, as is our nutrition. But there are shocking exceptions. In parts of equatorial Africa, HIV now infects one-quarter of the population: average life expectancy has diminished from the sixties to the early forties; skilled labor is scarce because of the deaths of young adults; and there has been a massive increase in child mortality. Though patients with HIV in the United States and western Europe—especially middle-class males—are living much longer in reasonable health thanks to new drug treatments and early diagnosis, this is not true in poor areas of the world. What is our responsibility as Christians to provide assistance abroad? How do we avoid becoming complacent because of our own good fortune?

Mark 12:28-34   The great commandments to love God and neighbor are linked to the well-being of the people and the well-being of the land they inhabit. Covenant is a transformed relationship between God, humanity, and creation requiring a transformed heart. Christians understand baptism as the initiation into this transformation of heart and life. Mystic Meister Eckhart asks:

> What is the test that you have undergone this holy birth? Listen carefully. If this birth has truly taken place within you, then every single creature points you toward God. If the only prayer you say in your whole life is "thank you," that would suffice. This, then, is salvation: When we marvel at the beauty of created things and praise their beautiful Creator.

❦ *Proper 27*

1 Kings 17:8-16   The widow of Zarephath is saved from starvation because of her generosity to the prophet Elijah, in a time of famine when other poor people around her must have died. Centuries later Jesus was to comment that though there were thousands of lepers and cripples and tax collectors in his area, he was sent only to heal a few in order that God's will might be made known in particular ways and places. It is easy to believe God shows preference when some are healed and others not. We, after all, do not love everyone equally but have our favorites. Yet in the seventeenth century the poet Thomas Traherne wrote:

> By Lov our souls are married and sodderd to the creatures: and it is our duty like God to be united to them all. We must lov them infinitely but in God, and for God: and God in them. When we dote on the Perfections and Beauties of som one Creature: we do not lov that too much, but othr things too little. Never was any thing in this World loved too much, but many Things have been loved in a fals Way: and all in too short a Measure.

Hebrews 9:24-28   Here we have an image of the second coming of Christ "as a high priest of the good things to come." There is a lovely line in Jeffery Rowthorn's hymn describing the priestly people of God who "daily lift life heavenward...for earth's true glory."[18] By caring for the creation we make it and ourselves a more perfect offering to be lifted back to the Creator in thankfulness.

Mark 12:38-44   The poor widow is singularly blessed for offering her two coins, but her gift is costly. She risks starvation for acting rightly, while a rich donor risks only inconvenience. Who pays the most for the preservation of the environment—or for its destruction? Toxic waste sites are disproportionately located in poor neighborhoods among Americans of color. Communities with political and economic clout have the influence to practice NIMBY (Not in my backyard!). There is a huge difference between free gift and extortion. Disposing of our own toxic byproducts should be the responsibility of those with more resources who can cope with the ramifications rather than a burden placed upon the poorest among us.

🌿 *Proper 28*

Daniel 12:1-13 The prophet Daniel has a series of striking visions. Dreams and visions are among the most ancient and universal vehicles for divine revelation: ancient Egypt and Babylon, Mesopotamia, Greece, and Rome all recognized them as crucial to religious experience and useful for planning future action. Almost every significant figure of the early church through Augustine considered dreams to be one important way God spoke to human beings. In *A Treatise on the Soul* Tertullian claimed, "Beyond a doubt the greater part of mankind derive their knowledge of God from their dreams."

In our modern era, dreams have been understood as warning, direction, insight, analysis of the past, neurological phenomena, and self-healing; many of us pay them no mind whatsoever. It is entirely consistent with Christian tradition to take our dreams seriously, examine them, and ask whether God might have a word for us through them. How have your dreams informed you and enlarged who you are?

Hebrews 10:31-39 You need endurance to do the will of God, says the author of Hebrews. If we find endurance to be arduous, consider the monarch butterfly. A hundred million of these lovely, fragile insects migrate as far as 4000 miles each year in search of winter warmth and summer food and mating. Some insects have been clocked traveling 80 miles in a day, tiny as they are. They assemble and roost at the same sites each year preparatory to migrating, sometimes crowding trees so that they appear to be in gold blossom.

Mark 13:14-23 "This is the way the world ends: not with a bang but a whimper," wrote poet T. S. Eliot. The latest round of the great debate among astronomers as to whether the universe will collapse in on itself in a big crunch, or go on expanding endlessly, has been won by the expansion crowd. Data from a huge telescope in Chile detected the light of a supernova about halfway to the edge of the visible universe and showed that the expansion rate was faster than previously measured. Further data supports the expectation that the universe will continue to expand like rising bread, all its elements moving away from its center and each other, until a thousand billion years from now the stars have burned all their fuel and wink out, and even the black holes evaporate—leaving cold darkness. Signs and portents of the end times! But are we worried? Who, after all, has the universe in hand?

🍂 *Proper 29*

Daniel 7:9-14 The Ancient One is depicted on a wheeled throne. It took the clear sight of a Sunday school child's drawing to show me the obvious: an image of God as an old African American grandfather in a wheelchair—startling, expansive, fresh. For a fully-abled person, it might seem incongruous to picture the perfect God with a disability, but from the perspective of an elder in a wheelchair such an image offers a vision of wholeness. I remember, too, Ezekiel's vision of wheels within wheels. Imagine what resurrection a wheelchair might signify to one previously immoblilized in a bed or a chair.

Revelation 1:1-8 God is the Alpha and the Omega, creator and destiny of the universe. There is great strength and comfort in this knowledge. Theologian H. Paul Santmire writes:

> Would it not be possible to envision the end of the universe. . . not as an omega-point, but as an omega world, a commonwealth of creaturely being, where the light of the divine fire unites and permeates all things. . . where a genuinely cosmic peace is finally established, where God is truly all in all?[19]

In this evolving creation we are students learning our way, and creation gives us feedback about our progress. "All of creation God gives to humankind to use. If this privilege is misused, God's justice permits creation to punish humanity," wrote Hildegard of Bingen in the eleventh century.

John 18:33-37 "My kingdom is not from this world," says John's regal Jesus. At times Christians have used this as justification for dismissing the material world as unimportant or irremediably fallen, worthy of scorn or exploitation. The reign of Christ is not of the world, but is *for* the world, and, in the language of the gospels, it is also among us. In the incarnation God has come "usward" to lift us Godward, to paraphrase Lancelot Andrewes, and with us the whole creation—sanctified, restored, and made new.

ENDNOTES FOR YEAR B

❧ Advent

1. "Rising," Wendell Berry, *Collected Poems 1957-1982* (New York: North Point Press, 1984), 244.
2. See J. Robert. Wright, ed., *Readings for the Daily Office from the Early Church* (New York: Church Hymnal Corporation, 1991) and A. M. Allchin, *The Joy of All Creation* (Cambridge, Mass.: Cowley Publications, 1991).

❧ Christmas

1. Quoted in J. Philip Newell, *The Book of Creation* (New York: Paulist Press, 1999), 12-13.
2. From "Changing Government" in Oliver Davies and Fiona Bowie, *Celtic Christian Spirituality* (New York: Continuum, 1995), 184-85.
3. John Sanford, *Dreams and Healing* (New York: Paulist Press, 1978), 21.

❧ Epiphany

1. *The Book of Common Prayer,* 392. The Ash Wednesday litany (267 ff.) offers some particulars.
2. Carl Sagan, *Cosmos* (New York: Random House, 1980), 331.
3. Anne Wilson Shaef and Diane Fassel, *The Addictive Organization* (San Francisco: Harper & Row, 1988), 57.
4. Robert Jay Lifton and Greg Mitchell, *Hiroshima in America* (New York: G. P. Putnam's Sons, 1995), 353-54.
5. Rudolf Bultmann, *Jesus Christ and Mythology* (New York: Charles Scribner's Sons, 1958), 65.
6. Agnes Sanford, *The Healing Light* (New York: Ballantine Books, 1972) 3, 4.
7. J. Robert Wright, ed., *Readings for the Daily Office from the Early Church* (New York: Church Hymnal Corporation, 1991), 79.
8. John Snow, *Mortal Fear* (Cambridge, Mass.: Cowley Publications, 1987).
9. A good science resource that speaks of the complex relationships between human and animal evolution and extinction is Richard Leakey & Roger Lewin, *The Sixth Extinction* (New York: Doubleday, 1995).
10. Julie Meservey, *The Inward Garden* (Boston: Little, Brown & Co., 1995).

❧ *Lent and Holy Week*

1. As reported in the *Saint Louis Post Dispatch* (19 September 1999).
2. From the foreword by William O. Douglas in Yoshikazu Shirakawa, *Eternal America* (Tokyo: Kodansha International, Ltd., 1969), 8-10.
3. Alice Miller, *Prisoners of Childhood* (New York: Basic Books, Inc., 1981).
4. *The Hymnal 1982*, Hymn 528, words by Jeffery Rowthorn.

❧ *Easter*

1. Freeman Dyson, *Disturbing the Universe* (New York: Harper and Row, 1988).
2. *New Scientist* (21 August 1993): 30.

❧ *The Season After Pentecost*

1. "Why" in Oliver Davies and Fiona Bowie, eds., *Celtic Christian Spirituality* (New York: Continuum, 1995), 230.
2. Alan Guth, *The Inflationary Universe* (Reading, Mass.: Addison-Wesley Publishers, 1997).
3. Robert Van de Weyer, ed., *Celtic Prayers* (Nashville: Abingdon Press, 1997), 30.
4. A good resource for such accounts is Ray Moody's *Life After Life* (New York: Bantam, 1975).
5. John Snow, *Mortal Fear: Meditations on Death and AIDS* (Cambridge, Mass.: Cowley Publications, 1987), 11.
6. As quoted in F. Pearce, "Give the Fault Its Due," *New Scientist* (10 October 1998).
7. Caspar Henderson, "Small is Still Beautiful," *New Scientist* (4 January 1997).
8. Ian Melbourne, "Toilets to Go," *New Scientist* (11 April 1998): 11.
9. *The American Journal of Genetics* 63: 1175.
10. Pierre Teilhard de Chardin, *Hymn of the Universe* (New York: Harper & Row, 1961).
11. Jonathan Kozol, *Rachel and her Children: Homeless Families in America* (New York: Fawcette Columbine, 1988), 81.
12. Londa Schiebinger, *Nature's Body: Gender in the Making of Modern Science* (Boston: Beacon Press, 1993), 3, 13.
13. Chris Butler, "Myths about Woman Abuse," *For Shelter and Beyond* (Boston: Massachusetts Coalition of Battered Women Service Groups, 1992).
14. John Polkinghorne, "Is Science Enough?", *Sewanee Theological Review* 39:1 (December 1995), 15.
15. Arian Hough, *God Is Not Green: A Re-examination of Eco-theology* (Herefordshire, England: Gracewing, 1997), 137.
16. Roy Baumeister, *Evil* (London: W. H. Freeman, 1997).
17. John Polkinghorne, "Can a Scientist Pray?", *Sewanee Theological Review* 39:1 (December 1995): 38.
18. *The Hymnal 1982*, Hymn 528, words by Jeffery Rowthorn.
19. H. Paul Santmire, *The Travail of Nature* (Minneapolis: Fortress Press, 1985), 172.

YEAR C

ADVENT

❧ 1 Advent

Zechariah 14:4-9   The prophet graphically describes the sliding of plates along a fault line during an earthquake. Innovative research is underway to find new ways to predict earthquakes. A Greek physicist has discovered that electrical currents in the earth's crust may signal impending earthquakes; by measuring small voltage changes along fault lines he has successfully predicted three quakes in Greece. He has also demonstrated the connection between rock stress and electricity in the laboratory by duplicating the stresses on rocks that produce tiny amounts of current before breaking.[1] How do we live and pray with the uncertainty of the future? How do we cope with our feelings of helplessness in the face of all we that we cannot predict?

1 Thessalonians 3:9-13   Thankfulness comes naturally to some people, but for many of us it must be learned and cultivated as a habit of heart and mind. Mystic Meister Eckhart describes a thankful heart as the sign of baptismal regeneration:

> What is the test that you have undergone this holy birth? Listen carefully. If this birth has truly taken place within you, then every single creature points you toward God.... If the only prayer you say in your whole life is "thank you," that would suffice.... This, then, is salvation: When we marvel at the beauty of created things and praise their beautiful Creator.

Luke 21:25-31   Signs in the sun, moon, and stars must not be ignored. By mid-July of 1998, over 50 people had died in the United States because of the sweltering heat across much of the country. At the same time, politicians were arguing whether to stop government funding for climatic change research or continue it. The previous year our Senate voted against limiting emissions of greenhouse gases unless the same restrictions were imposed on nations of the developing world. Some legislators have fought hard to prevent the United States from implementing international agreements on environmental protection such as the Kyoto Accord. Although many scientists agree that global warming is a real and novel phenomenon caused in large part by human activity, our country continues to resist cooperating with poorer and more vulnerable nations. Where do our gospel calling and politics overlap? How are we to read the signs of our times?

❦ 2 Advent

Baruch 5:1-9   Creation celebrates the joyful return of the exiles of Israel. The woods and forests are a sign of God's protecting goodness. Much of Israel has been deforested over the centuries. In response, modern Israelis are developing a holiday called *Tubat Shevat* that celebrates the environment as a gift of God, and encourages Jews around the world to help plant trees in Israel for the renewal of its forests. Our own forests have not been faring much better. In California, 99 percent of the native riparian forest of the Great Valley was cut in less than a century to make way for farms and artificially channeled rivers. Marshlands that watered the woodlands were drained for development, and native species of birds and salmon have disappeared. Conservation efforts are underway to replant some small areas of forest in the Kern River preserve and the Cosumnes River valley, but such efforts are tiny compared to the lost forest and its inhabitants.[2] How are forests being protected in your region? How might conservation be understood as prayer in action?

Philippians 1:1-11   The fruits of righteousness are seen in the abounding of love. In this passage, as in Baruch, there is an effusion of grace spilling over in loving action, a kind of unity shaped by love, bringing forth a harvest of righteousness. And what is the alternative to a community governed by love? One governed by fear, perhaps, or anger?

> Every gun that is made, every warship launched, every rocket fired signifies, in the final sense, a theft from those who hunger and are not fed, those who are cold and are not clothed. This world in arms is not spending money alone. It is spending the sweat of its laborers, the genius of its scientists, the hopes of its children. . . . This is not a way of life at all in any true sense. Under the cloud of threatening war, it is humanity hanging from a cross of iron.[3]

Luke 3:1-6 The "voice of one crying in the wilderness" has become a catch-phrase for those who persist in delivering an unpopular message to their culture. In 1972 geophysicist James Lovelock published a paper advancing the Gaia hypothesis—a theory that there is a complex interrelationship between biological and physical systems on earth in which all work together to maintain the health of the whole planet. For many years a vital link seemed missing, and many scientists dismissed the possibility that organisms could have evolved in such a way that they have a role in regulating such planetary systems such as weather.

An Oxford team of scientists has now developed an understanding of the relationship between marine algae and weather that supports Lovelock's thesis. Lovelock observed that marine algae produce a gas called dimethyl sulfide (DMS) that reacts with oxygen in air at the surface of the sea to form minute solid particles, around which water vapor condenses to form clouds. These Oxford scientists theorize that algae have developed a means to disperse their offspring around the globe much in the way fungi and plants use air to carry spores and pollen over a wide area. Aloft in the clouds, the DMS antifreeze may help the algae survive; it also forms ice crystals that may help the cloud release its moisture and rain the algae down again to the surface of the seas.[4] How might we express in our prayer the wholeness of earth's ecosystems?

🌿 3 Advent

Zephaniah 3:14-20 I will bring you home and cast out your enemies, says the Lord. In a time of trial, the people of God look toward a hopeful future of restoration—a refrain that occurs again and again in scripture. I was cheered to hear an interview with a group of British ecologists about their research on "brownfields." These are areas of urban wasteland, including old quarries, slag heaps, crumbling walls and foundations, gravel pits, and alkali dumps from soda manufacturing. Some environmentalists have called for their cleaning and development, but these researchers testify that the strange man-made habitats have, over many years, become unique ecosystems that house many rare species: insects, orchids, and other wildflowers among them.

Brownfields are a fitting metaphor for our interior landscape, too. Though all of our lives may be littered with the ruins of the past with wasteland qualities that are painful and toxic, they may yet produce qualities of soul that are rare and beautiful. God loves us, even in our brownfields, and sees us, tarnished as we are, as fertile gardens.

Philippians 4:4-9 "Have no anxiety about anything" is an injunction easier said than done. When we are anxious or worried, our autonomic nervous system turns up its responsiveness; blood pressure, pulse, and respiration rate increase; and the brain becomes less sensitive to its stress modulating chemicals. Among chronic worriers there is excess activity in the cingulate cortex portion of the brain, and it is possible that there may be a genetic component to some chronic anxiety.

Edward Hallowell, a doctor of psychiatry and author of *Worry*, cites a number of contributing causes to persistent anxiety, including social isolation and lack of intimacy, and masked grief. He suggests that we can often retrain the brain by intentional behaviors that modify thoughts and attitudes, interrupting worries with positive thoughts.[5] "Whatever is true, honorable, pure, gracious, lovely, excellent—think about these things": this is the apostle's version of cognitive therapy. The epistle reminds us that God stands ready to hear and support us in times of anxiety, and to invite us into the peace which passes our understanding.

Luke 3:7-18 Trees that do not bear good fruit are good for nothing. Early in the fifth century, John Chrysostom preached:

> Do you see how sturdy, fair, well-shaped, graceful, and magnificent are the trees that do not bear fruit? Yet if we have occasion to possess a garden, we prefer pomegranate and olive trees filled with fruit. Sterile trees are there for appearance rather than utility; and if they can be useful, it is only in a very limited way. Such are those persons who consider only their own interest. And such persons do not even attain this end, for they are good only to be rejected, whereas the trees can be used to build houses.[6]

❧ 4 Advent

Micah 5:2-4 The shepherd feeds the flock. A modern-day shepherd writes that raising sheep is "an efficient way to convert grass into food and clothing for humans." Yet in poor pasture only one or two sheep may find adequate food on an acre of ground. Sheep like to feed on fresh grass that has not been trodden down; they prefer to wander as they feed, or to be pastured on rotating fields. Depending on age and reproductive cycle, a sheep can consume over a pound of grain a day, or the equivalent.[7]

The shepherds of old in the arid lands of Palestine must have been constantly exploring and evaluating new grounds. In moving their flock through unfamiliar terrain, they needed to be alert for predators and poisonous plants, as well as fresh water. Since these sheep were not penned in lush fields, active skills were required to keep them in motion, safe and nourished. How might these shepherding skills be applied to today's flock?

Hebrews 10:5-10   God takes no pleasure in sacrifices and burnt offerings; we no longer bring these to the altar. Now we bring "ourselves, our souls and bodies," as Paul says. We bring tokens of the whole work of our lives. A kindly deed, the use we have made of the hours of our week, a new manuscript, the bitter and critical words we refrained from saying, the patient waiting and forbearance of a hard time in relationship—we bring all of these to the altar, too. There, assembled upon the corporal as it unfolds like the gate of heaven to receive us, the whole of creation is carried forward in our prayer and offered back to its author.

Luke 1:39-56   Elizabeth, the elderly mother, would have raised some eyebrows in her time. A woman nearing sixty recently gave birth to a child conceived with a donated egg. There was great controversy about whether she should have been allowed access to reproductive technology at her age. Critics argued that she would probably not live into her child's adult years. Does any parent have this guarantee? The Bible contains several stories of God hearing the plea of older and barren women to conceive babies; their children often become wondrous heroes. Though the ancient authors of scripture went to great lengths to differentiate the Hebrew God from fertility deities of the Near East, God has always been connected with marvelous fruitfulness, and with the fulfilling of deep human desires to be creative and generative.

CHRISTMAS

🕯 *Christmas Day III*

Isaiah 52:7-10   "Beautiful feet upon the mountains": when I was a child I found this a very odd phrase. Few of us think of our feet—those poor, walked upon, callused and corned extremities—as being beautiful, even if they are the feet of a messenger bringing good news! Once I broke a tiny chunk off the tip of one of the bones in my ankle. When I came out of the plaster and began to put weight on my foot again, the ankle was stiff and flat. For the first time I appreciated the marvelously sensitive way the ankle joint tips and swivels to compensate for irregularities in the ground without our having to think about it. Even the smallest ridge or stone underfoot requires an ankle adjustment if we are not to tumble. I gained a new respect for the beauty of my otherwise unlovely feet.

Hebrews 1:1-12   This prayer from one Celtic community hymns Christ the cosmic one, image of the Creator, who upholds the universe:

> It is you who makes the sun bright, together with the ice
> it is you who creates the rivers and the salmon all along the river.
> That the nut tree should be flowering
> O Christ, it is a rare craft.
> Through your skill too comes the kernel, you fair ear of our wheat.
> Though the children of Eve ill deserve the bird flocks and the salmon
> it was the Immortal One on the cross
> who made both salmon and birds....
> Besides this, what miracle is greater?[1]

John 1:1-14 The universe begins as God speaks the Word. Astronomer David Darling addresses the various arguments about how the universe began:

> The biggest deal of all is how you get something from nothing. Don't let the cosmologists kid you on this one. They haven't got a clue either.... "In the beginning," they will say, "there was nothing—no time, space, matter or energy. Then there was a quantum fluctuation from which...." Whoa! Stop right there. You see what I mean? First there's nothing, then there is something.... I may not have been born in Yorkshire but I'm a firm believer that you cannot get owt from nowt. Not a universe from a nothing-verse, nor consciousness from a thinking brain.[2]

There is every reason to believe that the something from which the cosmos came is God, the consciousness God's own. Jewish mysticism offers an image of God who was everything and everywhere, contracting Godself to make hospitable room for creation's coming. Or as comic Terry Pratchett facetiously put it, "In the beginning there was nothing. And the Lord said: 'Let there be light' and there was still nothing, but now you could see it." How do you reconcile theories of cosmology and the existence of God?

❧ 1 Christmas

Isaiah 61:10–62:3 The prophet speaks of the Lord's springtime for the people. It is hard to think of spring in January when much of North America is still snowbound. The season of sprouting shoots brings to mind New England's vernal pools. From March through early June the snow melts, the rains come, and depressions in the woods and meadows fill up to make temporary ponds. These seasonal pools are the major breeding habitat for thousands of species around the world. Salamanders and toads lay eggs in them since they are generally free of predatory fish, and the snakes have not yet stirred. Male woodfrogs often start to sing when there is still ice rimming the ponds; they mate by the hundreds in a tiny pool. A month or so later tadpoles hatch and feed on the growing algae. Water beetles and dragonfly nymphs are the main threat to amphibian eggs and hatchlings.

Spring brings a mad dance of life, and then the growing amphibians become land-dwellers; the pools dry to sticky mud and finally disappear in the August sun. There is little to protect these vernal pools from the pavement of land developers who may not even know they are a regular feature of the seasonal landscape. I think of the song of joy to which the prophet refers as the wild chorus of frog voices that start as if by signal from a conductor one early spring night.

Galatians 3:23-25, 4:4-7   We were under a schoolteacher until our time of redemption. Now our discipline must come from ourselves—our own adult consciences. Conservationist Kent Redford writes:

> There are no cost-free feats of legerdemain to spring us from the contradictions inherent in promoting both economic development and environmental conservation. Through their actions, human beings are increasingly becoming dominating ecological actors and virtually all human development is done at ecological cost. Recognizing these costs sets the stage for evaluating what are acceptable compromises between economic development and conservation.[3]

How can we best discern acceptable compromises, and make conscientious decisions for the good of all creation?

John 1:1-18   A stunning suggestion about creation's origins comes from scientist Michael Grady, who has been shaping his theory for nearly two decades. He hypothesizes that the universe began as four dimensions of space and one of time filled with a supercooled liquid. A minute triggering event then seeded a crystal that expanded at lightning speed in all directions—physicists refer to this as a phase nucleation event. Grady suspects we are on the three-dimensional solid outside surface of a four-dimensional growing crystal bubble. His idea explains some of the puzzles of conventional cosmology—such as how disparate parts of the universe can have the same temperature, and how the universe seems balanced between endless inflation and a slow recollapse. If there are other similarly formed universes, he envisions these might collide like soap bubbles. His theory could explain the odd foamy nature of the cosmos and the quantum fluctuations of space.[4]

🌿 2 Christmas

Jeremiah 31:7-14   The prophet likens the abundant life of God's promise to "a watered garden." So consider that water upon which we rely. Nearly all of earth's water—97.3 percent—is in its oceans. Of the 2.7 percent that is fresh water, 2.2 percent is frozen at the earth's poles. Some surprising statistics have been gathered about the remaining half of one percent—some of which falls on the United States as rain and snow. We use only 7 percent of this precipitation for our cities, factories, and irrigated crops. Nature distributes 23 percent onto nonirrigated farms and ranges, and 16 percent onto forests and wilderness areas; 22 percent returns to the oceans, a portion of it carrying our diluted sewage or fertilizer runoffs; and a huge 32 percent of rainfall evaporates or is transpired by plants into the atmosphere. So there are water resources we have not yet begun to tap—even in a world where fresh water is scarce—once we gain an understanding of how to do so wisely.[5]

Ephesians 1:3-6, 15-19   Can our wisdom, our knowledge grow quickly enough for us to have an enlightened understanding about the intricate ways creation has been wrought? Consider the delicacy of relationships in tropical forests around the world that produce a familiar fruit, the fig. Fig trees bear large amounts of fruit over a long season and are thus a dietary mainstay for huge numbers of animals: some species eat nothing else. These trees rely on wasps to pollinate their blossoms: each of the 900 known fig species has its own unique species of wasp pollinators.

The loss of one wasp species could set off a chain of extinction beginning with the fig tree and moving to insects, birds, monkeys, peccaries, turtles, and bats—all of whom rely on figs for food. Without monkeys and peccaries, jaguars would disappear. With each species lost, the chance of losing many other species intensifies. So if one of our actions—a crop pesticide, a deforestation, an introduced predator—endangers one sort of wasp, an entire natural system may be lost. It is vital that we invest resources into expanding our knowledge of the web of life, for it sustains us and all creatures.[6]

Luke 2:41-52   We glimpse Jesus the twelve year old. One text on psychological development describes the child of latency age like this:

> Toward the end of latency, there is a brief period during which marked emotional and social changes occur without much biological change. The child is often touchy, defiant and resentful toward his parents. His behavior may seem disorganized, even to the point of vagueness and unintelligibility of speech. . . . [Children] turn critical of their parents and of parental values. They seek the company of non parental adults, and seek experiences which exclude their parents.[7]

All of this gives us great sympathy for Jesus' frantic parents, rushing back to the city to look for their missing child, and reminds us, in the words of the old Christmas carol, "day by day like us he grew."

EPIPHANY

❧ *The Epiphany*

See entry in Year A, page 12.

❧ *1 Epiphany*

Isaiah 42:1-9 "New things I now declare," says God. A new idea about the universe is gaining currency among astronomers. Some now argue that the universe is clumpy, having a fractal quality, with recurring patterns of unevenly distributed matter at every scale. Others believe that the universe is fractal on a small scale, but homogeneous on a large scale. These ideas challenge the majority view that the universe is a homogeneous, smooth entity—the underpinning for theories of the big bang and the uneven distribution of galaxies across the cosmos. There is as yet no theory to explain how a fractal universe might have come into being. As probes measure further distances and thereby learn more about the universe's history, data should accumulate to support or weaken this theory. Scientists tend to react to radically new theories with excitement, even if they are skeptical about them. New questions invite us to look at everything we know from a changed perspective, to push out the limits. In this season we remember how the early Christians pushed out the limits of thinking about God as they spread the gospel.

Acts 10:34-38 The message of the gospel spread throughout Judea, most often carried on foot and by word of mouth. It is fun to speculate about what it would have been like if our forbears had had access to electronic communications. Who would have spread the word about Jesus? Who would have received it? How would the reliabilty of the news have been tested? A wonderful range of communication technologies are available to spread the gospel, and we have barely begun to use them imaginatively. How might these media change our thinking about religious authority? About who interprets Christian belief and what credentials we require for this task? How might an individual congregation pass along the good news in the new millennium?

Luke 3:15-16, 21-22 Jesus is baptized. The Orthodox church in this season observes the Great Blessing of Water at Epiphany, and its prayer declares:

> Today the nature of the waters is sanctified,
> The Jordan bursts forth and turns back the flood of its streams,
> Seeing the Master wash himself.[1]

What does it imply to say the nature of water is sanctified?

❧ 2 Epiphany

Isaiah 62:1-5 "You shall be called My Delight is in her, and your land Married." Displaced as most of us are from a life closely connected with the land, it is a stretch for us to imagine the bond that our agrarian forbears—especially those of Native American ancestry—understood intimately: a marriage with the land in a spirit of complete mutuality and devotion. Yet the preservation of our world seems to require that we recapture some part of that covenant connection with the land. Martin Soroos writes:

> In resource terms the atmosphere is an example of a global commons, a status it shares with the ocean and the seabed, outer space and Antarctica. A global commons may be loosely defined as a domain that is beyond the exclusive jurisdiction of any one nation but one that all nations may use for their own purposes (such as extracting resources or discharging pollutants). Without effective controls, the use of a commons may increase to the point that it becomes severely depleted, contaminated, or degraded, a tendency Garrett Hardin refers to as the "tragedy of the commons."[2]

Like those small squares of common grazing land in the center of colonial villages, our atmosphere is a limited resource that can be sustained for the benefit of all only if *all* cooperate in using and caring for it.

1 Corinthians 12:1-11 There are varieties of gifts given for the upbuilding of the community. In an achievement-oriented culture, we are under some pressure to try to be good at everything, and to conceal our weaknesses. The apostle Paul makes clear that both strengths and weaknesses are given for the benefit of the whole community; we collaborate in the work of the gospel. Consider this tale of St. Columba:

> Once, it is said, when Columba was at sea a great storm arose, with gusts of wind blowing from all sides, and his boat was buffeted by great waves. Columba tried to help the sailors bail out the water that came into the boat, but they said to him, "Your doing this does very little to help us in this danger. You would do better to pray for us as we perish." Columba stopped bailing water, and began to pour out prayers aloud to God. Marvelous to relate, as soon as he stood up in the prow and raised his hands to God the wind ceased and the sea stilled. The crew were amazed and gave glory to God.[3]

This insightful old story suggests we do well to stick to our gifts and not to try to be expert at the tasks given to others, heeding the testimony of our neighbors about the discernment of our gifts and callings.

John 2:1-11 Wine for a wedding—gallons and gallons of it! These ancient partyers were not afraid of a little inebriation during a festival that might last days—and did not have to worry about drinking and driving. Jesus was not a teetotaler.

Why does alcohol intoxicate the brain? Researchers have found a molecule on the surface of nerve cells that responds abnormally to a sedative drug, but also restores sobriety in drunken laboratory rats, and they suspect it may determine the effect that alcohol has on people. Some animals seem to have cells that are particularly susceptible to alcohol and sedatives; these can interfere with muscle control in the cerebellum and cause staggering and poor coordination.[4] How might the church teach moderation?

❦ 3 Epiphany

Nehemiah 8:2-10 Ezra reads from the book of the law in the city square, and "the ears of all the people were attentive." We do not often think about what a wonder our sense of hearing is. Today about one person in ten has impaired hearing, 28 to 30 million people in the United States alone. Most hearing loss is in the higher frequencies, an essential component of the consonants of human speech. Hearing aid technology to date has focused on detection and amplification of sound. The next generation of hearing aids may use insect biology to focus hearing on particular sounds in the high frequency range, separating them from the background din. A common fly, *Ormia ochracea,* has the ability to detect the song of crickets from among all the insect calls and other sounds of summer, allowing it to locate the cricket so it can become an unwilling host to the larvae of the fly. The fly's tiny head does not allow detection of the delay in sound waves between one ear and the other, as in large-headed animals; this fly has ears on its chest, two tiny membranes barely wider than a human hair, connected by a flexible bridge. The two ends vibrate with incoming sounds at different instants, allowing the insect to locate the source of sound and find its cricket in the field. For new hearing aids, nanotechnology will provide micro components, and the power source may be mechanical, like the fly's "ear," rather than battery-supplied.[5]

1 Corinthians 12:12-27   All the parts of the body are necessary for its healthy function, even those hidden from view—like the pineal or adrenal glands. What if we also understood our planet as a body in which all parts are necessary for health, full of wonder and potential value? Deep beneath the surface of the earth, hidden body parts play an intricate role in creation that we have hardly begun to fathom, yet threaten by our actions. Two thousand feet below the ground surface of south-central Texas aquifers are home to a surprising diversity of unique creatures. Some of them are relics of animals that lived millions of years ago at the surface when Texas was covered by ancient seas. So far over 40 species have been found living in the dark and at great pressure, feeding on bacteria and fossil organic material. Scientists are astonished at the number and diversity of species in such a restricted environment. As more and more water is mined from aquifers, what will we lose as these ecosystems are destroyed before we learn what role they may play in the matrix of creation?

Luke 4:14-21   How can the acceptable year of the Lord be *any* year of our debased human history, including those of Jesus' adulthood—years of Roman domination, war and rebellion, injustice and crime? The remarkable pronouncement of the prophet Isaiah leads in two directions. First, we see how the whole creation has been hallowed by God's redeeming love and made acceptable, despite its sin, through the incarnation. Second, the inner movement of the Holy Spirit is toward a joyful awakening to the way an individual's vocation connects to the whole work of God in renewing the face of the earth. Mechtilde of Magdeburg wrote:

> The day of my spiritual awakening was the day I saw—and knew I saw—all things in God and God in all things.... Do not disdain your body. For the soul is just as safe in its body as in the Kingdom of heaven.

4 Epiphany

Jeremiah 1:4-10 "I am only a boy," protests the prophet. In 1998 an eleven-year-old researcher published results of a seventh-grade science project in the prestigious *Journal of the American Medical Association.* With some writing assistance from her mother, a registered nurse, Emily Rosa developed a method of testing the effectiveness of touch-therapy. She found no data to support the practice of forms of touch-therapy in which practitioners move their hands a few inches above a patient's body to "manipulate their energy fields" or "auras."[6]

If Emily's story were told in every elementary school classroom, a whole new generation of scientists might be encouraged to undertake some research, unintimidated by their age. This is a good lesson for churches who tend to infantilize young members, disbelieving that they have gifts and callings to ministry even as children and teens. How can we equip our youth with real skills and information, and provide sound mentoring to help them fulfill their vocations?

1 Corinthians 14:12-20 Spirit and mind together are needed for effective prayer and evangelization. In healing, too, attentiveness to spirit and mind, to the biological and the psychological/spiritual dimensions of treatment, forms a mature, holistic approach. Physicians in the United States have been slower to accept this understanding than those in some other parts of the world. A review of Lynn Payer's book *Medicine and Culture* offers this insight:

> To Europeans, the appearance of disease signals predominantly a lowering of resistance and the need to shore up defenses with, for example, a trip to the spa or the use of hydrotherapy. Americans consider themselves to be naturally healthy; if they become ill, they assume there must be a cause, preferably external. They want something done, fast. So, American physicians attack the environmental agent, using antibiotics for often trivial infections, Cesarean section for normal childbirth...[out of] our basic image of the body as a machine. If there's something wrong, let's fix it.[7]

How do we understand the interplay of body and spirit in the healing prayer of the church? In anointing? In the eucharist?

Luke 4:21-32 No prophet is acceptable in his own country. Take Missourian Harlow Shapley, an American prophet who ruffled more than a few scientific and theological feathers. His original intention was to study journalism at Princeton, but due to a delay in that school's opening he wound up studying astronomy. In the 1930s at

Mount Wilson Observatory he noticed that globular clusters in our galaxy are centered around a distant point in the constellation Sagittarius—a radical conclusion:

> The young researcher boldly reasoned that this point must be the true hub of the Milky Way disk, not the region around the Sun. The new model put the Sun decidedly off to one side, about two-thirds of the way to the outer edge. His shifting of the Sun from its pivotal location was a feat that could only be matched by Copernicus's earlier removal of the Earth from the center of the solar system.... It would take a sharp-eyed farmboy, born and bred in the heart of America's Midwest, to banish the solar system from its regal position at the center of the known universe and place it in a more rural location.[8]

Who are the prophetic voices among today's scientists? Are we prepared to hear their teachings?

❧ 5 Epiphany

Judges 6:11-24 I love the directness of Gideon's response to the angel: If God is with us, why have all these terrible things happened to us? Why is God not living up to God's reputation? On bad days I find myself asking the same thing. The physical world is beset with suffering. Christians who take God's creation and incarnation seriously cannot, like Buddhists, simply insist suffering is illusory. In pondering why God lets sin exist, fifteenth-century mystic Julian of Norwich concluded that all the suffering produced by sin moves us to a longing for Christ, "that we set our heart on that 'pass-over'—over from the pain we now experience to the bliss we trust in." God "shall make all that is wrong to turn out for the best." How can we balance our distressed response to evil and tragedy with a deep-seated trust in God?

1 Corinthians 15:1-11 Christ's resurrection draws the whole creation into new life. The ancient icons of the east show the risen Christ bending down to pull Adam and Eve from their graves after him. The theologian Anselm understood that resurrection was a cosmic event:

> Heaven, stars, earth, waters, day and night, rejoice now for a new and ineffable grace given them through Christ, for all things were as if dead, buried by oppression and tainted by being used in the service of idols; but now are raised to life and praise God.

Luke 5:1-11 Full fishing nets: will farmed fish be the food of the future? So far, farmed fish are fed on live smaller fish or fishmeal, often consuming four times their own market weight. The next crop of the future may be zooplankton: tiny marine animals that can be cultivated in lagoons and filtered from the water by sea-going combines to use as fish food. Though far from a cost-effective solution to date, perhaps someday it will be.

⚜ 6 Epiphany

Jeremiah 17:5-10 A "salt land" is the image of an uninhabitable, deathly place to live, fit for those "whose hearts turn away from the Lord." Yet ironically, salt is necessary to life and was an important trade commodity of the Dead Sea region. Ir-hammelah was the ancient city of salt at the head of the Dead Sea, its economy fueled by deposits at Mount Sodom along its side. Fluctuations in water level left thick deposits of salt to be scraped off rock and sand. Perhaps a particular mineral formation became associated with the story of Lot and his unfortunate wife, who was turned into salt.

1 Corinthians 15:12-20 Some say there is no resurrection of the dead, sighs the apostle. True in our time, too! But is anything impossible for God? In Colorado's most arid, environmentally hostile lands can be found tiny round worms called nematodes. These worms should not exist at all, since in times of drought they excrete all but 10 percent of the water in their bodies. They curl up into tight spirals, becoming extremely small, and shut down their life systems. For all intents and purposes, these creatures die, and can blow about like grains of dust on the wind or lie for decades without movement or activity. But when rain finally comes, the nematodes begin to swell and uncurl; once again they begin to eat, excrete, reproduce, and generally return to life until the next drought. If we can believe the extraordinary life cycle of the nematode, one of God's humblest creatures, perhaps it is not such a stretch to believe God is capable of raising us from the dead in grander fashion.

Luke 6:17-26 Blessings and woes reverse the assumptions of the world. Look beneath the surface, Jesus says to us, for the radical, transformative work of God. Marjorie Stoneman Douglas spent her long life studying, loving, and advocating for the protection of the Florida Everglades, her home. She catalogued their social and environmental history, and mourned their modern decline, drained and polluted, dammed and developed—the victim of growing agriculture. She said simply, "There are no other Everglades in the world." Of their settlers, who lived oblivious to the complexities of this swamp environment, she remarked:

> It was too soon to expect that all these people would see that the destruction of the Everglades was the destruction of all. They had cried for help in times of extreme wetness and extreme dryness, as if they could not realize that they lived under a regular alternation of extremes.[9]

How do we also misread our apparent blessings and woes? Can we understand that our small local discomforts have their place in the larger context of the planet?

❧ 7 Epiphany

Genesis 45:3-11, 21-28 Famine drives Joseph's family to Egypt. Many of us remember graphic television footage of starving people in famine-afflicted Ethiopia and Somalia some years back. Though there are still areas of deep hunger, like the Sudan, in many parts of Africa sustained effort by skilled farmers has led to robust sustainable agriculture. Now Asian countries have taken the lead in childhood malnutrition—notably India, Pakistan, and Bangladesh, where nearly half of all the malnourished children on the planet live. Sadly, child starvation in these areas is not blamed primarily on scarcity of food, but on the low social status of women, who lack equal access to food, education, and health care, and therefore give birth to underweight, ill infants. One-third of the children in south Asia weigh less than 2.5 kilograms at birth, and after breastfeeding ceases, these babies lose ground rapidly.[10]

1 Corinthians 15:35-50 Defining the end of our physical existence has not been an easy task, and we still have not reached a consensus on just what constitutes death. What criteria can be used for determining brain death in an otherwise living body? An irreversible coma without independent respiration—deep unconsciousness, unresponsivity, and not breathing spontaneously—is one; in Great Britain the criteria include the loss of the capacity for consciousness and the loss of ability to breathe, constituting brainstem death. And yet the heart may go on beating unassisted for hours, sometimes days, after complete brainstem death, and while most would say this individual is not alive, few would argue to go ahead with the burial until the inevitable stopping of the heart occurs, and some argue against organ donation until the heart ceases. All these criteria become critical in making decisions about the prolonging of life through medical intervention, and the donation of organs for transplantation. What does the church have to contribute to this discussion?

Luke 6:27-38   "Be merciful." Is altruism an adaptive quality in human evolution? Scientists used to think so—but what of those individuals who cheat to get ahead and often prosper at the expense of others? What is advantageous for the individual may not be for the group, which survives best if all or at least most of its members care for others within the group. Yet how does a group become altruistic? Sociobiologists have no firm answer for just how the altruism of the few can become the social standard of the many. Perhaps more pressing a question for our time is this: How do we form new Christians who value being generous simply for Christ's sake in a culture where altruism is often seen as weakness and foolishness, and exploitation a sign of success and streetsmarts?

❧ 8 Epiphany

Jeremiah 7:1-15   Caring for the vulnerable and doing justice is a mark of those who genuinely worship God. What then do we say of ourselves as we engage in economic warfare? In Iraq, where we are currently enforcing an economic embargo, a major hospital has run out of supplies for testing the blood sugar of diabetic patients. In Cuba it is impossible to obtain at any price the one medicine effective against a certain kind of childhood leukemia.[11] United Nations agencies estimate that between 1990 and 1997, sanctions against Iraq contributed to the deaths of 200,000 children in that country. Embargoes impoverish and sicken the poorest individuals long before they bankrupt governments. Are these not a form of biological warfare, under the polite title of economic constraint?

1 Corinthians 15:50-58   Paul contemplates the perishable and the imperishable. As a young person backpacking in the White Mountains, I was shocked to read that orange peels in the fragile environment above the timber line can take seven years to decompose! Those same environmental guides to the White Mountains and Appalachians wryly reminded me that the Vibram soles on my hiking boots would likely survive a nuclear holocaust and remain for a virtual eternity in some landfill. It may be useful to meditate on what we use and discard that is—relatively—imperishable and how we might substitute material that is perishable. Decomposable coffins to go with our blessedly decomposable bodies might be a place to start.

Luke 6:39-49   A large portion of human civilization is built upon fragile coastal land that may cease to exist if global warming continues its present trends. One of the earliest and most recognizable consequences of a warmer earth may be rising sea levels in much of the world: as greenhouse gases thicken and the planet's surface warms, glaciers and ice caps melt more rapidly and the warming water of the seas expands. Sea levels over the millennia have fluctuated, but currently seas are rising—as much as .15 meters this century. Some 1 billion people, 20 percent of the earth's inhabitants, live on lands likely to be inundated or changed by rising oceans. Huge numbers of environmental refugees—many of them in the world's poorest nations—would be forced to migrate. While wealthy nations would suffer some losses—the Mississippi delta is our most vulnerable region—they could also mobilize their resources to build bulkheads, dams, levees, and pumping systems to protect coastal cities in vulnerable nations as well as in their own.[12]

❧ *Last Epiphany*

Exodus 34:29-35; Luke 9:28-36   Moses has a shining face, as does Jesus on the holy mountain. As a priest I often look out on the congregation and glimpse the glow of transfiguration in them all. In the words of the poet Walt Whitman:

> Divine I am inside and out, and I make holy whatever I touch,
>   or am touched from.
> . . . .
> Why should I wish to see God better than this day?
> I see something of God each hour of the twenty-four, and each
>   moment then,
> In the faces of men and women I see God, and in my own face
>   in the glass;
> I find letters from God dropped in the street, and every one is
>   signed by God's name.[13]

1 Corinthians 12:27–13:13   Gandhi described the power of love as the foundation not only of human community in God, but of the whole creation.

> The law of love will work, just as the law of gravitation will work, whether we accept it or not.... The more I work at this law, the more I feel the delight in life, the delight in the scheme of this universe. It gives me a peace and a meaning of the mysteries of nature that I have no power to describe.[14]

If love is the greatest gift, how can we better encounter it at work in *all* of creation?

LENT

❧ *Ash Wednesday*

See entry in Year A, page 24.

❧ *1 Lent*

Deuteronomy 26:1-11   When I first saw the region of the Jordan where the Israelites had ventured over the arid hills into an incredibly lush valley of fruit trees and grass, I could imagine their excitement and sense of blessing: the contrast is extraordinary. We might think of the territory of the soul's journey with God in terms of the ocean instead of the desert for a change, for it, too, can be a terrifying wilderness, full of danger. And the oceans also have pockets of life with extraordinary lushness and abundance.

Contemporary oceanographers believe there is just one world ocean, an interconnecting body of over 142 million square miles covering nearly three-quarters of our own planet misleadingly called "Earth."[1] From this territory also we are called to offer firstfruits, to receive everything as gift from God. The particular habitats that foster most of the life of the oceans—sandbanks, reefs, estuaries, kelp beds, and the like—are finite "promised lands" of abundance within the sparsely populated open oceans; these too require our special gratitude and care.

Romans 10:5-13   In the heights of heaven, in the abyss of space, physicists and astrophysicists have been scanning the skies for MACHOs (massive compact halo objects) and the subatomic world for WIMPs (weakly interacting massive particles).

They are trying to account for the extra gravity we observe at work in the rapid movement of galaxies—too rapid for the matter we have been able to identify so far. The missing source of this gravitational force has been dubbed "dark matter."

Though hotly debated, many physicists believe that WIMPs predominate in dark matter. They have named two sorts of hypothetical WIMPs: axions and neutralinos. Each particle is believed to have a superparticle symmetrical pair-partner: electrons have selectrons, quarks have squarks, photons have photinos, and neutrons have neutralinos; if so, these would come close to supplying the amount of matter believed missing from the universe. The Large Hadron Collider under construction near Geneva will be the most powerful particle accelerator ever built and should be able to create WIMPs, thereby providing experimental evidence for this theory.[2] We may soon know just what is very near us and causing such big gravitational effects. We do not need to venture into remote realms to find Christ, yet even in their mysteries we can find Christ at work.

Luke 4:1-13   Jesus is tempted with false visions of power. Physicist Jeremy Bernstein worked at Los Alamos as a young man and was invited to witness one of the aboveground nuclear bomb tests in the Nevada desert in the 1950s.

> At zero there was a flash. I counted and then turned around. The first thing I saw was a yellow-orange fireball that kept getting larger. As it grew, it turned more orange and then red. A mushroom-shaped cloud of glowing magenta began to rise over the desert where the explosion had been. My first thought was, "My God that is beautiful!"... It now appears that these tests have caused deadly illness, both in the soldiers who had been deployed to witness them— some from as close as a mile from the explosion—and the civilian population surrounding the site.... Proximity to absolute power can make fools of any of us.[3]

What are our temptations to power? Our denials?

❦ 2 Lent

Genesis 15:1-18   "A slave born in my house shall be my heir." The aging Abraham laments his childlessness and has a hard time believing God's promise that he will father offspring. Texan millionaire Miller Quarles is offering a prize of $100,000 to the person who discovers a cure for the disease of old age. He is 81. In old age, we accumulate ancient cells damaged by wear, and slow or stop producing many new ones. Old cells are more likely to contain and pass along defective genes that can produce cancer and other diseases. Some researchers are studying telomeres, the end sections of chromosomes that tend to snap off in aging cells so that the chromosomes cannot replicate, or suffer mutation and turn cancerous. The enzyme telomerase seems to control these processes, and might one day be a key to extending life. Critics argue that producing more cancers is just as likely an outcome of tampering with telomerase in the human body. How might we practice entrusting God with our futures? How might we lay aside our fears of aging, of accomplishing less, perhaps, than we had hoped when young?

Philippians 3:17–4:1 Our commonwealth is in heaven; through Christ we are knit into a unity that is as yet far from realization on earth. The naturalist Henry Beston makes a similar lament:

> Under today's disorders there is something at work among the nations whose great importance has not yet been adequately realized—the need of men for a community to live in and live with. The hope is vague, unsaid, and unformulated, but the need is great, and there is something in our hearts which troubles us that we have lost what was once so beautifully called "the commonweal." I suspect that if this open wound is to heal, it will have to heal like all wounds from the bottom, and that we shall have to begin at the beginning with the family and its obligations, with the village and its responsibilities, and with our universal and neglected duty to the earth.[4]

Our churches are called to be little schools for community, for commonweal, in a society that is losing its skills for building these. To this end we preach discipline, constancy, care, forbearance, forgiveness, and lovingkindness—the virtues which underpin common life, rooted in the earth.

Luke 13:22-35 Jesus mourns Jerusalem with the metaphor of the mother hen with chicks. Centuries later, Anselm of Canterbury develops that same image:

> And you, Jesus, are you not also a mother? Are you not the mother who, like a hen, gathers her chickens under her wings? Truly Lord, you are a mother; for both they who are in labour and they who are brought forth are accepted by you.

This is a difficult metaphor for modern urban dwellers who know chickens chiefly as a plastic-wrapped collection of parts, or through documentary images of wire-penned, identical hordes of factory-farmed animals. Those who raise a few chickens for eggs tell another story: how they become tame, have distinctive personalities (even if no intellectual gifts), and social groupings. Did the holy family keep chickens? Did the young Jesus have a particularly warm association with a broody hen sitting on her nest with chicks under her wing? The pelican is another classic poultry image for Jesus' motherly love. It was once believed that the pelican plucked breast feathers to soften the lining of the nest for her offspring, and even fed them with drops of her own blood. Do you have a bird experience that might offer a metaphor for some aspect of the spiritual life?

❦ 3 Lent

Exodus 3:1-15   The burning bush is a wonderful image of creative light, reminding Moses that *this* very place in creation is holy ground—the ground on which he is already standing—and here is the place of his encounter with God. Writer Lawrence Kushner describes an experiment conducted by the young biochemist Stanley Miller to determine whether or not life could have originated on his planet:

> He took the molecules assumed to have been plentiful in the earth's infant atmosphere: hydrogen, methane, ammonia, and water vapor—the incubating soup—mixed them in a kind of blender, and turned it on. He then subjected the simmering broth to regular electric charge, approximating as nearly as possible the action of lightning. By the end of a week the concoction had parented amino and nucleic acids, the building blocks of life. . . . Again and again it is light that initiates. Light that rearranges the molecules so that they might produce life. "Let there be light." And how is it that the unknown author of the first creation account of Genesis knew to begin with light? Perhaps our penchant for returning to and reverencing lightning is—like the story of the great flood and amniotic waters—more like memory than fantasy. From whence could such wisdom come if not from beings who themselves are created by light? Filled with light. Made conscious by it.[5]

1 Corinthians 10:1-13   The ancients drank "from the spiritual rock that followed them," which Paul identifies as Christ. Water from rock seems the epitome of impossibility. Yet rock—even barren, frozen, summit rock—nourishes our souls with life. What do rocks signify to you? Sir Edmund Hillary wrote of great mountains:

> Above soar knife-sharp saw-toothed ridges—the final defenses before the ultimate summits. They are always changing as the moods of nature change. A bit-

ter wind blows a plume of snow off a lofty mountain brow; sunset transforms the snow and rock to crimson and gold; a fierce storm clothes the mountains in a cloak of purest snow....As he looks at the mountains the climber's heart swells with joy and pain! It is so beautiful and yet so inaccessible.[6]

Luke 13:1-9   Jesus tells the parable of a fruitless fig tree in need of manure. Adding manure can bring about transformation in a garden or orchard. There are dozens of soil additives we can buy, but sometimes older and simpler is better! Researchers in England have discovered that garden compost can combat crop diseases. Compost is a rich stew of microorganisms: some prey upon disease-causing bacteria and fungi, some compete with these for necessary nutrients and water, and some actually manufacture antibiotic chemicals. So the addition of organic material that otherwise might be discarded yields a fruitful outcome. Jesus provides an apt metaphor for a healthy community: we can be one another's compost.

❦ 4 Lent

Joshua 4:19–5:12   Joshua bids the elders to set up stones of memory for their descendants. I think of childhood expeditions into the wilds of New York state with my eighth-grade geology class in search of fossils. We found a coral reef standing like a low wall covered by pine needles in the middle of a wood. We could see the crinoid stems like ancient flowers (though these "flowers" were marine animals), and shells that littered the ocean floor in the Ordovician Period some 450 million years ago— an unimaginable amount of time. We cracked off chunks of limestone in a gorge that contained cabbage-like algae fossils from the Pre-Cambrian time over 600 million years ago, among the oldest preserved living things. Touching the stones conjured the memory of the planet itself, its long record of life evolving over the most recent tenth of its age. Vertebrates are relatively new arrivals, from the Ordovician Period on. Amphibia, the first land vertebrates, did not appear until the Devonian Period some 350 million years ago. Of all this unfolding process of creation, stones of memory remain. We may hold the past in our hands as a record of the ongoing process of creation, and give thanks.

2 Corinthians 5:17-21   We are a new creation in Christ. Further, together we are part of a larger new creation of all that God has made. Sallie McFague describes a radical metaphor for the church:

Where human beings...create communities embodying concern for the basic needs of the life-forms on earth, aware of their profound interdependence as well as individuality, *here* is the church from the perspective of the organic model....The church as institution is called to live out the new creation *in its body*.[7]

How might we preach the new creation as God's love for the whole cosmos of which we are part, without denigrating the dignity of human nature or responsibility?

Luke 15:11-32   The prodigal son cannot enter into and enjoy his father's love when he is young and strong and naive. Only when he separates himself from family and familiar experiences and matures through failure and trouble does he come into the vulnerable state in which love can touch him and break open his own heart—a journey the older brother has yet to make.

> Most of all, God is in the embattled, broken-down layers [of yourself] because God has a long history of loving the poor and the weak. This is where to look for God most in yourself—where you are broken and vulnerable. Where you are scarred and need God's healing. Look for God where your defense is weakest. At the break in the wall, the crack in the earth, the ground shifting out of control. God lives in the wide sweep of your inner geography and in the smallest molecule of your history. It is time to come home.[8]

❦ 5 Lent

Isaiah 43:16-21   "The wild beasts honor me," says God. How is it that animals honor their creator? Eighteenth-century Anglican poet Christopher Smart was a mystic who seems to have also suffered some mental imbalance. Among his extraordinary religious poems is "Jubilate Agno," a complicated hymn of praise from the creation to God. In its surprising images, Isaac kneels with his camels, Jacob and his speckled drove adore the good shepherd, Nimrod the hunter binds a leopard to the altar, and a menagerie of curious animals that resemble the patriarchs of old offer tribute to God along with humans:

> Let Abishai bless with the hyena—the terror of the Lord and the
>   fierceness of his wrath against the foes of the King and of Israel,
> Let Ethan praise with the Flea, his coat of mail, his piercer, and his
>   vigour, which wisdom and providence have contrived to attract

observation and to escape it.
Let Heman bless with the Spider, his warp and his woof, his subtlety and
industry, which are good,
Let Chalcol praise with the Beetle, whose life is precious in the sight of
God, tho' his appearance is against him.
Let Darda with a Leech bless the Name of the Physician of body and soul.[9]

Philippians 3:8-14 Pressing on toward the goal, the person of faith strives like an
athlete.

All running, all exercise—all work, for that matter—is a dance with fatigue:
manipulation of it, experimentation with it, and finally acceptance of it. What
training is for is to pull its teeth. . . . Even purely recreational runners can thus
come to know what racers know: that the most enjoyable times in running
come when you are teetering on the edge of fatigue but hang on a moment
longer, and a moment longer, and at some point discern not only that you can
bear it, but that you can even pick it up a bit.[10]

How do we train for our baptized ministry? How do we counteract our fatigue and
even pick up our pace?

Luke 20:9-19 To be wise tenants of the vineyard earth, and to honor the creation
as an extension of Christ's body—the incarnate, material expression of God's love for
us—we are surely called to keep it clean. This requires discipline, commitment, and
imagination. Rather than simply stacking up our trash legally or illegally, planet
hygiene demands that we reduce it. One encouraging example: fifteen-sixteenths of
a discarded tire can be recycled. Dumped tires are a major fire hazard and provide a
breeding ground for mosquitoes and the diseases they carry. Since 1990 Missouri has
prohibited dumping tires in landfills, and placed a fifty-cent fee on the sale of each
new tire to pay for recycling. Tires are chipped and burned as fuel in some of the
state's power plants, reducing sulfur emissions. Ground "crumb" rubber, separated
from the metal and polyester ingredients of tires, can be sized and used to manufacture new tires, adhesives, shoes, toys, auto parts, and many other useful items, or as
a surfacing material for paths, athletic fields, and playgrounds. Rubber scrap can also
be used to make asphalt for paving.[11]

❦ *Palm Sunday*

Isaiah 45:21-25 In the verses before these, the prophet reminds the people that God did not create the cosmos "a chaos" (*tohu*), or "a void" (*bohu*)—using the first of the pair of words from Genesis 1:2. Rather, the earth was made orderly and habitable. In the mechanistic models of the Newtonian world, decay was deemed the inevitable future of all systems, hurried along by disruption. The new science reminds us that order and chaos are in a more complex relationship than our ancestors understood; chaos is part of the effective functioning of creation. Reporting on the new science of chaos theory in 1987, James Gleick wrote, "Pattern born amid formlessness: that is biology's basic beauty and its basic mystery. Life sucks order from a sea of disorder."[12] A new optimism has been born in the business world because of chaos theory science: "This was a world where order and change, autonomy and control were not the great opposites that we had thought them to be.[13] The irrepressibility of the divine life seems written even in the physical operations of the cosmos in ways we had never imagined.

Philippians 2:5-11 What might it mean for us to understand ourselves as servants of the earth? Over the centuries Christians have emphasized human dominion and control. Even "stewardship" has been seen as our right and responsibility to dispose judiciously of the resources of nature, to "use them wisely." It stings our pride to think of ourselves truly as servants who, in the model of Christ, empty ourselves of godlike power and privilege to bend down and tenderly minister to the land, the air, the water, even the stones of our home planet. Do human needs and wants always come first, ahead of the needs of other creatures?

Luke 22:39–23:56 In Luke's gospel the entire cosmos participates in the passion of Jesus. The women of Jerusalem are warned of coming days when they will regret having borne children. As Jesus dies the curtain of the temple is torn, probably by a great earthquake; creation is fractured down the middle at its most sacred point. The sun goes dark and remains so for a prolonged period as creation hides its face. That which dies with him shall also rise with him.

❦ *Maundy Thursday*

Exodus 12:1-14 The Passover meal is food for the journey—just enough, nothing extra, to be prepared with precision according to God's command. We reflect often on the great abundance of God's providence. This is a season for considering its restrictions: sometimes, as for the Israelites fed with manna in the wilderness, there is just enough and it must be stewarded properly. In the rain forests of Brazil, the Manau people have relied for centuries on fish from the Amazon River for protein and for most of their total diet. When the river floods each year, the fish follow the rising water into the forest and feed on seeds, fruit, and displaced insects floating among the tree trunks.

By the time authorities understood that the fish supply depended upon the flooding of the forests, all the large forests within 100 kilometers of the Manaus had been cut down, and the fish were dwindling. Fish, in turn, were found to be the major dispersers of seeds in the forest, so once the fish were gone, the rising waters no longer reseeded the deforested land. The ecosystem has collapsed and its human inhabitants may follow.[14]

1 Corinthians 11:23-32   "For I received from the Lord what I also handed on to you." In the 1980s Richard Dawkins coined the word *meme* to describe a complex of ideas, skills, habits, stories, and behaviors—everything learned that is passed from one person to another by imitation. Supporters of the concept of memes believe these little packets of memory follow all the laws of evolution: they are "inherited" by the process of imitation; they can be modified by the individual's choice or lapse of memory; and while some are passed on, others are not—a process of selection. Pushed to its extreme the meme theory is extremely deterministic: all our behavioral choices are laid at its door. But if we are not simply the tidy selves we think we are, then who and what are we? How shall we then think about our relationship to God, as we hear again the meme of the institution of the Lord's Supper?

Luke 22:14-30   Jesus takes bread and says, "This is my body which is given for you. Do this in remembrance of me." What we *do* with our bodies, with our bread, with the material creation, matters crucially to God. It literally brings God to the cross on our behalf and into resurrection glory after. We are not merely educated in our religious heritage, we are *formed* in it. Our lives, our selves are made and shaped like a Japanese bonsai tree—through nourishment, training, discipline, pruning, and sometimes even repotting. Even our sense of time is retuned according to a sacred calendar of story. Our ordinary actions take on a sacred significance as we put on Christ in the context of our faith community. As we pray, we become; what we do, we are. Our life of discipleship is not simply about inner states, but about how we put the bread of our own lives on the table of God, how our own blood is poured out for the covenant with creation that God renews in Christ.

❦ *Good Friday*

Wisdom 2:1, 12-24   It is well-known that war degrades the environment. A less well-known but now compellingly documented reality is that environmental damage helps cause wars. Deforestation, erosion, and population growth probably triggered the fighting in Chiapas, Mexico, that began in 1994. Armed conflict between Senegal and Mauritius grew over disputed newly-irrigated agricultural land in 1989. On the infamous Gaza strip in the Middle East, conflict is brewing over scarce water in a depleted aquifer: the Israelis are drawing upon it and limiting access to Palestinian residents. Damaged land can greatly increase already unstable political situations and produce waves of economic refugees who become easy targets of hostility. Economic aid from wealthy nations for the restoration of the environment in poor ones may be money well spent to avert the greater cost and damage of war in the future. How then shall we help take down the broken body of the earth from its cross and anoint and restore it for its resurrection? How shall we see the care of land and water far distant from us as part of the care of the whole of humanity and the creation?

Hebrews 10:1-25   Through Christ the people of God are made a transformed priesthood that no longer need to offer blood sacrifice. We stand together, consecrated through God's actions in Jesus, in a fresh dignity of humanity—called to self-giving but not to blood-letting, to compassion but not to masochism. Such an understanding requires that we make careful moral discernments in our life together. For example, prompted by the Environmental Protection Agency, a panel including bioethicists, toxicologists, and chemists convened in 1998 to debate whether it is ethical to test pesticides for safety and toxicity on human subjects.[15] Human beings are exposed to pesticides in agriculture and even in urban environments, so accurate data is essential. No one is sure if current safety standards based on animal testing are adequate since humans may be more sensitive to the chemicals than lab animals.

All agreed that if human tests are done, there are ethical requirements, yet when subjects agree to take money for putting their health in jeopardy, does poverty constitute a coercive factor? Does the value of new pesticides to society outweigh the potential danger to subjects? Should those who manufacture and profit from pesticides be among the subjects?

John 18:1–19:37   As we enter the new millennium, creation hangs on the cross with Christ. This image comes through graphically in the photographs taken from space of the island of Madagascar, as astronaut Karl Heinz wrote:

Madagascar is still green with tropical forest but probably not for long. The ocean around that island is colored a thick bloody red by the silt that is being eroded from recently deforested areas. And how much desert there is on the Earth. Over Africa I never saw a great expanse of green tropical rain forest.[16]

Madagascar is home to the greatest species diversity on earth. Eighty percent of its 8,000 known plant species exist nowhere else on earth. Half of its 200 bird species are unique, as are most of its animals and insects. Today only 10 percent of the island's forests remain, and the cutting continues.[17] It seems to me that this precious island of life bleeds with the wounds of Christ. Good Friday is a day for mourning all that we put to death by human ignorance, fear, greed, foolishness, anger, and desperation.

Holy Saturday

See entry in Year A, page 33.

❧ EASTER

❧ *The Great Vigil of Easter*

See entry in Year A, page 34.

❧ *Easter Day*

Acts 10:34-43 God raised Jesus on the third day. At Easter God's resurrecting nature pervades our sense of the entire universe—the whole of creation that God is busy raising up in Christ. One Christian naturalist notes:

> The paradox of Easter is the paradox of rebirth. Yet the death and rebirth of a community is not paradoxical. An individual sandhill crane is born, matures, and dies; but the community of cranes returns century after century to the same meadow at the foot of the sandhills along the North Platte River in southern Nebraska. It is this truth, the transcendence of the species over the individual, the way in which a community endures and accumulates a history, despite the frailties of the creatures who inhabit it that we celebrate when we stand in awe before the great seasonal migrations. The story of Easter is not paradoxical either, if we will think of it in the same way: If we will think not of individual existence which is fleeting, but of the continuities in the human community.[1]

Do we bear witness to and celebrate God's resurrecting power in our daily lives? In the rhythms of the creation?

Colossians 3:1-4 "Your life is hidden with Christ in God." Lancelot Andrewes describes the resurrection as a kind of childbirth: Jesus comes out from the body of the earth, and we too are birthed from old to new life. In his words from an Easter Day sermon:

> [Christ] made the grave as a womb for a second birth, to travail with us anew, and bring us forth to life everlasting; made *cor terrae ventrum ceti,* the heart of the earth to us, as the belly of the whale was to Jonah, which still did not retain him. The very term *the heart of the earth* was well chosen. There is a heart in it. For if the earth has a heart, there is life in it, for the heart is the fountain of life, and the seat of the vital spirits that hold us in it.

Luke 24:1-10 As a hospital chaplain, I often found myself helping the nurses wash and wrap the body of a patient who had died to prepare it to go to the morgue. Often this mundane, unpleasant task is carried out with great reverence and tenderness. Touching the dead is a poignant experience. The very feel of a corpse communicates the absence of the person: the flesh becomes cold and first stiff, then flaccid. The skin color changes as the blood slows and stops, and body fluids may be loosed as muscles lose their holding tone. The corpse both triggers the memory of the person and signals his or her absence in a way that is fearful and wonderful.

Preparing the body is, properly, the last act of physical kindness we can offer. It is also an act of reverence and honor to creation: the body belongs to the earth and is returned to it in one way or another—its atoms will be recycled into new life and energy—but the person is returned to its Creator. We might all be encouraged to reclaim at least a part of this holy task, washing and wrapping our beloved with prayers and goodbyes, caresses and tears, and learning, by touching absence, the resurrection.

❧ 2 Easter

Job 42:1-6 "I have uttered what I did not understand, things too wonderful for me, which I did not know," cries Job after God recounts the marvels of creation beyond human understanding. Creation stirs in us a profound humility before the astonishing imagination of God. Essayist Wendell Berry writes of the wilderness:

> No place is to be learned like a textbook or a course in school and then turned away from forever on the assumption that one's knowledge of it is complete. What is to be known about it is without limit, and it is endlessly changing.

Knowing it is therefore like breathing: it can happen, it stays real, only on the condition that it *continue* to happen. As soon as it is recognized that a river—or, for that matter, a home—is not a place but a process, not a fact, but an event, there ought to come an immense relief: one can step into the same river twice, one can go home again.[2]

What sort of knowing does creation open to you? How have wild places taught you—perhaps even places you have never visited?

Revelation 1:1-19   A kingdom of priests to serve our God is a radical new vision emerging among Christians. In ancient Jewish practice, an inherited temple priesthood was passed down among the Cohen (Hebrew for "priest") family from fathers to sons since the time of Aaron.[3] Since the priesthood among Jews was passed down in the male line, Jewish geneticist Karl Skorecki wondered whether DNA studies could demonstrate an actual familial link between all the Cohens now living who are believed to be descendants of the single Jewish priestly family of old. His research demonstrates that indeed there are Y-chromosome characteristics in common in this group. Jews today celebrate this venerable heritage of priestly people, long after the temple has vanished. For Christians, on the other hand, "familial" identity is established through baptism as "adoption"; genetic inheritance has no significance. Rather, we are summoned into the priestly role of lifting all of life to God in thanksgiving, praise, and intercession.

John 20:19-31   When I see the barren slash of a strip mine, the stubble of a clearcut forest, or an oil slick gleaming across acres of ocean, I see the print of the nails in Jesus' hands. For the incarnation was not a sending of Jesus into the void, but a sending of the God-made man into the God-made earth, and the bleeding wounds of the planet caused by selfishness and greed, hate and indifference, are of a piece with the nail-wounded hands of the Healer and Savior. These wounds I am invited to touch—to put my fingers in their imprint, investigate closely, and understand in all their violence. So perhaps when we desire to go on retreat and pray, we should not be heading for the unblemished countryside, but to the strip mall or the toxic dump—all those places where Jesus' wounds in the body of the home planet are held out to us. There we may know God's love and its cost, and study how to hold back our hands from the hammer.

❦ 3 Easter

Acts 9:1-19 Saul's conversion reminds us that the one most despised, the greatest enemy, may through grace become the strongest ally. God has endless power to turn enemies to allies, evil toward good. Epidemiologists point out that Bubonic plague, the dread vermin-carried disease that wiped out much of the population of Europe throughout the Middle Ages, has yielded a useful protein that can quiet the painful, disabling inflammation of arthritis, and may be helpful in treating other inflammatory diseases. Thalidomide—the drug that pregnant women took for nausea in the 1950s, producing devastating birth defects—has just been approved for use in treating patients with *erythema nodosum leprosarum,* a skin condition related to Hansen's Disease (leprosy) and the wasting caused by AIDS. Where can we find evidence of evil turned toward good in our own lives? In our corporate life?

Revelation 5:6-14 To those who are adult urban dwellers, Christ the Lamb seems an exotic metaphor. There is little we can see about a sheep, or for that matter a lamb, that seems God-like; cute perhaps, not very bright, soon dirty and dingy, pretty single-minded about grass—surely not divine. Yet as a child, something about this lamb image touched me deeply. In "The Lamb," poet William Blake captures the tender fellow-feeling that Jesus the Lamb conveys, respite from all the white-haired grandfather pictures and words. A child asks a lamb, "Does thou know who made thee?" and answers:

> Little lamb, I'll tell thee....
> He is called by thy name
> For he calls himself a lamb:
> He is meek and he is mild,
> He became a little child:
> I a child and thou a lamb,
> We are called by thy name.
> Little lamb, God bless thee.

The child recognizes the lamb as a fellow new, small, mild creature who is also holy—the creature of the Creator known as the Lamb. So to the child, God is not a frightening stranger, for God shares the meadow with the child and the lamb. The poem's trinity of God, child, and lamb hints at the intimate relationships of the holy Trinity that inform them. The lamb invites us to that fresh image of worship and love when our world was new.

John 21:1-14   A net full of fish is a metaphor both for God's abundance and the task of fishing for disciples. A contemporary fishing method offers a more troubling metaphor for our times. An estimated 2 million pounds of cyanide have been loosed into Philippine waters since the 1960s to stun fish for capture. Crystal cyanide is ground up and mixed with sea water, then squirted onto coral reefs where fish are in hiding. Smaller fish may be killed by the chemical and left to decompose on the reef, while larger targeted fish are taken. Cyanide weakens harvested live fish; many of them die in transit, requiring larger harvests to sustain trade. The risks of eating these fish—particularly the internal organs where the poison is concentrated—are unknown. As yet few countries have laws to control cyanide fishing, though the Philippines has made strides in eradicating the practice and recruiting local fishers as "front-line marine stewards." The aim of conservationists is not to prevent all live-fish harvesting and trade, but to advocate sustainable non-devastating methods and levels of harvest while protecting the health and livelihood of local fishers.[4]

🌿 *4 Easter*

Acts 13:15-39   In his short sermon Peter lays out the intricacy of God's plan for salvation. The events of history, the words of scripture, the invitation to forgiveness and new life—all are seen connected as a whole: one story, one redeemed creation. From the fact of interrelationship comes an ethic of compassion for all life. One of my childhood heroes was the Jewish photographer and naturalist Roman Vishniac. Among the pioneers in filming microscopic creatures alive and unfolding that hidden world to the public, he wrote:

> I was watching a mosquito's head one night under the 200 power magnification and I was astounded by the loveliness of the eyes.... It was so beautiful that I loved this mosquito. But I watched too long. I had no water cell before the lamp, and I didn't realize the strength of the light. Suddenly it was killing him. One by one the colors of his eyes went out like lights being turned off back of the windows, and through the microscope I saw the death of this mosquito. And I can tell you it is such a terrible thing—death.[5]

I smash them by the dozen while weeding my garden, these mosquitos. But because of the holiness of Roman Vishniac, I recognize this carnage as choice and loss. In the ambivalent relation of human and insect—of predation and disease, of mosquitos feeding the swallows and bats and toads of my urban garden—is a tiny square of the great quilt which is God's *peace,* the design at the heart of the universe. Compassion is the heart's response to glimpsing the pattern, as part of it.

Revelation 7:9-17   The white-robed army of the resurrection waves palm branches in joy before the throne of Christ the Lamb, the cosmic ruler ushering in the salvation of the universe; animals, people, stars, angels, waters all join in a hymn of glad praise (5:13-14). On a physical level, the chemical constituents of our bodies were "forged in the furnace of the stars." The atoms of our bodies are endlessly recycled: we are made up of the very stuff of the saints. And atoms of granite, a grizzly bear, Red Sea water, the child down the street who died of asthma, Missouri primrose, and the triceratops—they, too, are among our atoms, part of our bodies. Even on the macrocosmic level, our bodies are shared with other creatures: mites live in our eyelashes, flora and fauna of astonishing ingenuity inhabit our guts. We could not live without some of these, though others sometimes kill us. Our outer environment is populated by creatures so numerous and diverse and knit together that we can barely understand how they interrelate and support one another's life and our own. Visionaries among us, from St. Francis and St. Thomas Aquinas to Chief Seattle, name this our brotherhood and sisterhood with all creatures.

John 10:22-30   "My sheep hear my voice," says Jesus. How selective is our hearing? I camped last summer on a hilltop near the edge of the Ozarks in a large forested state park. In the dark of a moonless night, I could hear dogs barking from a distant farm. The wind purred through the oaks and hemlocks. A half-mile below there was a faint water sound, only audible in the wee hours when the distant traffic had stilled. There were occasional rustlings of night creatures—mice perhaps, under the leaf litter. Crickets sang, and the last few cicadas with their electric whine. All the sounds I had barely noticed on the day's hike were magnified into a wonderful changing chorus; it seemed to me the Creator's voice saying, "Hear: This is good. This is mine." The sheep who hear the shepherd in the cacophony of the modern world are the sheep who attend, who pick the Creator's voice out from the background din and strain to hear the words of love: "All these things—yes and you, too—are mine."

🌱 5 Easter

Acts 13:44-52   The scene: a city square, crowds, bad temper... pigeons. In my town, pigeons have been upsetting some people in public places like mall parking lots and town squares. A wave of chemical poisonings has distressed others, including naturalists, who believe pigeons add minimal disease risk and are smart and peaceable cleaners of urban debris, undeserving of a cruel death.

> If you're protecting the spires of a Gothic cathedral, you might have to design an elaborate barrier system. But if you're starting from scratch, all you have to do is factor the inevitable pigeons into the design. "Pigeons are a part of the environment the way cold weather is," remarks [Canadian naturalist] MacKay. "We build structures to expand in the cold, but we don't engineer with any thought to wildlife." We probably never will. By definition, "wildlife" falls out of civilization's purview—except as something to tame, evade or hunt. Senegalese poet Baba Dioum writes, "In the end, we conserve only what we love."[6]

How shall we deepen our love of wild things and our commitment to protect them?

Revelation 19:1, 4-9   The four living creatures—the elders of the animals, perhaps—seem to be symbolic of the whole animal realm. They depict, too, the four directions from which the creatures, along with the multitude of peoples, stream toward the throne of the cosmic Christ with a victory shout. It is like a recapitulation of the Noah story: the fruitful multitudes of earth's animals return to give praise to their Creator. In the thirteenth century Thomas Aquinas wrote, "Each creature is a witness to God's power and omnipotence; and its beauty is a witness to the divine wisdom.... Every creature participates in some way in the likeness of the Divine Essence." How would our relationships with the creatures of the earth change if we truly believed this?

John 13:31-35   Loving one another is not merely a state of mind and heart, but is measured by how well we do justice to one another, how we live in mutuality and respect. The command is sweeping and huge, but we implement it by small actions. Just as our sins often begin with small infractions that begin to add up, justice and love, too, begin with discrete behaviors that gain momentum, transforming community as they multiply.

> People rarely intend to create environmental problems.... Rather, most environmental ills simply emerge inadvertently from the sum of myriad, seemingly minuscule individual actions occurring at small scales, but around the globe.... Motive is irrelevant to environmental impacts. It applies only to dealing with the aftermath.[7]

How then do we become more conscious of our small acts and their potential impact? More believing of their power for ill or good?

❧ 6 Easter

Revelation 21:22–22:5   The river of life flows through the holy city and the trees' leaves are for healing. The city is no longer at odds with the rural realm, but is itself a perfect ecosystem for sustaining and healing life. What would it take for us to have a clean and drinkable river flowing through the heart of our city? For air and soil clean enough that medicinal plants could be grown between city streets?

Acts 14:8-18; John 14:23-29   Christ's peace in John's gospel has a mystical and almost abstract quality—a peace from beyond the world for a band of disciples who understand that they are called to be separate from the world in its debasement. Yet in the book of Acts we hear the apostles preaching to their Greek audience that they are not minor deities and emissaries from a supernatural realm, but flesh and blood men who proclaim a living God, creator of "the heaven and the earth and all that is in them," bountiful giver of rain and harvest, food, joy, and healing.

❧ 7 Easter

1 Samuel 12:19-24   The prophet prays for the people. Can one be a rational, scientific thinker and believe in the power of prayer—specifically, in asking God to accomplish some particular effect? Physicists examining the quantum world have discovered that we cannot observe something without affecting it, for our universe is profoundly interactive. They also observe that the tiniest action can produce a chain of reaction that is unpredictable and complex. The famous example used to introduce chaos theory is that of a butterfly flapping its wings in one corner of the earth and causing a weather system in another. Physicist John Polkinghorne suggests:

> What is happening is not fully determined by the causes of which we first thought!...I am going to guess that this exquisite sensitivity and unpredictability are signs to us that the physical world is more subtle, more flexible, and more open to the future...than we previously supposed....If you think there is anything in the picture of the openness and flexibility of the universe that I have described, and of God's providential interaction with that universe, then it does make sense to ask God to do particular things. A scientist *can* pray—and many do.[8]

Revelation 22:12-20 I am the Alpha and the Omega, the beginning and the end, creator and destiny of all. Theologian Elizabeth Schüssler-Fiorenza writes:

According to Revelation, final salvation does not just pertain to the soul and spiritual realities. It is the abolishment of all dehumanization and suffering and at the same time the fullness of human well-being... a rectification of the great tribulation with its sufferings of war, peacelessness, hunger, and inflation, pestilence, persecution, and death.[9]

John 17:20-26 We have been loved from before the foundation of the world. Mystic Julian of Norwich wrote:

See! I am God. See! I am in everything. See! I never lift my hands off my works, nor will I ever. See! I lead everything toward the purpose for which I ordained it, without beginning, by the same Power, Wisdom and Love by which I created it. How could anything be amiss?

⚜ The Day of Pentecost

Joel 2:28-32 Prophecies, dreams, and visions are all states of altered consciousness a little suspect to modern rationalists. Some specialists believe that our minds use the same cognitive system in dreams as in our waking thought, and that the dreams of individuals are no more or less imaginative and fanciful than their normal cognition.[10] People who go blind as adults continue to have visual dreams, while those born blind have dreams that utilize their other senses. Most dreams are so mundane that they are often erased upon waking; we tend to remember the strange dreams more easily. Contrary to popular opinion, we dream in all phases of sleep, not only during REM (Rapid Eye Movement). Children under five dream relatively little, then at ages eight to nine there is a spurt in dream activity. Scientists still do not know just why we dream—to release stress or work out problems, or because of changes in brain chemistry. We modern westerners are among the first known generations of people who tend to disregard the significance of dreams for our lives, and who often dismiss visions as the product of psychopathology. Have you inquired about dreams, revelations, and visions among your congregation? What are the hallmarks of authenticity in these?

Acts 2:1-11   Linguists warn that of the some 6000 languages spoken on earth today, one-third are in danger of dying out within a century. Half of the world's population now speaks just five major languages. Some languages are spoken by just a handful of native speakers: in Ethiopia alone there are 90 tiny language groups. It is argued that a spirit of world unity and efficiency would be enhanced if a majority of people were to speak the same few languages. Yet a language is the storehouse of a people's accumulated wisdom, metaphors, culture, and experiences—part of the lovely diversity of the human race. Languages encapsulate particular ways of knowing and learning. Greenlanders, for example, have dozens of different words for particular kinds of snow. Linguists believe that the ability to evolve and change, adopting some vocabulary from other tongues and some through popular culture, allows a language to thrive over time. While purists fret over mutation and innovation, these are often healthful adaptive signs for a language. Hearing about "God's deeds of power" in their own native language was a sign of the unity of the Spirit for the early church. How might we celebrate the diversity of tongues within that unity in our own time?

John 20:19-23   While planning a camping trip in a state park with an urban youth group, one youngster confided in me his absolute terror of spending a night outside in the forest—this tough little boy who walks to school every day through gang territory. He sounded much like the exurban businessman who had spoken about his fear of coming into the heart of the city for a church meeting. We tend to fear the landscapes that are foreign to us, to imagine them as far more hazardous than they are, and to withdraw our care from them, locking ourselves in. At Pentecost we hear the Spirit's challenge to set aside fear and open the door. Only what we know will we care for. So it is imperative that urban children go out into the fields and forests of the country, and that rural children come into the city, so that we may love the whole of our planet and minister to all of it with tenderness and compassion.

❒ *Trinity Sunday*

Isaiah 6:1-8   "Holy, holy, holy…the whole earth is full of God's glory." The Celtic Christians recognized a "white martyrdom" of exile and pilgrimage, an asceticism informed by leaving home or monastery and wandering with no fixed destination for the glory of God. These religious travelers were not primarily evangelizing, though they won converts as they went; they were "guests of the world," seeking God whom they believed could be found afresh everywhere they went in an earth "full of God's

glory." Columba, one of the most famous of these *peregrinati,* spoke of being "crucified on the blue wave." He wrote:

> Let us concern ourselves with heavenly things, not human ones, and like pil-
> grims always sigh for our homeland, long for our homeland...our theme
> song: "When shall I come and appear before the face of my God."

These saints attested that while loving the world and enduring its hardships, the
Christian is a citizen of another homeland. I think of the gospel of Thomas and its
cryptic teaching: "Be Passers-by."

Revelation 4:1-11 "Worthy is the Creator." There are experiences of the creation
that change our hearts and lives, that impress us in an instant, or over a stretch of
time; we sense the near hand of God still at work with artistry and love. Naturalist
Henry Beston spent a year in a tiny cabin on the outermost dunes of Cape Cod:

> Some have asked me what understanding of Nature one shapes from so strange
> a year? I would answer that one's first appreciation is a sense that the creation
> is still going on, that the creative forces are as great and as active today as they
> have ever been, and that tomorrow's morning will be as heroic as any of the
> world. *Creation is here and now....* It is as impossible to live without reverence as
> it is without joy.[11]

John 16:5-15 The Spirit of Truth, the Counselor, takes what is God's and makes it
known, declares it plainly. Of course we are very good at ignoring what is declared to
us plainly. Every year in spring and summer, as midwestern crops are fertilized and
the Mississippi carries the nitrogen runoff down to its delta, a dead zone as large as
the state of New Jersey forms in the Gulf. Nitrogen causes an explosive growth of
algae that consumes all the oxygen in some 7,000 square miles of ocean. Shrimp,
crabs, fish, and other marine life either flee or die. The Mississippi dead zone is the
largest of over 50 coastal dead zones around the world. Though costly, restoration of
10 million acres of new wetlands could reduce nitrogen in the Gulf dead zone by as
much as 20 percent and would also recover wildlife habitats, restock fisheries, and
create attractive open space.[12] This is not new information: the destruction of the
Gulf fisheries has been underway for two generations. How do we become ready to
receive the truth that is plainly declared to us?

THE SEASON AFTER PENTECOST

☙ *Proper 1*

Jeremiah 17:5-10   A tree planted by the water is the sign of the person rooted in God and therefore durable and fruitful. Consider the *Moringa Oleifera* tree, a common species in Africa and Asia. Its seeds have a remarkable property: when ground up and thrown in polluted water they cause particles of contaminants to stick together and settle to the bottom, fulfilling the same role that expensive chemicals like aluminum sulfate do in water treatment plants. This technique has been known and used for many centuries; it removes most of the bacteria and viruses infecting tropical waters and makes them safe to drink. Perhaps like the *Moringa Oleifera,* the righteous person is a detoxifying presence, one who can unmask hidden evil and strip it of its power to cause disease in the community.

1 Corinthians 15:12-20   Through Christ's resurrection, everything has been changed. Twentieth-century mystic Teilhard de Chardin understood this transformation as ongoing in the trajectory of the natural and human history of the world, and issued a call to proper creaturely humility:

> Because the term towards which the earth is moving lies not merely beyond each individual thing but beyond the totality of things; because the world travails, not to bring forth from within itself some supreme reality, but to find its consummation through a union with a pre-existent Being; it follows that man can never reach the blazing center of the universe simply by living more and

more for himself nor even by spending his life in service of some earthly cause however great.[1]

Neither the abasement of humanity in the Holocaust, nor the nuclear threat, nor the law of thermodynamics that sees all systems devolving toward dispersion of energy and increasing chaos need lead us to pessimism. For Christ has been raised from the dead, and in him all things are made new.

Luke 6:17-26   Jesus exuded a power that healed. Though in some other gospel passages we hear that Jesus was sent to heal only some individuals as a sign of the reign of God, here crowds seem to be experiencing healing poured out abundantly. Sallie McFague writes:

> Jesus' healing stories are extremely valuable in a time of ecological deterioration and destruction such as we are experiencing. They refuse any early and easy spiritualizing of our salvation; they force us, as Christians, to face the deep sickness of the many bodies that make up the body of God.[2]

How can we remind ourselves that the whole earth is "the body of God"?

❧ *Proper 2*

Genesis 45:3-11, 21-28   The story of Joseph is a delightful tale of reversals and growth. The despised and pitied brother has made good in the land of his exile and now supports his family in their time of famine. Lands infamous for famine in the sixties and seventies—Ethiopia, Somalia, and the Sahel in Nigeria—have quietly become prosperous agricultural regions now exporting food to others, thanks in part to the expertise of local farmers, who have successfully employed traditional and inventive techniques to breed their domestic grains and rise above subsistence to prosperity.

When such good news is told alongside the bad news of new areas thrown into starvation by drought, land degradation, and war, those who have abundance are more likely to feel moved to share. The message is that misery is not permanent, and that those who may need aid today are not simply "helpless victims" but skilled individuals who can help both themselves and others. How can we stir up a tireless compassion that collaborates rather than offers an imperial "charity," and that warms our hearts toward people in need who are strangers in a strange place far from us?

1 Corinthians 15:35-50   For Paul, the two Adams point to a polarity between the unredeemed, fleshly life and the life of the resurrected spiritual body. And yet to see the two as prototypes of opposed worlds, earth and heaven, is to run the risk of derogating the creation God has made. Physicist Richard Feynman addresses the polarity of the physical and metaphysical from another perspective:

> The sciences, and not just the sciences but all the efforts of intellectual kinds, are an endeavor to see the connections of the hierarchies, to connect beauty to history, to connect history to man's physiology...and so forth....To stand with evil and beauty and hope, or to stand with the fundamental laws, hoping that way to get a deep understanding of the whole world, with that aspect alone, is a mistake. It is not sensible for the ones who specialize at one end, and the ones who specialize at the other end, to have such disregard for each other....The great mass of workers in between, connecting one step to another, are improving all the time our understanding of the world.[3]

How can church become a place where the physicist and metaphysicist, the physician and the artist, the bricklayer and the theologian experience the connectedness of their callings, the wholeness of creation and its sanctity?

Luke 6:27-38   "A good measure, pressed down, shaken together, running over, will be put into your lap." Here is an image of extraordinary abundance, providential supply that is ours for the asking. Yet instead we grasp and fear and lose the very thing for which we hunger. In the words of poet Wendell Berry:

> To destroy that which we were given in trust: how will we bear it?
> It is our bodies that we give to be broken, our bodies
> existing before and after us in clod and cloud, worm and tree,
> that we, driving or driven, despise in our greed to live, our haste
> to die. To have lost, wantonly, the ancient forests, the vast grasslands
> is our madness, the presence in our very bodies of our grief.[4]

How shall we contain our greed and our need so that we may enjoy God's generosity? How shall we cultivate a heart that knows its abundant supply?

❧ *Proper 3*

Jeremiah 7:1-15 "Amend your ways and your doings," cries the prophet. Local acts of justice are needed to restore relationship with God. Jeremiah calls the people to a justice that is not an unattainable ideal; it is required of us, step by step.

> In a Peruvian wildlife preserve that covers half the land area of the city of San Francisco live 545 species of birds, 100 kinds of dragonflies, and 792 types of butterflies. Twenty to 50 percent of the plants there have yet to be named. Nearly 1,500 species of birds—that's 16 percent of all the species of birds in the world—nest in the rainforests of Indonesia.... Already, half the world's tropical forests have been burned, bulldozed, and obliterated. The rest are being wiped out at the shocking rate of 35.2 million acres a year. That's 67 acres a minute—a football field a second.... Tropical deforestation wipes out 17,000 species of animals and plants per year.[5]

Such a litany of alarming facts can make us feel powerless. How can consumers protect tropical forests? Buy only hardwood products that are harvested sustainably and avoid endangered species. Press Congress to pass a law requiring imported meat to be labeled as to country of origin. (Much foreign beef comes from rainforest areas; a four-ounce hamburger of tropical beef likely deforested an area the size of your kitchen.) Buy products whose makers support rainforests. Consider where your tourist dollars might support and not damage forests. Recycle paper and conserve energy at home. Join a protection organization. These small concrete actions begin to set justice right on earth and put us right with God.

1 Corinthians 15:50-58 Consider how we often invest energy into providing for the perishable part of us while neglecting the imperishable part of us! We over-package our mortal remains at death in concrete bunkers and brass caskets. Cremation releases dioxins, metals, hydrochloric and hydrofluoric acid, and sulfur dioxide to pollute the air and carbon dioxide to warm it. There is good news afoot: Memorial Ecosystems will bury you in an environmentally friendly way, without excess or nondegradable packaging, in its South Carolina cemetery that doubles as a wildlife habitat.[6] Even in making plans for our perishable bodies we can be wise stewards of the earth.

Luke 6:39-49 The speck in our brother or sister's eye is always easier to see than the log in our own. A Brazilian agronomist told a western journalist:

You are all in Brazil to try to stop us exploiting the wealth of the Amazon. What arrogance! You've already destroyed all the forests in your own nations and so you come and lecture us about the environment! For once let me give you a lecture. . . . Imagine that the Renaissance, the explosion of scientific knowledge and the agricultural revolution had not taken place in Europe but in one of the tropical countries. . . . Instead of your ecologists coming here with their romantic nonsense, it is our ecologists who would be handing out unwanted advice. We'd visit the vast prairies of the United States, like you visit the Amazon, and tell you that there was no chance of ever building farms out there, that the winters were too hard and there were not enough nutrients in the soil to support regular harvesting. . . . We'd tell you that to try anything different would destroy the ecosystem forever. . . . We're not going to listen and we're going to develop the Amazon.[7]

🌿 *Proper 4*

1 Kings 8:22-43   "Will God indeed dwell on earth?" asks Solomon. Millennia later, Anglican poet Christopher Smart answers eloquently:

God all-bounteous, all creative,
Whom no ills from good dissuade,
Is incarnate, and a native
Of the very world he made.[8]

Are we inclined to expatriate God from the daily round of our lives? How can we better know God as a native?

Galatians 1:1-10   "Some are confusing you with a contrary gospel," Paul warns the Corinthian Christians. In the sphere of environmental science, "false gospels" are also promulgated and passed along. According to public opinion, reducing pollution is more important to climatic change than increasing energy conservation; "greenhouse gases" consist of air pollutants; and damage to the ozone layer precipitates significant climatic change. In fact, carbon dioxide, a major greenhouse gas, is not a pollutant, nor does it damage the ozone layer. It is arguable that human activities play relatively minor roles in global weather patterns. The term "global warming" misleads some into believing that warmer temperatures are or will be the main result of the greenhouse effect. But for scientists the term includes a variety of changes in weather, including altered storm patterns, shifts in ocean currents, a rise in sea level, shifts in ecological zones, and alterations in agricultural conditions.[9] How can we better sort out fact from fallacy, and responsibly question those who offer themselves as voices of authority?

Luke 7:1-10 We see Jesus healing the centurion's slave by long-distance power. Jesus is acting with command authority as a sign of God's imperium. Our modest human version of long-distance healing may be medical video technology that links doctors with distant patients: an assistant on site guides the camera and follows the physician's directions, allowing the patient to be closely examined—and often treated—from afar. Within operating rooms, physicians guide robotic instruments by fiberoptic viewing systems inside the body to perform microsurgery. Soon these technologies may be combined so that a physician in one place can conduct surgery on a patient elsewhere while watching a projected image of the patient's body. All our power for healing derives from the power of God, and we experience it as a kind of "divine long-distance healing" even though God is very near to us.

❧ *Proper 5*

1 Kings 17:17-24; Luke 7:11-17 Resurrecting the widow's sons is a sign of God's power. We have the ability, if not to raise those dead and buried, then to extend the hour of our dying through medical technology in ways our ancestors could not imagine. A greater wisdom is required in knowing when to use these treatments and when to refrain from using them. Mary S. was a 97-year-old woman I visited as chaplain in a hospital ward for long-term care. She lay on her side in a frozen fetal position, unable to move without assistance, her eyes staring, apparently seeing nothing. Her last family member had died some years back and she had no visitors save hospital staff. She was incontinent and had to be spoon-fed small quantities of pureed food. One night her heart stopped. The team on call resuscitated her with CPR because no legal guardian had signed a "do not resuscitate" order.

Resurrection life is more than breathing, heartbeat, or digestion. It is a fullness of life governed by the promise that in our dying as in our living we rest in God's hand: we have nothing to fear. How, then, do we employ this knowledge in our care for one another? How can it influence the policies of our institutions who treat patients of diverse religious beliefs?

Galatians 1:11-24 Paul describes the gospel apprehended through revelation. We often think that scientists and mystics are at opposite ends of a spectrum. Physicist Albert Einstein suggests the contrary. Though Einstein lost his youthful belief in a personal Judeo-Christian understanding of God, he retained a belief in a God revealed in the harmony of all that exists. He defined God as a "deep intuitive conviction of the existence of a higher power of thought which manifests itself in the inscrutable universe."[10]

> The most beautiful experience we can have is the mysterious. It is the fundamental emotion which stands at the cradle of true art and true science....A knowledge of the existence of something we cannot penetrate, our perceptions of the profoundest reason and the most radiant beauty, which only in the most primitive form are accessible to our minds—it is this knowledge and this emotion that constitute true religiosity.[11]

Is this not also a voice describing revelation? Or are revelation and intuitive conviction entirely different?

❦ *Proper 6*

2 Samuel 11:26–12:15 David steals Uriah's "ewe lamb." For the powerful to steal from the poor is particularly odious in God's sight. In the competition of nations for the world's resources there is, perhaps, an equivalent. The rich world biotech companies are vying to patent as many new products and sources of products as they can, a practice that may close developing countries out of new technology and limit research into disease prevention. Ironically, even products and methods originating in poor countries are being snatched by wealthy ones. Turmeric, a spice used in Asia for millennia as a seasoning and a medicine, has been found to have active ingredients against disease that a western company is trying to patent. This is just the latest form of colonialist looting in a long history of theft by the rich from the poor.

Galatians 2:11-21 "If you, though a Jew, live like a Gentile, how can you compel the Gentiles to live like Jews?" Here is a classic example of "Do as I say, not as I do," of expecting others to conduct themselves better than one conducts oneself. Consider how the language of environmentalism has been employed to conceal who is bearing the real burden of global recycling of toxic materials. The United States, Canada, and several of the most prosperous western European countries—the largest waste exporters—have taken the lead in refusing to ratify treaties that would prevent the export of toxic wastes to the developing world. Recycling processes in poor nations often result in dangerous residues and emissions, but the "recycling" name, and all it implies, makes the export of materials to these companies acceptable. Africa is one of the prime destinations for waste that most western communities would not accept in their own neighborhoods. How might religious communities confront the dynamic of "NIMBY"—not in my backyard?

Luke 7:36-50   The woman with the alabaster ointment comes to Jesus from the ostracism of her sin and offers a small act of kindness, making a transgressive connection. Seeing this, he knows she is forgiven. The apparent isolation of things—yes, even one's own felt isolation—is an illusion. The cosmos is about connection: the spattered stardust from the ancient explosion of a solar core now resides in the molecules of the body of your cat—or Tom Cruise! As Ephesians more eloquently tells it, this connection is "according to God's purpose set forth in Christ as a plan for the fullness of time, to unite all things in Christ, things in the heavens and things on earth."

Genetics researcher John Moore writes that "all belief systems tend to close the mind."[12] To the contrary, belief and expanding knowledge can open one another outward endlessly. It is usually fear that closes minds, and isolation breeds fear as connection dissolves it. The lesson for our life in community is this: our smallest choices, our sins and little acts of kindness, do not happen in a vacuum. We are entangled and connected at every level with all the rest of creation.

✸ *Proper 7*

Zechariah 12:8-10, 13:1   A fountain for the cleansing of sin is to be opened for the city—and they will look at what they have done and mourn. I was thinking about sin while digging in my garden where some oak logs had decomposed. The delicate white and yellow web of threads of mycelium—the underground structure of a patch of morel mushrooms—had eaten away the wood as the fungus spread. Mushrooms are the fruiting bodies, the reproductive structures, that lift themselves out of the ground from the mycelium. Miles of mycelium may give rise to one or two mushrooms, or a "fairy circle" of tiny toadstools that pop up after spring rain in grassy places. In much the same way, sin is pervasive among us: we can gather a community of basically decent, faithful, and caring people and sooner or later there will be jealousy, bigotry, anger, dishonesty, or indifference to suffering among us. This mycelium of sin creeps and spreads in subterranean fashion; the evil act that no one sees or seems to mind, even the socially acceptable one, just spreads the spores of sin further abroad. It matters. It finally affects everyone.

Galatians 3:23-29   There is neither Jew nor Greek, slave nor free, male nor female in Christ. This unitive vision—much like the peaceable kingdom imagery of Isaiah—has implications for the whole creation. At present a gulf remains between the rest of creation and humankind; in our self-preoccupation it seldom occurs to us that Christ is a bridge between us and creation as well as between us and God. Joan McIntyre, head of Project Jonah, offers an example from her field:

> The whale is a split in our consciousness: on the one hand viewed as product, as resource, as an article, an object to be carved up to satisfy the economic imperative; on the other, a view almost lost now, as the great leviathan, the guardian of the sea's unutterable mysteries. Ever since we discovered the awesome abilities of our hands to fashion the world to our making, we have dishonored the unknown, until instead of inspiring us, it merely seems an inconvenience.... Now we find ourselves at the threshold of approaching the sea as we did the land: creating boundaries, carving up territories, dividing—in the name of nations—the waters that still flow in our veins and link each living thing to every other.... We are bound to a vision that leads us further away from nature, and further away from each other.[13]

How can we cultivate a vision that breaks down walls and barriers between us and God's creation?

Luke 9:18-24   Whoever loses life will save it. Resurrection calls us to surrender our selves, our old life, to God in order to enter the greater life prepared for us. The mystic and military priest Teilhard de Chardin wrote:

> Death will not simply throw us back into the great flux of reality, as the pantheist's picture of beatitude would have us believe. Nevertheless in death we are caught up, overwhelmed, dominated by that divine power which lies within the forces of inner disintegration and, above all, within that irresistible yearning which will drive the separated soul on to complete its further, predestined journey as infallibly as the sun causes the mists to rise from the water on which it shines. Death surrenders us completely to God; it makes us pass into God. In return we have to surrender ourselves to it, in love and in the abandon of love.[14]

❦ *Proper 8*

1 Kings 19:15-21   Elijah hands over the prophetic mantle to Elisha. A glorious fiery chariot will come to carry the old prophet to heaven; we will most likely face a less distinguished passage from this life. In the 1970s, when the population was roughly half what it is today, the wise naturalist Lewis Thomas wrote:

> The obituary pages tell us of the news that we are dying away while the birth announcements in finer print, off at the side of the page, inform us of our replacements, but we get no grasp from this of the enormity of the scale. There are 3 billion of us on the earth and all 3 billion must be dead, on a schedule, within this lifetime. The vast mortality, involving something over 50 million of us each year, takes place in relative secrecy.[15]

We do well to treat each other with great tenderness and compassion, as we do the best we can in the midst of so much loss. We worry about those who are ill or frail with age and calamities that might befall our children or ourselves. How do we go on loving one another, and loving God wholeheartedly, in the middle of our dying? How do we love our sagging, aging, slowing selves and accept our shocking dependence on one another in our mortality? How do we go on pouring our energies into loving afresh and relishing change when the people we love keep leaving, and the communities we love keep evolving into new and strange forms?

Galatians 5:1, 13-25   The desires of the flesh can be mastered by self-control, argues the apostle. In his studies, behavioralist Mark Muravan has determined that will power can fatigue when over-challenged, just like a muscle. A barrage of temptation can wear down the resolve to resist. In one exercise, subjects were asked to write about times they had succeeded or failed at trying to control their emotions. Reports of controlling emotions successfully were correlated with feeling either calm or energetic, while reports of failing to control them were correlated with depleted capacity caused by exhaustion, stress, or intoxication. Researchers suspect that self-control grows stronger with practice but diminishes with disuse.[16]

Luke 9:51-62   "Foxes have holes, and birds of the air have nests; but the Son of Man has nowhere to lay his head." Even a small child can grasp the poignancy of the image: the little fox curled in its den, the birds nesting on their eggs or tucked away in their birdhouse on the back lawn, but the child homeless.

In comparison with the world of Jesus' time, the birds and foxes have far fewer places in most of our towns to lay their heads. Ambivalent about St. Francis' Day and the blessing of pets in his rural area where wild land is being swallowed up for construction, a colleague preached a sermon that highlights the dilemma:

> I do wish we could expand that awareness of ours to the many other creatures we have impact upon, for instance, wild life whose habitat our sprawling development destroys. Not far south of where I live, developers are bulldozing five acre tracts of trees and brush and are driving out the many animals and birds which inhabit these acres. Episcopalians then put up a big house and three acres of chemically-treated turf on which we run a single spaniel, and we ask the Creator to bless that spaniel. Is not some nearsightedness here?[17]

How then shall we bless wild nature, acknowledging how we are blessed by it, and teach the same loving care for wild creatures as for our domestic ones?

❦ *Proper 9*

Isaiah 66:10-16   This passage is filled with rich imagery of mourners nursing from the "glorious bosom" of Jerusalem. "As a mother comforts her child, so I will comfort you," says the Lord. God the breastfeeding mother sounds like a modern image but it is an ancient and recurring one. St. Anselm in the Middle Ages found Jesus to be the motherly person of God, and described him on the cross feeding humankind on milk from his pierced side—a shocking and compelling image of vulnerability transformed into strength.

Galatians 6:1-18   What we sow we shall reap; everything we do, for good or ill, brings its consequences, and for these we bear responsibility. In the past decade, the size of factory hog and chicken farms has dramatically increased. At one time, liquid hog manure could be disposed of by spraying it on fields as fertilizer; its pervasive aroma was a sign of spring. Now the volume of waste far surpasses the ability of the soil to absorb it and break it down, so excess waste is collected in huge cesspools that leach or spill into ground water and waterways. In 1995, 35 million gallons of animal waste entered North Carolina waterways, three times the amount of oil spilled by the crash of the tanker Exxon *Valdez*. Environmentalists are working to pass legislation creating responsible standards for handling animal waste.[18] As our wells become polluted, we reap the consequences of what we have sown in low consumer costs and long indifference to environmental care among factory farmers. The *real* costs of our pork and poultry include the cost of waste disposal, clean-up, and the development of new ways to treat manure and render it harmless.

Luke 10:1-20   "The kingdom of God has come near to you," says Jesus. We all have perhaps had experiences in which we have, by grace, come near to God's reign:

> I stopped there in my field as looked up. And it was as if I had never looked up before. I discovered another world. . . . It was as though, concerned with the plow and harness and furrow, I had never known that the world had height or color or sweet sounds, or that there was a *feeling* in a hillside. I forgot myself, or where I was. I stood a long time motionless. My dominant feeling, if I can at all express it, was of a strange new friendliness, a warmth, as though these hills, this field about me, the woods, had suddenly spoken to me and caressed me. It was as though I had been accepted in membership, as though I was now recognized, after a long trial, as belonging here.[19]

At what moments in our lives do we experience with astonishing clarity that the kingdom of God has come near to us?

🌿 *Proper 10*

Deuteronomy 30:9-14; Colossians 1:1-14   The word is very near to us; the gospel is bearing fruit among us. The word of God speaks to us in the creation, hallowed and renewed in the Word-made-flesh. Just as Jesus is, in Anton Boisen's term, a "living human document," so too the earth, the cosmos is also a living document of God's love for us, resonant with meaning. Paul Gruchow explores this analogy, one that had been dear to Thomas Aquinas before him:

> But we will not come to any deep understanding of our place in nature except as we delve into its basic documents, and these documents are our wild places. Decimating a natural environment is in this sense exactly like burning all the copies of some book essential to the history of our culture. And when we destroy some entire ecosystem, as we have nearly done with our prairies, for example, it is like eliminating whole sections of our libraries.[20]

Which documents of nature have been your most compelling teachers?

Luke 10:25-37   "Who is my neighbor?" asks the parable. Demographers tell us the world has 5,000 ethnic groups but only 190 countries. Since 1945, about 15 million people have been killed in ethnic warfare around the world. Sub-Saharan Africa contains 1300 language groups in 42 countries; three-quarters of these have had coups or civil wars following decolonization.[21] Quite simply, if humankind is unable together to understand that there is no one—no individual or nation—who is not "my neighbor," then the world will devolve toward anarchy and pandemic war. Journalist Robert Kaplan, in a chilling account of his travels to nations that are unraveling, concludes that no global elite will be able to "engineer reality from above" or rescue areas that are collapsing through foreign aid or military force.

As a species we can imagine justice and harmony. But how can justice and harmony be possible for much of humanity, given the evidence of history, plus the inflammatory potential of a fourfold increase in population since the nineteenth century, with antennas rising from mudhuts that allow the poor to see how the rich live? To escape the world is folly—we tried that before each world war. As AIDS shows, Africa's climate and poverty beget disease that finds its way to the wealthiest suburb. We are the world and the world is us.[22]

❦ *Proper 11*

Genesis 18:1-14 Abraham's three visitors receive generous hospitality, for life in desert places requires a gracious collaboration among people if travelers are to survive its harshness. Water is the first essential for life; without it, we perish. In severe situations our ancestors would have died, but we modern desert travelers can be rescued in an emergency by an intravenous drink that combines the right mixture of salts and sugars. It seems likely that the virtually universal custom of offering a visitor a beverage upon arrival derived from the necessity of replacing fluids to preserve health and life while traveling in dry regions. A cup of cold water is the first gesture of care and hospitality (a cup of hot tea in the cold regions I come from!), and this was what Jesus asked the disciples to give in his name to all in need.

Colossians 1:21-29 The gospel is preached to every creature under heaven—we humans are not the only beneficiaries. Poet Christopher Smart was extraordinarily sensitive to this message: he wrote mystical, hymnodic, and strange poetry about God's good news to all the creatures, common and exotic, that he so loved. A scholar of distinction in the eighteenth century, Smart suffered financial catastrophes and an apparent religious mania that at times led him to fall on his knees and pray aloud on the public street, or wherever else he happened to be. During a decade of incarceration in mental asylums, he wrote some of his greatest religious poetry, some of it modeled after the psalms, in the Celtic tradition of praise poetry. Perhaps best known is the endearing poem he wrote about his cat:

For I will consider my Cat Jeoffrey.
For he is the servant of the Living God duly and daily serving him.
. . . .
For he keeps the Lord's watch in the night against the adversary.
For he counteracts the powers of darkness by his electrical
   skin and glaring eyes.
For he counteracts the Devil, who is death, by brisking about
   the life. . . .
For he purrs in thankfulness when God tells him he is a good cat.[23]

Perhaps in a more tolerant age religious eccentricity—ecstasy even—and the extraordinarily attentive love a poet has for the creation of God's making might be viewed more charitably.

Luke 10:38-42   Mary is commended for her contemplative attention to Jesus. Naturalist Henry Beston spent a year in a tiny cabin on the outer dunes of Cape Cod—on a spot now washed away. His account of that year, *The Outermost House,* has become a classic, calling modern urban dwellers to the possibility of a contemplative life lived in awareness of the natural world. He wrote:

> Whatever attitude to human existence you fashion for yourself, know that it is valid only if it be the shadow of an attitude to Nature. A human life, so often likened to a spectacle upon a stage, is more justly a ritual. The ancient values of dignity, beauty, and poetry which sustain it are of Nature's inspiration; they are born of the mystery and beauty of the world. Do no dishonour to the earth lest you dishonour the spirit of man. . . . Touch the earth, love the earth, honour the earth, her plains, her valleys, her hills, and her seas; rest your spirit in her solitary places. For the gifts of life are the earth's and they are given to all, and they are the songs of the birds at daybreak, Orion and the Bear, and dawn seen over ocean from the beach.[24]

How shall we hold out our hands over the earth as over a flame?

❧ *Proper 12*

Genesis 18:20-33   Abraham pleads for Sodom. Jewish writer Elie Wiesel has described this stance—a man pleading with God for the sake of his neighbors—as the essential human act of faith. When we grow weary of long intercessions for all those in desperate need, both near at hand and in the news from around the world, we might remember Abraham pleading for the doomed city. He did not throw up his hands and say, "What will be, will be, it is God's will," but bargained hard and long to save life. We learn later in the text that Abraham does not get everything he asks for in this debate with God—but because of his persistence a few are spared who would otherwise have perished. Perhaps our persistence may bear some small fruit also, God willing.

Colossians 2:6-15   The elemental spirits of the universe (*stoichaeia*) are seen in rivalry with Christ.[25] It is important to distinguish between pantheism—a doctrine that exalts parts of, or the whole, creation as a god—and panentheism, one that perceives God as always and everywhere present and active in creation. God is our element, the fundamental power of the universe. Christ is our connecting line, toppling all false claimants to power, all pretenders to "fundamental" or "primary" status. In Christ, all things hold together in the One: the cosmos, its ecosystems, humankind, and the creatures. The elements fire, air, earth, and water—believed to be fundamentals in ancient times, and lifted up anew by much New Age spirituality—are composed of the same constituent elements of the Periodic Table of Elements, the same subatomic particles with their energies. While the four are poetically rich and descriptive of one level of human experience easily recognizable to everyone, they are not fundamental elements of creation. How do we generate a rich, poetic theological language that is contemporary and informed by science and reason to speak about God among quarks and bosons, black holes and cosmic strings?

Luke 11:1-13   Give us this day our daily bread. Between 1950 and 1984 world grain production rose robustly with new varieties, along with new fertilizers, pesticides, and irrigation methods. From 1984 to1988 production fell, then rebounded in 1989. Such fluctuations are common in the history of food production and will continue in the twenty-first century. We cannot count on steady growth trends as population continues to rise. While new technologies improve stock and productivity of land in the short run, genetic diversity of species, fertile soil, and clean ample groundwater are the capital upon which all growth rests. We cannot rely on improvements in the former to compensate for the destruction of the latter. It is immensely difficult to predict the effects of climatic change on food production, so upturns in the yearly trend should not lead us to false optimism for the future.[26] The concept of daily bread reminds us to eat within our means and collaborate with the Creator who supplies our food.

🌿 *Proper 13*

Ecclesiastes 1:12–2:23 All is vanity, mourns the world-weary philosopher. That is one way to look at mortality and transience, at all we cannot control in our lives and the universe. But there are other vantage points. Writer Annie Lamott describes her neighbor, who has been living for several years with metastatic lung cancer:

> He usually drives by our house a couple of times a day and seems to be in a quietly good mood most of the time. I just do not understand this conceptually. Several weeks before this latest flu, when I had a simple head cold, I pounded on his windshield when he attempted to drive by and said, "Why are you doing this to me? Look at me—I'm *congested.*" He smiled. He loves me, loves my emotional drag-queeny self.... He's so savoring the moments of his life right now, so acutely aware of love and small pleasures that he no longer feels that he has a life-threatening disease: he now says he's leading a disease-threatening life.[27]

How might we find ways to pause and savor the moments of our lives?

Colossians 3:5-17 The virtues of a renewed human nature are detailed for a growing Christian community with an enthusiasm that suggests they are achievable with a little effort. For better or worse, social change tends to be driven by principles only when supported by pragmatics. Environmentalist and journalist Mark Hertsgaard traveled the developing world asking how issues of poverty and environmental protection are related. He finished his description of the journey with these words:

> I see two principal reasons for hope. First, most people want to do right by the environment and, if given the chance, they will—as long as they are not being penalized economically for it. Second, far from being enemies, economic and environmental health can reinforce one another. In fact, if humans are smart, repairing the environment could become one of the biggest businesses of the coming century.[28]

As the church, our theological position calls us to build up the creation for God's sake, for humanity's sake, and for the dignity inherent in the creation itself as God's loved work. How should we balance this with a pragmatism that is "wise as serpents," that recognizes the work as good business?

Luke 12:13-21 As mortality threatens, our tendency is to build bigger barns. At the end of 1998 hurricanes devastated several small countries in Central America. Months later, the United States government was still unwilling to grant debt reduction to these nations, even though much of their infrastructure, agriculture, and environment had been demolished and they were forced to rely on foreign aid to begin rebuilding. Yet nations in deep debt cannot grow in prosperity, build up business, or improve public health and education; they only become more dependent on outside help. Where is the logic in keeping the poorest nations indebted to the wealthiest, except in the illusion that by so doing our barns will be bigger and our surplus will increase? This hardly sounds like wisdom. In 2250 B.C.E., Babylonian king Hammurabi developed a sophisticated body of law that included this provision:

> If a man owes a debt, and the storm inundates his field and carries away the produce, or if the grain has not grown in the field, in that year he shall not make any return to the creditor, he shall alter his contract and he shall not pay any interest for that year.

We have yet to achieve his level of wisdom with regard to debt management.

🍃 *Proper 14*

Genesis 15:1-6 "Number the stars," God tells Abraham as a measure of the abundance of God's promise. Who could look at the stars and *not* be overwhelmed by the vastness of God's creative power—stars and galaxies beyond our counting. Star Watch, U.K. reports that a survey of high-school-age children in one of the more densely populated counties of England revealed that only about one child in ten had ever seen the hazy light of the Milky Way, so pervasive was the light pollution in their area.[29] It is possible to shield streetlights from spilling radiation upward to the night sky, but the public needs to demand it. Does it matter to us that we see the stars and planets at night, or are they expendable in the cause of safer streets and low-cost lighting? Will our children be able to look up and try to count the stars, filled with wonder at God's greatness?

Hebrews 11:1-16 We are "strangers and exiles" on the earth, seeking a homeland. Journalist John Tierney identifies a new American phenomenon he names "explornography"—the exploitation of wild places by the privileged for titillating pseudo-adventures.[30] Author Barry Lopez goes further beneath the surface and identifies a fractured sense of geography behind this corrupted relationship with wild land:

In the wake of this loss of personal and local knowledge, the knowledge from which a real geography is derived, the knowledge on which a country must ultimately stand, has come something hard to define but I think sinister and unsettling—the packaging and marketing of land as a form of entertainment. An incipient industry, capitalizing on the nostalgia Americans feel for the imagined virgin landscapes of their ancestors, and on a desire for adventure.[31]

These attitudes are, perhaps, the occupational hazard of immigrant peoples toward the earth, and are woven into our Judeo-Christian story. How might our relationship with the earth change if we were to listen carefully to our neighbors whose relationship to the geography of this country has been indigenous for millennia? How can we become minimal impact travelers on the earth, aware of the cost of our presence?

Luke 12:32-40 Ready servants will have done the work of preparation and will be equipped for the moment of God's arrival. Quite a number of the great scientists have described reaching a breakthrough in a thorny problem after years of painstaking thought and investigation in a flash of insight—sometimes when their minds were engaged with something entirely different. In 1865 German chemist August Kekulé vonStradonitz had been wrestling with models of the structure of the chemical compound benzene. Ruminating in front of a fire, he experienced a revelation:

> Again the atoms were gamboling before my eyes. This time the smaller groups kept modestly in the background. My mental eye, rendered more acute by repeated visions of this kind, could now distinguish larger structures, of manifold conformation; long rows, sometimes more closely fitted together; all twining and twisting in snakelike motion. But look! What was that? One of the snakes had seized hold of its own tail, and the form whirled mockingly before my eyes. As if by a flash of lightning I awoke.[32]

VonStradonitz had arrived at the structure of the benzene ring. The moment of joyful discovery does not devalue the discipline of preparation—in the life of the spirit or the life of the mind—for it is to the well-ordered mind that such dramatic insight is most likely to come.

✺ *Proper 15*

Jeremiah 23:23-29; Luke 12:49-56 The followers of Jesus are scolded for forecasting the appearance of the sky, but not the signs of the times. Jeremiah warns against false dreams and prophecies that cloud the people's memory of God. How do we discern what sort of cognitive process is suitable to use in charting our lives, and what sort is not useful or reliable? Some ways of knowing that were dismissed as "occult" or fantastic a few years ago are now receiving the attention of neuroscientists. The function of intuition—just as much a male as a female cognitive process—is one of them.

Every day we make decisions and assessments based on hunches, or for reasons we cannot explain but feel to be right. Scientists have demonstrated that even when the conscious mind remembers cues incorrectly, another part of the brain has stored accurate nonverbal memory. Intuition may be fallible at times, but it is not mere fantasy: information is simply taken in by the senses without the awareness of the analytical part of the brain. While western cultures have not always valued and cultivated the intuitive process, other cultures have developed meditative techniques that quiet conscious thought and allow unconscious connections to rise into awareness. Consultants offer training in practicing intuitive knowing to develop this underutilized skill.

Hebrews 12:1-14 God disciplines the one God loves. The Greek is graphic: this passage speaks of corporal punishment and has been used over the centuries, and is still used, to support its use in child-raising. Modern medicine disagrees. Philip Greven has written a comprehensive overview of corporal punishment and its religious rationales and consequences. He observes:

> Being assaulted violently in the name of discipline invariably produces anger and often rage.... Unfortunately, it does not disappear, but is transformed with time into a more or less conscious hatred directed against either the self or substitute persons, a hatred that will seek to discharge itself in various ways permissible and suitable for an adult.... The parent who hurts a child while imposing discipline is teaching a lesson in indifference to suffering as well as one in obedience.... It is hard to love life fully when one has been hit and hurt.[33]

Corporal punishment conditions children to disregard their own feelings, and can lead to depression and hardness of heart as they grow up. When children are hit in the name of upholding God's discipline, they learn to hate God as well as their parents and themselves.

Proper 16

Isaiah 28:14-22 A covenant of humankind with death threatens the destruction of the whole earth. Few examples of humanity's covenant with death are as compelling, vast, and horrifying as the abuses of Nazism in the twentieth century, with its systematic, planned, and widely supported genocide against Jews, gypsies, homosexuals, people with disabilities, and other groups deemed unfit and subhuman by those in power. During the Nazi era scientists, too, lent their knowledge and power to the cause, conducting "research" founded on scant scientific rationale that produced a level of suffering tantamount to torture.

In response to these appalling medical abuses, the Nuremberg Code was developed by scientists and medical practitioners around the world to govern all medical research involving human subjects. The covenant upholds the essential dignity and value of every human being and the justice due to every person, and insists that those practicing research on human beings conform to certain basic principles. The Nuremberg Code remains the basis of subject protection in medical research around the world, and has been expanded and elaborated by research institutions as medical research has progressed.

Hebrews 12:18-29 "Our God is a consuming fire." Fire is a terrifying image, but one that carries the possibility of many benefits: refinement, purification, and removal of old stubble to make way for new growth. Whether to let natural forest and grass fires burn or to extinguish them, whether and when to set fires to clear away old debris—these questions have been newsworthy of late, particularly with massive blazes in Yellowstone Park and the foothills of California. Researchers are discovering that fire-dependent ecosystems are far more complex than one would expect. Burning of prairie grassland stimulates some organisms to multiply and others to decline, depending on the season of the fire and the year's rainfall and temperatures. Fire, whether human-made or caused by lightning or other natural combustion, is a vital part of the prairie and forest ecosystems. We have only begun to understand how to manage it for the best outcome.[34] In place of the image of utter destruction that divine fire conjures, how might we consider the purging, seasonal fires of our lives as God's hand tending us?

Luke 13:22-35 The narrow door cannot be stumbled through unwittingly; it must be searched out with attention and care. In the lore of the ancient eastern church, it is said that old Father Nectarius was able to teach a whole convent of nuns on the island of Egina to hear the song sung by the trees. Not far from Egina lived Father Joseph, the most skillful grafter of trees, who attributed his grafting skill to his ability to distinguish between the songs of different saplings and trees: this enabled him to tell which graft would harmonize with the main stem. Father Joseph maintained that anyone who listens carefully enough can hear the vibrations of the sap circulating in the trees.

The contemplative way of prayer is a path of love and attention, much like listening to the song of the trees. There are no shortcuts to finding our way with God, to hearing God's song. Simply, we come again and again to be still and listen with love, careful not to overwhelm the song of others with our own strong melodies.

❦ *Proper 17*

Ecclesiasticus 10:7-18   We will inherit in death creeping things, wild beasts, and worms—a grim picture. During a long exile in Wales from the vagaries of seventeenth-century politics, Jeremy Taylor wrote of our dying:

> God having in this world placed us in a sea, and troubled the sea with a continual storm, hath appointed the Church for a ship, and religion to be the stern; but there is no haven or port but death. Death is that harbour whither God hath designed every one, that there he may find rest from the troubles of the world.... If all the parts of this discourse [about resurrection] be true, if they be better than dreams... then there is no reason but that we should really desire death, and account it among the good things of God.[35]

To our ears his devotional words seem as dour as the words of wisdom in Ecclesiasticus. And yet both passages are designed to bid the faithful not to love the ephemeral stuff of the world too much, but to embrace mortality as the teacher who disciplines our hearts toward proper reverence and love of God, and a deep humility with regard to our own imperfect nature.

Hebrews 13:1-8; Luke 14:1, 7-14   Brotherly and sisterly love is hospitable, writes the author of Hebrews. "Throw a feast for the poor who cannot repay you if you would be blessed," says Jesus in Luke's gospel. Today there is controversy about open eucharistic tables in which baptism is not a requirement and ongoing disagreement about women's ordination and the nature of priesthood. Are we spending our energy arguing about the most important things? I am persuaded by these strong words from a Roman Catholic theologian and missionary to the Philippines:

If the Eucharist symbolizes food and drink and sharing a meal in the memory of Jesus, who lived, died and rose from the dead, the most important challenge facing any celebration of the Eucharist today is not the legitimacy of the priest's orders, or the appropriateness of the liturgical text, but the fact that the Eucharist is today celebrated in a world where over one thousand million people are regularly hungry. Hunger, malnutrition, lack of opportunities to grow and harvest food, the erosion of the genetic base of our staple foods, the control of seeds by a few giant companies and the continual degradation of fertile croplands are all interrelated. One cannot celebrate the Eucharist today without being challenged to do something about this appalling reality.[36]

✿ *Proper 18*

Deuteronomy 30:15-20   "Use your free will to choose life," urges the writer of Deuteronomy. And in the epistle reading that follows, Paul instructs Philemon to use his free will to give freedom to the slave Onesimus. Dietrich Bonhoeffer, a Lutheran pastor and resister of Nazisim in Germany, explored the implications of our free will:

> In the free creature [man] the Holy Spirit worships the Creator, uncreated freedom praises itself in created freedom. The creature loves the Creator, because the Creator loves the creature.... Man is free by the fact that creature is related to creature. Man is free for man.... We do not rule [creation] because we do not know the world as God's creation, and because we do not receive our dominion as God-given but grasp it for ourselves. There is no "being-free-from" without "being-free-for." There is no dominion without serving God.... Without God, without his brother, man loses the earth. In his sentimental backing away from dominion over the earth man has always lost God and his brother. God, our brother, and the earth belong together.[37]

How can we better understand that our freedom is rooted in service—to God and to one another?

Philemon 1:1-20   "Receive him as you would receive me," writes Paul of Onesimus, the runaway slave. How might we live if we received the earth with the same honor, attention, and hospitality we would offer the apostolic teacher, or for that matter, Christ? The person of faith might pick up a leaf, a blossom, a stone—any creature of the natural world—and sit before it with full attention and reverence. What might such a creature show us about our Creator? How might it move us to pray?

Luke 14:25-33   Estimating the cost involves prudent foresight and self-restraint based on reliable data about resources and potential. In estimating the cost of a specific action on the environment and future generations, scientists consider sustainablity, which can be defined as "improving the quality of human life while living within the carrying capacity of supporting ecosystems."[38] *Critical limits* must be considered: since we require some natural assets for life that are irreplaceable, we must respect the limits their supply places on our patterns of consumption.

These critical limits may be hard to measure. For example, scientists may agree that biodiversity helps sustain a wetland ecosystem, but not on how important a particular species is to that process. A balancing of social, economic, political, and ecological goals—*competing objectives*—is required to reach a desired end. Human needs tend to be assessed subjectively. Sustainability reflects a concern for the generations that will follow us, and for maintaining some equity of resource use; it recognizes the immorality of some living well at the expense of others living poorly. How can we better exercise foresight and self-restraint as we estimate the cost of choices in our daily lives?

❦ *Proper 19*

Exodus 32:1, 7-14   Moses pleads for the people: he knows they are indeed stiff-necked, but he also knows of their struggles and possibilities. Well-known biologist Edward O. Wilson recently raised an optimistic voice for the role human beings can and do play in protecting their environment. He believes that we are by nature *biophilic,* with a passion for nature that moves us to conserve wild places and to migrate to them for rest and refreshment. Along with other conservationists, he maintains that community-based environmentalism holds the most hope:

> It's the challenge now and of the next century.... Right now we're pushing the species of the world through a bottleneck. We've got to make it a major moral principle to get as many of them through this as possible. And there's one good thing about our species: We like a challenge.[39]

1 Timothy 1:12-17   Grace overflowed for the sinner. The planet's systems are gracious of our sins, too. But as greenhouse gases increase, there are limits to how much imbalance the atmosphere can bear without producing a destructive chain reaction of damage to the planet's ecosystems, including human life.

Scientist Fred Pearce argues that our planet is "drowning" in nitrogen, this most common component of the earth's atmosphere. The level of nitrogen is increasing radically because we are using more fertilizer and leaving more crop debris, burning fossil fuels, draining wetlands, clearing brushland, burning forest, and planting legume crops whose roots fix nitrogen. Although nitrogen moderates carbon dioxide in the atmosphere and speeds the growth of plants, in excess it increases urban smog, algae blooms, tree death, the destruction of heathlands, and the leaching of nutrients from the soil. It is estimated that human beings have doubled the amount of available nitrogen on the planet; agricultural fertilization is the greatest culprit. There are many strong arguments for trying to reduce the imbalance we add to the system as both a moral and a sensible course of action.

Luke 15:1-10   God seems to be attracted to lost things: the lost sheep, the lost coin, and lost us! So I wonder what sort of metaphor we might make of the search for lost mass—the bulky physical sort of mass, missing from our universe. Astronomers have observed that spiral disks and galaxies move in strange ways as though affected by something we cannot see: they have labeled this "dark matter." Everything we *can* see with our best technology comprises only an estimated 5 to 10 percent of the matter that must be out there. Our own Milky Way is being drawn to its neighboring galaxy Andromeda at a rate that implies it has ten times the mass of the 100 billion stars we estimate are in it. Is there a bookkeeping problem? Are there lots of old, dim stars we cannot see? The popular theory is that there are some subatomic particles we have yet to find. One scientist muses:

> This is an idea that could give men and women a cosmic-sized inferiority complex. Just as they were adjusting quite nicely to the revelation that Earth was not the center of the universe, they suddenly have to hear that they might not be made out of the cosmos's predominant material.[40]

It is comforting to remember that what is lost to us is not lost to God.

🌿 *Proper 20*

Amos 8:4-12   The prophet warns against false measures. Land development often looks like an economic asset to a community, but increasingly conservationists are assessing the value of undeveloped land as a provider of services to the human community. Green space can shelter animals that pollinate crops and control pests. It can collect and retain moisture, regulate local climate, purify the air, replenish soil and keep it from eroding, provide useful materials—and be a place of beauty for all to appreciate. There are constructive, creative measures:

> New York City, for example, calculated that building a water treatment plant would cost between six and eight billion dollars. Instead the city will spend 1.5 billion dollars to keep development from overwhelming the Catskill and Delaware watersheds, which have filtered its water naturally for decades.[41]

How can we more effectively give voice to the benefits—both practical and spiritual—of conserving open spaces for those who will follow us?

1 Timothy 2:1-8 Timothy's author calls the church to thanksgiving for kings and officials, "so that we may lead a quiet and peaceable life in all godliness and dignity." Most of Jesus' teachings do not seem to summon us to a "quiet and peaceable life" but rather to leave comfort and complacency for the way of the cross. So we may have to push ourselves to seek that about the world order for which we do give thanks: the good public servant-leaders, the cooperation of citizens. And what of giving thanks for the *uncomfortable* parts of society and the world: a presidential scandal that presses us to converse about lying and truth-telling, public and private life, sex and power—or the way that some words and acts of hatefulness prompt passive people of good will to recognize their own roles in producing a climate of hate-tolerance?

Luke 16:1-13 "Whoever is faithful in a very little is faithful also in much." Being faithful in a little can begin by prayerful mindfulness in the doing of everyday tasks. These lines are drawn from a Celtic prayer for gardeners and farmers:

> All that I dig with the spade
> I do it in God the Three's aid.
> Each turning of the soil I make
> I do it for the Three in One's sake.[42]

Simple digging becomes a discipline of prayer. When I moved to Missouri and began a new garden, the first step was French-digging the flowers beds. After removing turf, a two-foot deep trench is dug, then a second trench adjacent to it whose topsoil is turned into the bottom of the first. A third trench is dug and its topsoil shoveled into the second, and at the last row, the top is put back in the first trench. Air has been added, and the soil loosened. Then compost is worked in, along with texture additives like sand and leaf mold. Every season the soil requires new additions to develop rich texture, balanced fertility, and the organisms that support growth and decay. Little by little the garden fosters new life, like the soul cultivated by prayer.

❦ *Proper 21*

Amos 6:1-7 "Woe to the complacent and rich" is Amos's bottom line. The following news comes as a sober reminder of our own role as Americans in the earth's environmental well-being. A 1998 report from the World Wildlife Fund for Nature published in Geneva ranked nations according to which are the most environmentally destructive. The study measured pressure on four natural resources: grain, ocean fish, timber, and fresh water; it also assessed each nation's contribution to global carbon dioxide emissions as well as the consumption of land measured by cement production.

Norway was ranked first: its primary impact is consumption of marine fish at ten times the world average. Following close behind were Taiwan, Singapore, Chile, and Denmark. The United States ranked sixth: Americans consume twice the grain of other world citizens. Bangladesh was at the lowest end of the scale. The report also pointed to a 30 percent decline overall in the health of the world's ecosystems over the past twenty-five years, and serious degradation of freshwater ecosystems worldwide. We tend to think of the "rich" as those wealthier than we are, yet in the world's eyes we, the majority of Americans, are "rich." How can we see ourselves as others see us? How can we respond constructively to Amos's message?

1 Timothy 6:11-19 God richly furnishes us with everything we enjoy, to stir our love. Julian of Norwich writes:

> I know well that heaven and earth and all creation are great, generous and beautiful and good.... God's goodness fills all his creatures and all his blessed works full, and endlessly overflows in them.... God is everything which is good, as I see it, and the goodness which everything has is God.[43]

Luke 16:19-31 The rich man and Lazarus are separated by a chasm. It is far easier to blame this reality on vast market forces, global banking practices, and unequal national resources than to claim our part in digging the trench that divides us from our poor neighbors.

It may be emotionally gratifying to blame corporations and governments for our environmental problems, and god knows they deserve it, but individuals cannot escape responsibility for their actions.... To fail to see this is to go on dividing the world falsely between guilty producers and innocent consumers.... No challenge will be more fundamental, or more difficult, than bridging the ancient gap between rich and poor.[44]

How do we keep shoveling fill into the chasm between us and our neighbor in need? How do we build the bridge and not grow weary?

❧ *Proper 22*

Habbakuk 1:1–2:4   War is about to become an instrument of God's justice in the eyes of the prophet Habakkuk. I suspect it has been a long time since Christians interpreted a wartime enemy as an agent of God's correction. Yet even today, our enemies may tell us something about the shadow-side of ourselves we need to hear. I wonder what our foreign policy might be like if our leaders responded to belligerent statements from enemy nations by saying, "It makes us angry to hear this, but under the rhetoric is there a true message about our conduct that could help us stand corrected?" or even, "Is there a divine message here?" If we then entered war with our enemies, would this practice of self-examination change the way we fought?

2 Timothy 1:1-14   The author describes gospel community as a network of trustworthy relationships in which the truth is told, tradition rightly conveyed, and steadfastness and self-control practiced. In the doctor-patient relationship, the concept of informed consent has evolved to support the values of justice and beneficence. Decisions are made in a climate of mutual respect. These beliefs have developed into legal doctrine for medical treatment: they obligate the physician to disclose to the patient in lay language a description of the proposed treatment and its inherent risks, expectations of recuperation or benefit, and other pertinent information, including alternatives. Some circumstances may allow variance from these standards, such as a patient's refusal to be informed, or an emergency situation. On rare occasions, information may be deemed in the physician's best judgment more injurious to the patient than its withholding. This last "therapeutic privilege" should involve consultation with a colleague and be motivated by compelling need.

All of this means that patients may be faced with quantities of written and oral information in a time of illness, and may be under some pressure to make hasty decisions based on complex data. Some argue that genuine informed consent under such circumstances is virtually impossible, or that the volume of information is more a burden than a help. Ultimately, once questions are posed and answers given, much of the patient's decision is still likely to rest on a trusting relationship between patient and doctor.

Luke 17:5-10 Faith as a mustard seed can change the world. And yet first and foremost it is our own hearts that are in need of change. In an Easter sermon, Augustine offers a lovely image of the baptized and regenerate ones as "a holy seed, a new colony of bees, the very flower of our ministry and fruit of our toil." What might our ministry look like if we were to play with these metaphors, and even live into them?

❧ *Proper 23*

Ruth 1:1-19 Orpah was right to go. She did exactly what society required of her, and none should think badly of her for it. But it is Ruth whom history remembers, the daughter-in-law who would not return home, who transgressed the social rules and clung to her old mother-in-law. She vowed to go wherever Naomi went, to follow her God and to be buried beside her—though as a foreigner in Naomi's homeland there was no hope of a husband or children, nor any promise of survival.

There is, then, for the faithful, a journey to be accomplished that mirrors these movements: detachment and trust, relinquishing and risking; investment and generosity, opening ourselves to what is unfamiliar and acting lovingly; and being led into new life and joy. We dance the steps of this journey in our individual lives, sometimes more than once, and also as communities of people. How do we live upon the earth as exile, sojourner, and homecomer?

2 Timothy 2:3-15 Do we still believe that the hard-working farmer should have the firstfruit of the crops? The next decade may see the end of the family farm in the United States. It is so easy to go to the supermarket and grab a package of meat off the shelf without a thought for the farmer. But this winter I have been passing by the pork and asking why the retail price is hefty while the farmer is going bankrupt. There are no good answers, but clearly those who stand to gain are factory farmers who can weather short-term losses that will wipe out their small competitors, and retailers who maintain the price at a good profit. In a society based on consumption, it is exhausting and confusing to be an informed and conscientious consumer trying to buy wisely, to obtain information discerningly, to enter into conversation about the common good, and to refrain from buying certain products for the sake of justice and lovingkindness to neighbors. What local consumer issues summon your congregation to perseverance, justice, and advocacy?

Luke 17:11-19 Lepers were still much feared in the fourth century. Gregory Nazianzus made an impassioned plea for their care:

> Those who have a particular right to our compassion are the sick who are affected by leprosy and whose flesh and bones are being eaten away...living corpses, mutilated in several parts of their bodies, so that some are now unrecognizable. To make themselves known they mention the name of their father, of their mother.... They tell us... "once upon a time you were my friend and intimate with me."... Part of them has departed before their burial; the other part will not have anyone to give them a burial. The very best and most charitable people are wholly indifferent in their regard.[45]

In our day a variety of diseases bring loss of identity—catastrophic burns and other disfiguring trauma, the dementia of Alzheimers and AIDS, to name a few. Gregory goes on to ask, "What then shall we do...we who are disciples of Christ, gentle and kind, of Christ who has borne our ills? What will our thoughts and attitude be toward those sick human beings?"

❧ *Proper 24*

Genesis 32:3-8, 22-30 Jacob envisions a ladder in the sky, with messengers racing up and down. If you photograph the stars through a telescope with a polished glass wedge placed in front of its aperture, their light will spread across a sheet of photographic emulsion as a rainbow-colored ladder. This technique is known as photographic spectroscopy. Colors from red to violet form bands of varied widths separated irregularly by black lines carrying information about the star's chemical composition; their size and position are as unique as a fingerprint. Cecelia Payne-Gaposchkin, a Harvard astronomer in the 1920s and one of the first women to brave a research science career, applied quantum theory to interpreting spectral data from the photographic plates in storage. She concluded that the composition of most stars is similar: stars contain a million atoms of hydrogen for every atom of calcium, and far more hydrogen than all other elements together. The composition of the earth, then, is in no way typical of the whole cosmos. The universe is more hydrogen-filled than anyone had imagined—hydrogen makes up 99 percent of all its atoms.[46] Does knowledge, perhaps, constitute a ladder toward heaven, helping our souls ascend?

2 Timothy 3:14–4:5 Inspired scripture versus myth: is this a true polarity? Only if one defines myth as fiction, and perhaps only if one defines divine inspiration as confined to literal facts. A new Bible in a "Pocket Canons" edition published in Scotland is causing controversy in church circles.[47] These paperbacks feature prefaces by a scientist, a bishop, and ten writers. Critics accuse them of blasphemy for arguing that the Bible can be read as literature—not only as the inspired Word of God. The bishop of Edinburgh cautions that language can describe but not be identified with God, and that it is helpful to read the texts as poetry and metaphor rather than dogma. The non-religious scientist introduces the Genesis edition by discussing the surprising continuity in human thinking about origins, free will, and language among both scientists and religious writers through history. If God can be poet as well as scientist, and truth stretches beyond hard facts to the emotional and spiritual experiences of human beings, we no longer need to set scripture against myth in a rivalry. Instead, we may find God communicating with us through word and story, data and statistics, melody and rhythm, sense and ambiguity.

Luke 18:1-8 The ears of the judge are worn out by the widow's continual pleas and finally her trouble is dealt with. Our ears grow weary from decades of debate over nuclear safety. How shall we keep listening? In ruminating on perseverance, we might consider the ongoing battle over nuclear waste disposal. Transmutation, a new technique under rapid development, may hold a key to converting the toxic remnants of nuclear waste into harmless elements. The premise is that technetium-99, a water-soluble waste product of uranium in fission reactors that accumulates in the food chain and has a half-life of 200,000 years, can be converted by the addition of a neutron into technetium-100. The latter decays in just under 16 seconds into the stable harmless element ruthenium. Dangerous isotopes would be broken down in repeated passes through a reactor undergoing a subcritical reaction, that is, one that is not self-sustaining.[48] Will opponents of nuclear power be able to adjust their thinking to allow for a type of nuclear reactor to be built that will still have some risk of accidents but might be able to detoxify a high percentage of waste? How might we pray about accepting risks in society for the sake of greater benefits?

✺ *Proper 25*

Jeremiah 14:1-10, 19-22　Drought is the constant terror of arid countries, and water the most precious resource—and therefore a potent symbol for God's sustaining of life. In the Thar Desert of western India, ancient methods of capturing water are effective enough to support sixty people per square kilometer, an amazingly dense number for desert land. Rain water falls so rarely there that it must be trapped and routed carefully if it is not to disappear under the sands. Little hand-dug dikes and ditches, piled stones, and depressions around the roots of plants catch silt and rain and hold them long enough to be absorbed by roots. Phoenix, Arizona was built over a complex ancient irrigation system engineered by the Hohokam tribe that carried Salt River water to crop growing areas. In Colorado the Anasazi harvested rain in the desert to grow grains and vegetables via systems of small dams that caught mountain runoff.

The ancient Persians built shallowly sloping tunnels called *qanat* deep into the earth that stretched for miles in Iran. For 2000 years these tunnels reliably supplied three-quarters of the country's people with water by a gravity-feed system. Now the digging of deep wells with pumps has begun to dry up these ancient water sources, spelling the end of sustainable irrigation. Many of the traditional water collection methods are cheaper, more accessible, more effective, and more sustainable than state-of-the-art modern engineering schemes.

2 Timothy 4:6-18　We who somewhat idolize physical fitness and compulsive exercise may find the image of finishing the race appealing. Regular exercise is good for the body, but athletic training that is too strenuous can impair the immune system. Olympic athletes who train up to forty hours a week may experience lowered antibody levels; some studies suggest higher rates of infectious disease in such persons, but scientists have yet to determine why. Strenuous exercise increases the number of white blood cells in many athletes, yet marathoners tend to have low lymphocyte counts, for reasons that are unclear. Mild exercise seems to be uniformly beneficial. A Chinese study of people over sixty who practice the slow, gentle exercise form of Tai Chi showed that they have a 40 percent increase in T-cells, which respond to infection. Perhaps moderate exercise could improve immune function in the elderly or people with immune impairment. Strenuous exercise might be used as a treatment to cool down the overactive immune systems of people with disorders like arthritis.[49] Could compulsive exercisers adopt the spiritual discipline of sabbath—a fast from the habit of working out—while the inactive seek a sabbath discipline of prayer through movement?

Luke 18:9-14 The Pharisee is oblivious of the double standard he maintains in devaluing another's life and prayers in comparison to his own. A debate is underway in medical research ethics over another double standard: does the poverty of the foreigner allow a different standard of care, simply because a different standard is usual for them? What should be the parameters for testing potential new vaccines for diseases, including AIDS, in countries where the diseases are endemic, but there is no funding for their treatment and prevention? Is it ethical to carry on these trials in countries where access to advanced treatment is impossible, limited, or delayed to gain information that would not be available in wealthy countries where treatment begins quickly? The Helsinki Declaration, reflecting the best judgment of many researchers, declares it is not. Even if those conducting the trial supplied treatment while it was running, who would supply it once the trial ended, and for the lifetime of the subjects? Will subjects sign up for trials simply to gain access to drugs they could not get otherwise, thus violating the prohibition that researchers must not "unduly influence" people to enroll in a trial? Those in poor countries or in places with repressive governments have no voice to protest, nor even to obtain full information about their disease and its remedies.[50]

❦ *Proper 26*

Isaiah 1:10-20 Come let us reason together, says God. Should emotion always be subordinated to reason in ethical decision-making? Many philosophers argue that reason is the highest function of human beings and that "sentiment" should not be allowed to intrude into the process of decision-making. Psychology professor Sidney Callahan presents a different point of view. She observes that emotion and thought interweave, neither simply causing the other, but each at times triggering and enhancing the other:

> Emotions are energizing and adaptive, and serve communicating, bonding, and motivating functions.... A lack of anxiety, guilt, empathy, or love devastates moral functioning.... Emotions energize the ethical quest. A person must be emotionally interested enough about discerning the truth to persevere despite distractions.

Both love and anger can constructively tutor moral reason by stirring attention and compassion, overcoming fear, and prompting beneficent action.[51] What if our emotions contradict reason? Then we are called to seek more data, expand our realm of thought, and enter into conversation with others to probe the discrepancy.

2 Thessalonians 1:1-12   In scripture, suffering generates a variety of theories about its cause and purpose: it is a test of character or faith, a contest between God and Satan, a punishment for sin, a consequence of the actions of those who went before, or an example to onlookers of the sustaining power of God. Theories are powerful tools for shaping human experience—the nature of our suffering is affected by what we believe about its origin and design.

Consider the theories of quantum physicists as they also seek to establish models to rationalize what they observe. Physicists speak of "seeing" the subatomic particles made in particle accelerators. In fact, as these particles pass through chambers filled with liquid hydrogen, interaction with the hydrogen produces small bubbles, and *these* are what we see. The particles are far too small to be observed directly. They are, in some sense, ideas rather than things, maps rather than terrain. In these terms, as physicist Niels Bohr remarked, the quantum world does not exist. A scientific theory is a set of approximations about natural phenomena, and might even be thought of as a variety of poetics, rooted in the observable universe. The best theories are economical, parsimonious—they have a simplicity along with a wide compass. How might we evaluate the various theories of suffering with similar criteria?

Luke 19:1-10   I wonder how long Zacchaeus hung around high in the branches of the sycamore waiting for Jesus to come by, watching the birds and insects and luxuriating in the shade of the wide canopy? In rainforests around the world today, tree-climbing scientists are lowered onto treetops by helicopters, hot-air balloons, and blimps, or are even placed on the green sea of branches in giant inflatable rafts to collect samples and study the ecosystem in the sky. Trees the height of twenty-story buildings house life of all kinds, and collect organisms that arrive on the wind or climb from below. From his bosun's chair swinging in the canopy, rainforest ecologist Mark Moffett writes:

> In my mind's eye, the great green bulk of one of the trees near me spins away, and these species hang in the air, forming a constellation packed with an intermingling of epiphytes, climbing plants, and animals large and small, each one holding up its own part of the ecosystem.... Refined over eons with millions of species packed in a space a hundred or more feet high and extending over thousands of square miles, rainforests are the embodiment of boundless information about death and life.... There is more feasting, more famine, more courtship and sex, more tender care of the young and of home, more combat and more cooperation in this arboreal realm than anyplace else on the globe.[52]

❧ *Proper 27*

Job 19:23-27 "My Redeemer lives!" cries Job in confidence, after everything he has endured. Job does not learn *why* he has suffered so, but he grasps that somehow his suffering is part of God's artistry in a larger magnificent fabric of redemption. That, for him, is enough. "God holds out his two hands toward his creation: the Son and the Spirit," wrote Irenaeus. I am reminded of that story of Jesus' baptism by John in the river Jordan, in which we see this process at work. God's voice booms from the opened heavens as at the beginning of creation. The waters of the Jordan are divided like the Red Sea for the deliverance of the people. The Son, the Word in which earth and heaven are joined, rises dripping from the womb of the deep in answer to the call. The Spirit, arcing down like the dove of Noah who brought back the twig announcing the renewal of creation after the flood, is the sign of the new creation accomplished in the Chosen One, the Christ. Like the Spirit brooding over creation, it hovers over the face of the deep. The mystery catches us in. It does not *explain* the whys and hows of God's purposes, but it reminds us that God is our redeemer, and redeemer of all, and in that confidence we may endure, and find rest.

2 Thessalonians 2:13–3:5 God is faithful. Hear the clarion words of Alan Billings, vice-principal of Ripon College, Oxford: "Christ came to redeem the whole world of matter and nothing less than the redemption of the whole world should be the concern of Catholics." Christ lifted up on the hard wood of the cross draws the whole world to himself, as the collect puts it. All matter is assumed by God in Christ in the incarnation; sin cannot wrench it from God's hallowing hands. The sacred is not separate from the secular or profane. There is no atom unaffected by God's grace and no human soul beyond God's redeeming power, living or dead; this redeeming work is ongoing, and it is also ultimately, everlastingly, breathtakingly hopeful. There is no room for pessimism, nor for quietism. The world and history may be apparently going to the dogs around us, but God is not and has never abandoned us or the world but is constantly renewing it. No one of us can bask in our redemption in isolation—as a person or a nation, a denomination or an ethnicity. God will not rest until all are saved, until the whole face of creation has been renewed. God is faithful; how then shall we be faithful in return?

Luke 20:27-38 The scholars of the law are asking Jesus the wrong question when they challenge him with the complexities of Levirate marriage. Their imagination is limited to seeing the reign of heaven as just an extension of the status quo. Jesus urges them to envision God's reign differently, beyond property and the need for protection and progeny. As we mature in our faith, formulating the right questions is just as important as arriving at accurate answers. How might we grow into better listeners, so that we ask questions that are meaningful and expansive?

❦ Proper 28

Malachi 3:13–4:6 The "sun of righteousness" with "healing in its wings" seems a natural metaphor for the therapeutic power of God, and for Christians the healing love of the "Son" of righteousness, Jesus Christ. The sun and the vitamin D that it brings us add to good mental and physical health. Yet we are also mindful of the risks attached to excess sun exposure, and have read how holes in the ozone layer of our atmosphere have brought added risk of skin cancer to residents in areas with increased ultraviolet light. Sunscreen preparations offer some protection from sunburn and some less dangerous forms of skin cancer. But research reported at the American Association of the Advancement of Science in 1998 indicates that they do not protect against melanoma, a skin cancer that results in 9,000 deaths a year in the United States. The EPA estimated in 1986 that the incidence of skin cancers would rise 2 percent for each 1 percent depletion of stratospheric ozone; plants and animals would also be adversely affected.[53] So for us, the sun is a more ambivalent metaphor than it was for our forbears. Are there other metaphors of healing that might be more apt for our prayers?

2 Thessalonians 3:6-13 Community members must work to eat—no idleness, no busybodies! This has the ring of damage control, of tedious and rather obvious advice given to a community in which some members are not acting responsibly, and the ethic of mutual service is unraveling. When we think of public service, the professions that come first to mind are safety workers like firefighters and police, medical caregivers, and perhaps educators. And yet among the greatest scientists are some of the world's greatest humanitarians and public servants. Albert Einstein considered Mahatma Gandhi a personal hero, and understood his own relentless search for the truth of the universe and its workings as an act of service. He wrote:

> Knowledge of truth alone does not suffice; on the contrary this knowledge must continually be renewed by ceaseless effort, if it is not to be lost. It resembles a statue of marble which stands in the desert and is continuously threatened with burial by the shifting sand. The hands of service must ever be at work, in order that the marble continue lastingly to shine in the sun. To these serving hands mine also shall belong.[54]

Luke 21:5-19   The end times are envisioned as a time of social and political turmoil where old relationships fracture and nature itself mirrors this upheaval. Are we entering end times, as some millennialists proclaim? Can we tell a fresh story about humankind that remains the gospel story, yet moves us beyond what Niles Eldredge calls our "slant on the living world"?

> It is all about people, a system set up by God for humans to control and to use as they please.... This vision has worked for 10,000 years primarily because there has until recently been enough room and resources to support unchecked population growth. Not until the last 100 years or so have the mutually resonating factors of industrialization, increasingly mechanized and chemically dependent agriculture, and out-of-control population growth come together in a horrible form of synergism to threaten the world's species, the world's ecosystems—and ourselves.... We need a new vision, a revised story of who we are and how we fit into the world.[55]

The danger of apocalyptic thinking is that it replaces a sense of responsibility for shaping difficult times by individual and corporate effort with a sense of helplessness and passivity in the face of overwhelming circumstances. How might we employ our thinking about "end times" to instead invigorate our commitment to care for the earth actively, while accepting the humility of what we cannot control?

🌿 *Proper 29*

Jeremiah 23:1-6   Bad shepherds and good shepherds: an analogy for governors who deal justly or unjustly with the people entrusted to them. The metaphor may also apply to physicians. The proportion of doctors who believe in telling patients the truth about their cancer and its prognosis has been increasing in recent years: a 1985 survey showed that 70 percent of physicians favor truth-telling, compared to 82 percent polled in 1961 who believed in *not* telling the truth to patients. Dr. Saul Tadovsky explores this landscape in an article entitled "Bearing the News." In his 30 years of practice, only 4 patients reacted to hearing the truth with persistent denial and anger, while the rest adapted and dealt with their illnesses constructively. Lying to patients about their prognosis often involves complicated conspiracies of silence with family members and other caregivers, and likely takes away decision-making power from the person affected. It also adds to the mistrust and isolation of the patient who sees her or his condition unfolding in a way that the physician has not disclosed.

In Tadovsky's view, physicians often lie to deny their own mortality or failure. He concludes that lying is simply wrong—a denial of dying as a basic element of living: "Not only as physicians but as human beings we have no right to deny someone the chance to survey his or her life in the context of the beginning definition of its end."[56] Within each profession of public trust and leadership, might one similarly define good and evil "shepherding" based on standards of justice, care, humility, truthfulness, and integrity?

Colossians 1:11-20 All things were created through Christ, and for Christ who indwells all things. In *Against the Pagans,* the fourth-century saint Athanasius wrote:

> He who is the good Word of the good Father produced the order in all creation, joining opposites together, and forming from them one harmonious sound...and gives order, direction and unity to creation....[God] did not want to see [the creatures] tossed about at the mercy of their own natures, and so be reduced to nothingness. But in his goodness he governs and sustains the whole of nature by his Word (who is himself also God), so that under the guidance, providence and ordering of that Word, the whole of nature might remain stable and coherent in his light....The almighty and most holy Word of the Father pervades the whole of reality, everywhere unfolding his power and shining on all things visible and invisible. He sustains it all and binds it together in himself.

Luke 23:35-43 "Save yourself!" shout Jesus' taunters. In our relationship with the world environment, this is, finally, what none of us can do. We cannot save ourselves; we can only collaborate in the saving of the whole. Those who tread lightly on the earth suffer along with those who exploit and exhaust it. Soil, water, and atmosphere know no political boundaries; they are our common gift from God and the common inheritance of Earth's children and grandchildren. Nor will God simply rescue us from our own destructive behavior and save the earth for us. We are partners with God through our calling in baptism to be "co-creators" in the intimate artistic enterprise of God's love. Whether we are partners for good or ill requires the conscientious application of all our reason, knowledge, vision, and reverence. We need one another's help and spirit of compassion to protect our planet and each other, and God asks of us nothing less.

ENDNOTES FOR YEAR C

🍃 *Advent*

1. Panayiotis Varotsos, *Journal of Applied Physics* 83:60.

2. Rich Reiner and Tom Griggs, "Restoring Riparian Forests," *The Nature Conservancy Magazine* (1989):10-16.

3. Dwight D. Eisenhower, from a speech before the American Society of Newspaper Editors, April 16, 1953.

4. For this paper on the web, go to http://www.unifi.it/unifi/dbag/eee/.

5. Edward Hallowell, *Worry* (New York: Pantheon Books, 1997).

6. J. Robert Wright, ed., *Readings for the Daily Office from the Early Church* (New York: Church Hymnal Corporation, 1991), 432.

7. Paula Simmons, *Raising Sheep the Modern Way* (Pownall, Vt.: Storey Communications, Inc., 1976), 28.

🍃 *Christmas*

1. Quoted in *Celtic Daily Light,* ed. Ray Simpson (London: Hodder & Stoughton, 1997), reading for May 5.

2. David Darling, "On Creating Something from Nothing," *New Scientist* (14 September 1996): 49.

3. Kent Redford, "The Question of Sustainable Development," *Nature Conservancy Magazine* (January/February 1995):15.

4. Marcus Chown, "Cosmic Crystal," *New Scientist* (13 February 1999):42.

5. Lloyd Darden, *The Earth in the Looking Glass* (Garden City: Anchor Press/Doubleday, 1974), 167-168.

6. G. John Roush, "The Disintegrating Web: The Causes and Consequences of Extinction," *Nature Conservancy Magazine* (November/December 1989):4ff.

7. Norman Cameron, *Personality Development and Psychopathology* (Boston: Houghton Mifflin Company, 1963), 98.

✺ *Epiphany*

1. Thomas Hopko, *The Winter Pascha* (Crestwood, N. Y.: St. Vladimir's Seminary Press, 1984), 154.

2. Martin Soroos, "The Thin Blue Line: Preserving the Atmosphere as a Global Commons," *Environment* (March 1998):6.

3. Ray Simpson, ed., *Celtic Daily Light* (London: Hodder & Stoughton, 1997), reading for April 18.

4. *Science News* 143 (30 January 1993): 70.

5. Scott Lafee, "Good Vibrations," *New Scientist* (4 October 1997).

6. *Journal of the American Medical Association* (1 April 1998).

7. Leonard A. Sagan, "What Language Does Your Doctor Speak?" *The New York Times Book Review* (17 September 1989).

8. Marcia Bartusiak, *Thursday's Universe* (New York: Times Books, 1986), 93-94.

9. Marjorie Stoneman Douglas, *The Everglades: River of Grass* (Sarasota, Fla.: The Pineapple Press, 1947, 1997), 383.

10. "Progress of Nations" (New York: UNICEF, 1996).

11. Richard Garfield, "Suffer the Innocents," *The Sciences* (January-February 1999):19ff.

12. "Coastlines and Rising Seas," *One Earth, One Future*, ed. Cheryl Silver and Ruth DeFries (Washington, D.C.: National Academy Press, 1990), 90-102.

13. Walt Whitman, *Leaves of Grass*, ed. Malcolm Cowley (New York: Penguin Books, 1959), 49, 83.

14. Mohandas Gandhi, *Satyagraha* (Ahmedabad, India: Navajivan Publishing Co., 1951), 384.

✺ *Lent and Holy Week*

1. Kenneth C. Davis, *Don't Know Much About Geography* (New York: William Morrow & Co., 1992.

2. Check the Los Alamos web site at www.xxx.lanl.gov/abs/hep-ph/9811284 and astro-ph/9810069 for papers by John Ellis and Dennis Zaritsky. For a review, see Stephen Battersby, "Space Oddity," *New Scientist* (16 January 1999):24ff.

3. Jeremy Bernstein, *Science Observed: Essays Out of My Mind* (New York: Basic Books, 1982), 135.

4. Henry Beston, *Northern Farm* (New York: Ballantine Books, 1948), 114.

5. Lawrence Kushner, *The River of Light* (Woodstock, Vt.: Jewish Lights Publishing, 1981), 91.

6. From the foreword by Edmond Hillary to Yoshikazu Shirakawa, *Himalayas* (New York: Harry N. Abrams, Inc., 1971).

7. Sallie McFague, *The Body of God* (Minneapolis: Fortress Press, 1993), 206.

8. Joan Sauro, *Whole Earth Meditation* (San Diego: LuraMedia, 1986), 61.

9. Christopher Smart, *The Religious Poetry* (Manchester, England: Carcanet/Fyfield Books, 1972), 30.

10. John Jerome, *The Elements of Effort* (New York: Pocket Books, 1997), 36-37.

11. Van Beydler, "A Tireless Pursuit," *Missouri Resources* 15 (Winter 1998-99): 7-11.

12. James Gleick, *Chaos* (New York: Viking Penguin Inc., 1987), 299.

13. Margaret Wheatley, *Leadership and the New Science* (San Francisco: Berrett-Koehler Publishers, Inc., 1992), 11, 2.

14. G. John Roush, "The Disintegrating Web: The Causes and Consequences of Extinction," *Nature Conservancy Magazine* (November/December 1989): 7.

15. This panel is reviewed by Jocelyn Kaiser in "EPA Ponders Pesticide Tests in Humans," *Science* (1 January 1999):18-19.

16. Kevin Kelley, ed., *The Home Planet* (Reading, Mass.: Addison-Wesley, 1988), 74.

17. Lydia Dotto, *Blue Planet* (New York: Harry N. Abrams, 1991), 15.

❧ Easter

1. Paul Gruchow, *The Necessity of Empty Places* (New York: St. Martin's Press, 1988) 29.

2. Wendell Berry, *Recollected Essays 1965-1980* (New York: North Point Press, 1987), 248.

3. John Travis, "The Priest's Chromosome," *Science News* 154 (3 October 1998).

4. C. V. Barber and V. Pratt, "Poison and Profits," *Environment* (October 1998): 4 ff.

5. Roman Vishniac, "Creativity: The Human Resource," from a brochure for an exhibition in San Francisco, 1979.

6. Jeanette Batz, "Pigeons Dropping," *The Riverfront Times* (13-19 January 1999): 18-23.

7. Stephen H. Schneider, *Laboratory Earth* (New York: Basic Books, 1997), xiv.

8. John Polkinghorne, "A Scientist's Approach to Belief," *Sewanee Theological Review* 39:1.

9. Elizabeth Schüssler-Fiorenza, *Invitation to the Book of Revelation* (Garden City, N. Y.: Image Books, 1981), 72.

10. C. Cavallero and D. Foulkes, *Dreaming as Cognition* (New York: Harvester Wheatsheaf, 1994).

11. Henry Beston, *Outermost House* (New York: Ballantine Books, 1928), 173.

12. William Allen, *St. Louis Post-Dispatch* (24 January 1999), C8.

❧ The Season After Pentecost

1. Pierre Teilhard de Chardin, *Hymn of the Universe* (New York: Harper Colophon Books, 1961), 150.

2. Sallie McFague, *The Body of God* (Minneapolis: Fortress Press, 1993), 188.

3. Richard Feynman, *The Character of Physical Law* (Cambridge, Mass.: The MIT Press, 1965), 124-26.

4. Wendell Berry, *A Timbered Choir* (Washington, D. C.: Counterpoint, 1998), 98.

5. Scott Lewis, *The Rainforest Book* (Los Angeles: Living Planet Press, 1990), 8-10.

6. See www.memorialecosystems.com.

7. Bob Holmes and Gabrielle Walker, *New Scientist* 21 (September 1996):26.

8. "Hymn XXXII," Christopher Smart, *The Religious Poetry* (Manchester, England: Carcanet/Fyfield Books, 1972), 99.

9. Willett Kempton, "How the Public Views Climate Change," *Environment* (November 1997):12 ff.

10. Quoted by G. J. Whitrow, *Einstein: The Man and His Achievement* (Cambridge: Harvard University Press, 1979), 138.

11. Albert Einstein, *Ideas and Opinions* (New York: Crown Publishers, Inc., 1982), 11.

12. John Moore, *Science as a Way of Knowing* (Cambridge: Harvard University Press, 1993), 94.

13. *Mind in the Waters,* ed. Joan McIntyre (New York: Charles Scribner's Sons, 1974), 8.

14. Pierre Teilhard de Chardin, *Hymn of the Universe* (New York: Harper Colophon Books, 1961), 150.

15. Lewis Thomas, *Lives of a Cell* (New York: Penguin Books, 1974), 98.

16. Reported in *Spirituality & Health* (Fall 1998): 10.

17. From "Beyond Pet Blessings," a sermon given by the Rev. Steven Weissman, in Louisiana, Missouri in 1998.

18. *Sierra* (January/February 1999).

19. From *Adventures of David Grayson* excerpted in *Great American Nature Writing,* ed. Joseph Wood Krutch (New York: William Sloane Associates, Inc., 1950), 219.

20. Paul Gruchow, *The Necessity of Empty Places* (New York: St. Martin's Press, 1988), 140.

21. Roger Doyle, *Scientific American* (September 1998): 30.

22. Robert Kaplan, *The Ends of the Earth: A Journey to the Frontiers of Anarchy* (New York: Vintage Books/Random House Inc., 1996), 437-38.

23. Christopher Smart, *The Religious Poetry* (Manchester, England: Carcanet/Fyfield Books, 1972), 43-45.

24. Henry Beston, *The Outermost House* (New York: Ballantine Books, 1928), 174.

25. For a discussion on the divinization of the elements see Walter Wink, *Naming the Powers* (Philadelphia: Fortress Press, 1984), 74.

26. Cheryl Silver and Ruth DeFries, eds., *One Earth, One Future* (Washington, D.C.: National Academy Press, 1990).

27. Annie Lamott, *Traveling Mercies* (New York: Pantheon, 1999), 118-19.

28. Mark Hertsgaard, *Earth Odyssey* (New York: Broadway Books, 1998), 328.

29. Find the Star Watch web site at http://www.u-net.com/ph/starw-uk/home.htm.

30. John Tierney, *The New York Times Magazine* (26 July 1998): 18 ff.

31. Barry Lopez, *About This Life: Journeys on the Threshold of Memory* (New York: Alfred A. Knopf, 1998), 135.

32. Quoted in Richard Morris, *Dismantling the Universe* (New York: Simon & Schuster, Inc., 1983), 166.

33. Philip Greven, *Spare the Child* (New York: Alfred A. Knopf, 1991), 8, 123, 126-27, 222.

34. *Fire in North American Tallgrass Prairies,* ed. S. Collins and L. Wallace (Norman, Okla.: University of Oklahoma Press, 1990).

35. Jeremy Taylor, *The Rule and Exercises of Holy Living and The Rule and Exercises of Holy Dying* (Wilton, Conn.: Morehouse-Barlow, 1981), 51, 57.

36. Sean McDonagh, *To Care for the Earth* (Santa Fe: Bear and Company, 1986), 171.

37. Dietrich Bonhoeffer, *Creation and Fall* (New York: Macmillan, 1959), 40.

38. Alex Farrell and Maureen Hart, "What Does Sustainability Really Mean?" in *Environment* (November 1998): 4 ff.

39. Virginia Morell, "In Search of Solutions," *National Geographic* (February 1999): 78.

40. Marcia Bartusiak, *Thursday's Universe* (New York: Times Books, 1986), 187-207.

41. *National Geographic* (February 1999): 80.

42. "Breaking New Land," *The Edge of Glory: Prayers in the Celtic Tradition,* ed. David Adam (Harrisburg: Morehouse, 1985), 29.

43. Julian of Norwich, *Revelations of Divine Love,* trans. Clifton Wolters (Middlesex, England: Penguin Books, 1966), 75.

44. Mark Hertsgaard, *Earth Odyssey* (New York: Broadway Books, 1998), 328, 334.

45. J. Robert Wright, ed., *Readings for the Daily Office from the Early Church* (New York: Church Hymnal, 1991), 79-80.

46. For a description of this research see Philip and Phyllis Morrison, *The Ring of Truth: An Inquiry Into How We Know What We Know* (New York: Random House, 1987).

47. The "Pocket Canons" series is reviewed in *The Economist* (3-9 October 1998): 95-96.

48. Michael Brooks, "Nuclear Lifeline," *New Scientist* (16 January 1999): 31-33. Or visit the web site at www.adtt.lanl.gov.

49. Craig Sharp and Mark Parry-Billings, "Can Exercise Damage Your Health?", *New Scientist* (15 August 1992).

50. *Science* 281 (3 July 1998): 22-23.

51. Sidney Callahan, "The Role of Emotion in Ethical Decisionmaking," *Hastings Center Report* (Hastings-on-Hudson: The Hastings Center, 1988): 9 ff.

52. Mark Moffett, *The High Frontier* (Cambridge: Harvard University Press, 1993), 176.

53. Cheryl Silver and Ruth DeFries, eds., *One Earth, One Future* (Washington, D. C.: National Academy of Sciences, 1990), 113-14.

54. Albert Einstein, *Ideas and Opinions* (New York: Crown Publishers, Inc., 1982), 59.

55. Niles Eldredge, *Dominion* (Berkeley: University of California Press, 1995), 166.

56. Saul Tadovsky, "Bearing the News," *The New England Journal of Medicine* (29 August 1985): 586-88.

INDEX OF SCRIPTURE

Joshua
4:19-5:12   4 Lent C
24:1-2, 14-25   Proper 16 B

Judges
6:11-24   5 Epiphany C

Ruth
1:1-19   Proper 23 C

1 Samuel
3:1-20   2 Epiphany B
12:19-24   7 Easter C
16:1-13   4 Lent A

2 Samuel
7:4-16   4 Advent B
11:26–12:15   Proper 6 C

1 Kings
3:5-12   Proper 12 A
8:22-43   Proper 4 C
17:8-16   Proper 27 B
17:17-24   Proper 5 C
19:9-18   Last Epiphany B
19:15-21   Proper 8 C

2 Kings
2:1-15   Proper 12 B
4:8-37   5 Epiphany B
5:1-15   6 Epiphany B; Proper 1 B

1 Chronicles

2 Chronicles
36:14-23   4 Lent B

Ezra

Nehemiah
8:2-10   3 Epiphany C
9:6-15   4 Easter A
9:16-20   Proper 13 A

Esther

Job
19:23-27   Proper 27 C
38:1-18   Proper 7 B
42:1-6   2 Easter C (alt)

Psalms

Proverbs
9:1-6   Proper 15 B

Ecclesiastes
1:12–2:23   Proper 13 C

Song of Solomon

Isaiah
1:10-20   Proper 26 C
2:1-5   1 Advent A
2:10-17   Proper 8 A
5:1-7   Proper 22 A
6:1-8   Trinity C
7:10-17   4 Advent A
9:2-7   Christmas Day (I) A, B, C
11:1-10   2 Advent A
25:1-9   Proper 23 A
25:6-9   Easter Day (2) B (alt)
26:2-9, 19   2 Easter B (alt)
28:14-22   Proper 16 C
35:1-10   3 Advent A

Amos

3:1-8　3 Epiphany A
5:6-15　Proper 23 B
5:18-24　Proper 27 A
6:1-7　Proper 21 C
7:7-15　Proper 10 B
8:4-12　Proper 20 C

Obadiah

Jonah

2:1-9　Proper 14 A
3:10–4:11　Proper 20 A

Micah

3:5-12　Proper 26 A
4:1-5　3 Easter B
5:2-4　4 Advent C
6:1-8　4 Epiphany A

Nahum

Habakkuk

1:1–2:4　Proper 22 C
3:2-6, 17-19　5 Epiphany A

Zephaniah

1:7, 12-18　Proper 28 A
3:14-20　3 Advent C

Haggai

Zecharaiah

9:9-12　Proper 9 A
12:8-10; 13:1　Proper 7 C
14:4-9　1 Advent C

Malachi

3:13–4:6　Proper 28 C

Matthew

1:18-25　4 Advent A
1:40-45　Proper 1 B
2:1-12　The Epiphany A, B, C
2:13-23　2 Christmas A, B, C
3:1-12　2 Advent A
3:13-17　1 Epiphany A
4:1-11　1 Lent A
4:12-23　3 Epiphany A
5:1-12　4 Epiphany A
5:13-20　5 Epiphany A
5:21-37　6 Epiphany A; Proper 1 A
5:38-48　7 Epiphany A; Proper 2 A
6:24-34　8 Epiphany A; Proper 3 A
7:21-27　Proper 4 A
9:9-13　Proper 5 A
9:35–10:15　Proper 6 A
10:16-33　Proper 7 A
10:34-42　Proper 8 A
11:2-11　3 Advent A
11:25-30　Proper 9 A
13:1-23　Proper 10 A
13:24-43　Proper 11 A
13:31-49　Proper 12 A
14:13-21　Proper 13 A
14:22-33　Proper14 A
15:21-28　Proper 15 A
16:13-20　Proper 16 A
16:21-27　Proper 17 A
17:1-9　Last Epiphany A
18:15-20　Proper 18 A
18:21-35　Proper 19 A
20:1-16　Proper 20 A
21:28-32　Proper 21 A
21:33-43　Proper 22 A

Luke (cont.)

12:13-21   Proper 13 C
12:32-40   Proper 14 C
12:49-56   Proper 15 C
13:1-9   3 Lent C
13:22-35   2 Lent C; Proper 16 C
14:1, 7-14   Proper 17 C
14:25-33   Proper 18 C
15:1-10   Proper 19 C
15:11-32   Lent 4 C
16:1-13   Proper 20 C
16:19-31   Proper 21 C
17:5-10   Proper 22 C
17:11-19   Proper 23 C
18:1-8   Proper 24 C
18:9-14   Proper 25 C
19:1-10   Proper 26 C
20:9-19   5 Lent C
20:27-38   Proper 27 C
21:5-19   Proper 28 C
21:25-31   1 Advent C
22:14-30   Maundy Thursday A, B, C
22:39–23:56   Palm/Passion Sunday C
23:35-43   Proper 29 C
24:1-10   Easter Day (2) C
24:13-35   Easter Day (3) A, B, C;
   3 Easter A
24:36-48   3 Easter B

John

1:1-14   Christmas Day (III) A, B, C
1:1-18   1 Christmas A, B, C
1:6-28   3 Advent B
1:29-41   2 Epiphany A
1:43-51   2 Epiphany B
2:1-11   2 Epiphany C
2:13-22   3 Lent B
3:1-16   Trinity B

John (cont.)

3:1-17   2 Lent A
4:5-42   3 Lent A
6:4-15   4 Lent B
6:24-35   Proper 13 B
6:37-51   Proper 14 B
6:53-59   Proper 15 B
6:60-69   Proper 16 B
9:1-38   4 Lent A
10:1-10   4 Easter A
10:11-16   4 Easter B
10:22-30   4 Easter C
11:1-44   5 Lent A
12:20-33   5 Lent B
13:1-15   Maundy Thursday A, B, C
13:31-35   5 Easter C
14:1-14   5 Easter A
14:8-17   Pentecost A, B, C (alt)
14:23-29   6 Easter C
15:1-8   6 Easter A
15:9-17   6 Easter B
16:5-15   Trinity C
17:1-11   7 Easter A
17:11-19   7 Easter B
17:20-26   7 Easter C
18:1–19:37   Good Friday A, B, C
18:33-37   Proper 29 B
19:31   2 Easter A
20:1-18   Easter Day (2) A
20:19-23   Pentecost A, B, C
20:19-31   2 Easter A, B, C
21:1-14   3 Easter C

Acts of the Apostles

1:1-14   7 Easter A
1:15-26   7 Easter B
2:1-11   Pentecost A, B, C
2:14-32   2 Easter A

1 Corinthians (*cont.*)

15:20-28   Proper 29 A
15:35-50   7 Epiphany C; Proper 2 C
15:50-58   8 Epiphany C; Proper 3 C

2 Corinthians

1:18-22   7 Epiphany B; Proper 2 B
3:4–4:2   8 Epiphany B; Proper 3 B
4:5-12   Proper 4 B
4:13-18   Proper 5 B
5:1-10   Proper 6 B
5:17-21   4 Lent C; Proper 7 B
8:1-15   Proper 8 B
12:2-10   Proper 9 B
13:5-13   Trinity A

Galatians

1:1-10   Proper 4 C
1:11-24   Proper 5 C
2:11-21   Proper 6 C
3:23-25; 4:4-7   1 Christmas A, B, C
3:23-29   Proper 7 C
5:1, 13-25   Proper 8 C
6:1-18   Proper 9 C

Ephesians

1:1-14   Proper 10 B
1:3-6, 15-19   2 Christmas A, B, C
2:4-10   4 Lent B
2:11-22   Proper 11 B
3:1-12   The Epiphany A, B, C
4:1-16   Proper 12 B
4:17-25   Proper 13 B
4:25–5:2   Proper 14 B
5:1-14   4 Lent A
5:15-20   Proper 15 B
5:21-33   Proper 16 B
6:10-20   Proper 17 B

Philippians

1:1-11   2 Advent C
1:21-27   Proper 20 A
2:1-13   Proper 21 A
2:5-11   Palm/Passion Sunday A, B, C
3:7-14   Last Epiphany A
3:8-14   5 Lent C
3:14-21   Proper 22 A
3:17–4:1   2 Lent C
4:4-9   3 Advent C
4:4-13   Proper 23 A

Colossians

1:1-14   Proper 10 C
1:11-20   Proper 29 C
1:21-29   Proper 11 C
2:6-15   Proper 12 C
3:1-4   Easter Day (2) A, B, C
3:5-17   Proper 13 C

1 Thessalonians

1:1-10   Proper 24 A
2:1-8   Proper 25 A
2:9-20   Proper 26 A
3:9-13   1 Advent C
4:13-18   Proper 27 A
5:1-10   Proper 28 A
5:12-28   3 Advent B

2 Thessalonians

1:1-12   Proper 26 C
2:13–3:5   Proper 27 C
3:6-13   Proper 28 C

1 Timothy

1:12-17   Proper 19 C
2:1-8   Proper 20 C
6:11-19   Proper 21 C

Baruch

5:1-9   2 Advent C

Ecclesiasticus

10:7-18   Proper 17 C
15:11-20   6 Epiphany A; Proper 1 A
27:30–28:7   Proper 19 A

Wisdom

1:16–2:1, 6-22   Proper 20 B
2:1, 12-24   Good Friday A, B, C (alt)
12:13-19   Proper 11 A

Cowley Publications is a ministry of the Society of St. John the Evangelist, a religious community for men in the Episcopal Church. Emerging from the Society s tradition of prayer, theological reflection, and diversity of mission, the press is centered in the rich heritage of the Anglican Communion.

Cowley Publications seeks to provide books, audio cassettes, and other resources for the ongoing theological exploration and spiritual development of the Episcopal Church and others in the body of Christ. To this end, it is dedicated to developing a new generation of theological writers, encouraging them to produce timely, creative, and stimulating publications of excellence, and making these publications available widely, reaching both clergy and lay persons.